Uncertainty in Policy Making

T0347335

Science in Society Series

Series Editor: Steve Rayner
Institute for Science, Innovation and Society, University of Oxford

Editorial Board: Gary Kass, Anne Kerr, Melissa Leach, Angela Liberatore,
Stan Metcalfe, Paul Nightingale, Timothy O'Riordan, Nick Pidgeon, Ortwin Renn,
Dan Sarewitz, Andrew Webster, James Wilsdon, Steve Yearley

Animals as Biotechnology
Ethics, Sustainability and Critical Animal Studies
Richard Twine

Business Planning for Turbulent Times
New Methods for Applying Scenarios
Edited by Rafael Ramírez, John W. Selsky and Kees van der Heijden

Debating Climate Change
Pathways through Argument to Agreement
Elizabeth L. Malone

Democratizing Technology
Risk, Responsibility and the Regulation of Chemicals
Anne Chapman

Genomics and Society
Legal, Ethical and Social Dimensions
Edited by George Gaskell and Martin W. Bauer

Influenza and Public Health
Learning from Past Pandemics
Edited by Tamara Giles-Vernick and Susan Craddock, with Jennifer Gunn

Marginalized Reproduction
Ethnicity, Infertility and Reproductive Technologies
Lorraine Culley, Nicky Hudson and Floor van Rooij

Nanotechnology
Risk, Ethics and Law
Edited by Geoffrey Hunt and Michael Mehta

Resolving Messy Policy Problems
Handling Conflict in Environmental, Transport, Health and Ageing Policy
Steven Ney

Uncertainty in Policy Making
Values and Evidence in Complex Decisions
Michael Heazle

Unnatural Selection
The Challenges of Engineering Tomorrow's People
Edited by Peter Healey and Steve Rayner

Vaccine Anxieties
Global Science, Child Health and Society
Melissa Leach and James Fairhead

A Web of Prevention
Biological Weapons, Life Sciences and the Governance of Research
Edited by Brian Rappert and Caitrìona McLeish

Uncertainty in Policy Making

Values and Evidence in Complex Decisions

Michael Heazle

First published by Earthscan in the UK and USA in 2010

For a full list of publications please contact:
Earthscan
2 Park Square, Milton Park, Abingdon, Oxfordshire OX14 4RN
711 Third Avenue, New York, NY 10017

First issued in paperback 2016

Earthscan is an imprint of the Taylor & Francis Group, an informa business

Notices
Practitioners and researchers must always rely on their own experience and knowledge in evaluating and using any information, methods, compounds, or experiments described herein. In using such information or methods they should be mindful of their own safety and the safety of others, including parties for whom they have a professional responsibility.

Product or corporate names may be trademarks or registered trademarks, and are used only for identification and explanation without intent to infringe.

ISBN 13: 978-1-138-98638-1 (pbk)
ISBN 13: 978-1-84971-083-1 (hbk)

Typeset by Composition and Design Services
Cover design by Susanne Harris

A catalogue record for this book is available from the British Library

Library of Congress Cataloging-in-Publication Data

Heazle, Michael.
    Uncertainty in policy making: values and evidence in complex decisions/Michael Heazle.
        p. cm.
    Includes bibliographical references and index.
    ISBN 978-1-84971-083-1 (hardback)
    1. Political planning–United States. 2. United States–Politics and government. 3. Policy sciences. I. Title.
    JK468.P64H43 2010
        320.6–dc22   2010005699

For Kazu, Alexi and Jake, and my parents

Contents

List of Figures and Tables

Figures

Tables

Foreword

Policy makers habitually portray the policies they make as flowing, directly and inexorably, from facts. Strong political incentives underlie such portrayals. The policy maker looks good in so far as he is perceived to be acting on facts rather than on beliefs, hunches or wishes. He looks informed rather than ignorant. He also is better able to muster support for his policy, which he depicts as a product of reality rather than ideology. Wars or other policy departures are presented as acts of necessity rather than of choice.

An outstanding example, one of those that Michael Heazle examines in this volume, was the adducing of supposed facts about unconventional weapons programmes as one of the chief rationales for launching a US-led offensive war against Iraq in 2003. The Iraq War was an extreme instance of an ostensibly fact-based case being used to sell a policy decision that was reached in other ways and on other grounds. The famously flawed intelligence analysis about Iraqi weapons that became associated with that war had not been requested (or, at the highest levels, even read) by the US administration of George W. Bush, which, in any case, had no process for examining whether initiating the war was a good idea. Whatever empirical input – flawed or accurate, on weapons programmes or anything else – that might have been relevant to Bush's war decision had no opportunity to influence it, at least as far as a formal governmental process was concerned. The war was the product of instinct, ideology and long-held wishes to remake the politics and economics of the Middle East. It did not stem from the ostensible, and mistaken, facts that were used to sell it.

Although the Iraq War was an extreme case, it was by no means the only instance of a policy issue being coloured, and even redefined, as an intelligence issue. The Cold War presented other examples, including ones involving the strategic arms race with the Soviet Union and Moscow's relations with violent revolutionary groups. Hard-fought battles in the 1970s and 1980s over intelligence assessments on these subjects, purportedly to establish an accurate factual basis for making policy, were really ideologically driven contests over the policy itself.

For the ideologically committed, depicting policy issues as factual or intelligence issues has the aforementioned advantage of salesmanship. For the less committed – or the less involved or less informed, such as members of legislatures who must vote on policies the wisdom of which they are unsure – this depiction offers a different attraction. It relieves (or rather, appears to relieve) the individual from making his own judgement about policy. My duty, he can say, is just to follow the facts.

This leads to yet another attraction, both for those ideologically driven to push for certain policies and those who would just rather not have to decide. When policies run awry, blame can be placed on getting the facts wrong. The fault is said to lie not with ideological misdirection or inadequate deliberation, but instead with bum information. Because the facts used to sell or to rationalize a policy do not originate with policy-makers, this conveniently deflects blame for failure away from the policy makers and toward the producers of the information. Most often this means directing it at an intelligence service.

Policy makers could not effectively play this game unless the notion of policy being driven by facts resonated with the general public. The public finds the notion comfortable, and comforting, for several reasons, one of which is that it conforms to an ideal model of how policy *ought* to be made. In this model, national leaders assemble all the available relevant information about a problem, carefully deliberate upon it, and choose a course of action based on that information rather than on any personal or political predilections. A belief that policy making really works something like that bolsters faith in the institutions of government.

The public draws further comfort from the idea that their leaders are working with facts rather than uncertainties. Uncertainty is disturbing, in countless ways that psychologists have documented. The public does not even need to absorb factual certainties itself as long as it believes that those making the policies have done so. A passenger on a bus can relax without knowing what lies on the road ahead, if he believes the driver knows.

If obstacles are encountered on the road and policy fails, a final source of comfort complements the policy makers' interest in deflecting blame for failure. If the problem was bad information, then it is reassuring to think that problems will not recur if the source of information is fixed. This is the chief basis for the unending interest in intelligence 'reform'. It is comforting to think that through bureaucratic tinkering we can prevent future policies from failing. It would be disturbing to think instead that even with such tinkering there still will be inevitable gaps in our knowledge, and that there will be inevitable policy dilemmas and obstacles even if our knowledge were perfect.

In short, strong interests and emotions sustain the belief that facts, or what are believed to be facts, drive public policy. The same interests and emotions sustain the belief that with properly working government institutions we will have the facts that we need, and that any important and relevant gaps in our knowledge will be filled.

The beliefs are untrue. Reality is far removed from the ideal model. There are many reasons for this, including the mundane limitations of policy makers' time and attention and the often-quirky ways in which political gamesmanship intrudes into the policy process. Two more fundamental reasons are especially pertinent to this book. One is that significant uncertainty relevant to many policy problems is inevitable. Policy makers will not know many important things.

This is partly because adversaries (and sometimes friends) withhold their secrets. It also is because the systems involved are too complex to analyse to the point of making good predictions. This is true of many natural systems – as with Heazle's other major case, climate change – and human systems such as unstable polities.

The second major reason the popular beliefs are untrue is that even perfect information does not point to a specific solution to many policy problems. Omniscient policy makers would still face difficult choices because of competing priorities, objectives and values – and some of the choices they make will appear in retrospect to have been wrong. Iraq and the issue of weapons of mass destruction is a prime example. Even a solid case that Iraq had programmes to produce such weapons would not have constituted an argument that an offensive war was the best way to deal with the problem – as indicated by the strong opposition to the war among many, in the US and elsewhere, who agreed with the Bush administration that Iraq had such programmes.

Michael Heazle's book insightfully and skilfully strips away the widespread misconceptions about how information and expertise do, and do not, play into the making of public policy. Drawing on theoretical perspectives and on the experience of American, Australian and British decision-making regarding Iraq and climate change, Heazle elucidates how substantive interpretations of policy problems flow from political preferences for certain solutions at least as much as solutions flow from the interpretations. His book makes several valuable contributions.

First, it expands our overall understanding of how public policy is made. It analyses the real world of decision making and not just the ideal world. In this regard it is an advance on scholarship that all too often merely plays off the unrealized ideal, searching for ways to obtain more accurate information or more profound expertise without considering the impact that either actually has on policy.

Second, the book provides insights on why bad policy gets made. It explores how mistaken and misleading images that are associated with misguided policies can be the products of ideology and politics. As such, Heazle's analysis is a welcome antidote to misguided efforts at reform.

Third, by demonstrating what expertise, either inside or outside government, cannot or does not provide, the book sharpens our understanding of what expertise *can* provide in support of policy making. It can furnish a lot, but only on specific empirical questions. Substantive expertise can and should be used – much more than it generally is – to inform policy making, but it cannot be a substitute for the difficult decisions policy makers must make.

Fourth, Heazle explains how competing values and objectives are at the core of most policy questions. Clarifying any one policy question means identifying the specific values and objectives at stake. In describing how politics intrudes into the policy process in ways that often diverge far from the ideal, Heazle is not arguing for taking politics out of the process. To the contrary: reconciling, or choosing among, competing values and objectives is what politics is all about. Policy making *should* be political, as long as the political issues are not disguised as factual ones.

Finally, the book explains why acknowledgement of uncertainty must be incorporated into policy making, far more than it commonly is. Deluding ourselves that we know what we really do not, and constructing strategies that would be sound only if a certain preferred image of the outside world proves to be true, is psychologically comfortable and politically attractive but not a prescription for successful policy. It is better to choose a course of action calculated to minimize the risk of harm and to maximize the chance of benefit no matter which of several possible worlds turns out to be the real one.

The messages that Michael Heazle presents in this book are by no means comforting or reassuring, but both scholars and practitioners would be wise to heed them.

Paul R. Pillar
Georgetown University
30 December 2009

Acknowledgements

While researching and writing this book over the last four years, I have been hugely fortunate. I have learned a great deal from the advice and guidance of many people who have been kind enough to take an interest in my ideas. Among my colleagues at Griffith University, I'd like to acknowledge firstly the wonderful support and guidance I have received from Associate Professor John Butcher, who has spent so much time reading various drafts and discussing my ideas with me. Without John's keen interest and patient input, my progress would have been far slower. I'd also like to thank Dr Michael Wesley, Professor John Kane and, in particular, Associate Professor Martin Griffiths for their excellent advice and willingness always to read drafts and lend a helping hand with my thinking. Other colleagues I'd like to acknowledge and thank include Dr Bjoern Dressel, Dr Steve McCarthy and Dr Tom Conley.

I also am indebted to a number of other people in Australia and abroad who so generously gave up some of their time to meet with me and answer my many emails. I would like to thank and express my sincere appreciation to John Morrison and Brian Jones in the UK; Paul R. Pillar, Jeff White, Greg Theilmann, Robert Gallucci, Branko Milanovic and Mike Eisenstadt in the US; Hans Blix and Rolf Ekeus in Sweden; Rod Barton and Frank Lewincamp, who met with me several times in Australia; and also Professor Ravi Kanbur (Cornell) who took time from a busy schedule to talk with me during a visit to Australia. I would like to thank Dr Paul Pillar (Georgetown) in particular for kindly agreeing to write the book's foreword. I also owe thanks to Dr Daniel Sarewitz (Arizona State) for his valuable advice on my analytical and conceptual framework; his own work on uncertainty in policy making has informed much of my thinking in this book.

I owe a special vote of thanks too to Meegan Thorley and Kathy Bailey at the Griffith Asia Institute, whose amazing administrative support helped in so many important ways; to Robyn White for getting the manuscript into shape; to Dan Halvorson for his tireless research assistance; and to the team at Earthscan for their wonderful editorial support. I especially would like to thank Alison Kuznets at Earthscan for making the book's publication a reality. Finally, a very big 'thank you' to my family – Kazu, Alexi and Jake – for *always* understanding and for just 'being there'.

This book's research was funded by a three-year post-doctoral research grant provided by the Australian Research Council. I thank the Council for its generous support. Some of my earlier publications and conference papers have contributed to the book's arguments and themes and several of the chapters draw on these. These works include: 'Scientific uncertainty and the International Whaling Commission: An alternative perspective on the use of science in policy making', *Marine Policy* (2004); 'Lessons in precaution: The International Whaling Commission experience with precautionary management', *Marine Policy*, (2006); 'Neoliberal idealism, state building, and the Washington Consensus: A story (still) under development', presented at *The 10th Annual Society for Global Business and Conference* (Kyoto, 2007) and the *5th International Conference of the World Association for Sustainable Development* (Brisbane, 2007); and 'Strategic assessment, decision making, and uncertainty', presented at *Australia's Strategic Futures* (Adelaide, 2008).

As usual, any shortcomings, flaws or errors in this work are the entire and sole responsibility of the author.

List of Acronyms and Abbreviations

ABC	Australian Broadcasting Corporation
AJPC	Australian Joint Parliamentary Committee
ANZUS	Security Treaty between Australia, New Zealand and the United States of America
AP6	Asia Pacific Partnership Group
APEC	Asia-Pacific Economic Cooperation
ASIO	Australian Security Intelligence Organisation
ASIS	Australian Secret Intelligence Service
BBC	British Broadcasting Corporation
BMD	ballistic missile defence program
BSE	Bovine Spongiform Encephalopathy
BW	biological weapons
CIA	Central Intelligence Agency
CW	chemical weapons
D&D	denial and deception
DIA	Defence Intelligence Agency
DIO	Defence Intelligence Organisation
DIS	Defence Intelligence Staff
DOD	Department of Defense
DSD	Defence Signals Directorate
EU	European Union
FDI	foreign direct investment
GCM	Global Circulation Model
GHG	greenhouse gas
GDP	gross domestic product
IAEA	International Atomic Energy Agency
ICBM	intercontinental ballistic missile
ICRW	International Convention for the Regulation of Whaling
IEA	International Energy Agency
IFI	international financial institution
IMF	International Monetary Fund
IPCC	Intergovernmental Panel on Climate Change
ISG	Iraq Survey Group

IWC	International Whaling Commission
MI6	British Secret Intelligence Service
NIE	National Intelligence Estimate
NGO	non-governmental organization
NW	nuclear weapons
OECD	Organisation for Economic Co-operation and Development
ONA	Office of National Assessments
PBS	Public Broadcasting Service
PJC	Parliamentary Joint Committee
PP	precautionary principle
RMP	Revised Management Procedure
RMS	Revised Management Scheme
SAP	Structural Adjustment Program
SRES	Special Report on Emission Scenarios
UAV	unmanned aerial vehicle
UGF	underground facility
UN	United Nations
UNFCCC	United Nations Framework Convention on Climate Change
UNMOVIC	United Nations Monitoring, Verification and Inspection Commission
UNSCOM	United Nations Special Commission
WDR	World Development Report
WG1	Working Group 1
WMD	weapons of mass destruction
WOT	War on Terror

1
Introduction: A Story of (Irrational) Great Expectations

Knowledge claims have long been used to legitimize authority and the use of coercion in society. Their sources, however, have waxed and waned over the course of human society's development. The secular logic of the ancient Greeks, its replacement by divine sources of knowledge and authority during the Middle Ages, and then the Renaissance rediscovery of classical antiquity[1] illustrate how notions of knowledge and authority have changed throughout Western history. The Renaissance shift from non-secular deduction to secular induction and Greek-derived notions of reason and logic (i.e. the basis of today's 'scientific method') laid the foundations for modern notions of knowledge and human progress. Indeed, it inspired the Enlightenment belief that people had the potential, if not yet the capability, to control and impose order on not only the natural environment, as Newton already had shown, but also their political environments by balancing and arbitrating the power of the state with the liberty of the individual.

This sea change in perceptions of knowledge, characterized generally in the West by the total separation in the modern era of 'science' (i.e. the natural sciences) and philosophy from theology, underpinned the contributions of Locke, Rousseau, Hume and others to the philosophical development of liberalism, legitimizing its adoption in Western Europe and the US as the formula by which the tensions between government, or the authority of the state, and liberty could be reconciled. Thus, in the modern liberal-democratic state, the actions of the state – as represented by the 'policies' and laws of the government of the day – must broadly be seen by the public as non-arbitrary and *rational* applications of state power and control that are focused entirely on what has come to be known as the 'national interest'. According to Bocking:

> [I]n areas ranging from economic development, to planning to education, [there] has been an ever expanding application of administrative rationalism: seeking, with the guidance of technological expertise, rational and efficient solutions to the problems of society, translating the authority of science into political power.[2]

The role of knowledge then has been a critical part of the entire liberal-democratic enterprise, providing as it does the means by which the often conflicting imperatives of 'freedom' and 'order' are reconciled in the making of 'policy'. As Yaron Ezrahi points out, the role of science and knowledge has been:

> as a source of authoritative constraints on [political] discourse and action ... to make the coercive powers of the state acceptable to people touched by modern consciousness, to institutionalize and validate public actions and claims in terms of liberal democratic values, and to overcome the tensions between the requirements of public action and the values of voluntary individualism.[3]

But, as Ezrahi also argues, the relationship between science and government in modern democracies is far less about the 'progressive rationalization of politics' than it is about the utilitarian employment of science and the knowledge it produces as a source of legitimacy for competing ideological view points.[4] Moreover, the standard rationalist criteria for legitimate policy making and political authority are becoming increasingly difficult to defend and justify as our attempts to better know and control our social and natural environments continue to produce as many questions and unwanted outcomes as they do answers and policy successes. The increasingly complex policy issues that science is expected to provide guidance on have progressively exposed both the limits of current human knowledge and also the prospects for its future growth.

Even the task of defining 'policy', in the sense of the state exercising authority for the public good at least, is complicated by the question of legitimacy, and its definition is often as controversial as the decisions to act or not to act it is intended to describe. Wayne Parsons, for example, explains *policy* in the modern English usage as 'an attempt to define and structure a rational basis for action or inaction'.[5] The important phrase here is *rational basis*, since policy makers, with few exceptions, accept that their decisions must be compatible with a broadly accepted, but again difficult to define, notion of 'rational': one that is idealized in the classical, positivist sense but ultimately determined by the majority values and predilections of a given society at any given time. Therefore, regardless of the actual or underlying ambitions and motivations of the policy makers for taking a particular policy decision (invade Iraq, refuse emission reductions, deregulate the economy/labour markets or oppose commercial whaling, for example), the policy must be presented and rationalized (i.e. justified) in a way that the wider electorate will find acceptable, particularly when the values/goals of the policy itself are controversial (e.g. former Australian prime minister John Howard's support for and participation in the Iraq war; his opposition to the Kyoto Protocol).

Whether or not the decision makers who determine what is or is not *policy* and on what grounds – that is, the executive *policy elite* – are simply reacting to what they believe to be a genuine policy challenge, or are creating policy challenges for the pursuit of ideological preferences – justified in the 'national interest' – the imperative is that they publicly state what they intend to do, how they intend doing it, and why. The act of publicly stating policy not only defines what *is* policy, but also reflects the strong link between policy and its justification. According to former US Secretary of State Warren Christopher:

> *In any given week as Secretary, I received dozens of memoranda advocating various particular policy directions. However persuasive their contents, they did not constitute US policy unless they were incorporated into a speech, public statement or formal government document. The challenge of articulating a position publicly compels leaders to make policy choices. Often decisions on what to do and what to say publicly are made simultaneously.*[6]

And it is upon this point, this intersection of what policy makers want to do and what electorates expect in terms of policy (i.e. 'rational' explanation and justification), that my analysis of uncertainty in expert advice and its significance in *justifying* as opposed to simply *informing* particular policy decisions is concentrated. The question of whether policy makers actually *believe* or subscribe to the policy justifications they put forward, or pursue policies for reasons other than what they publicly state, is unimportant since my argument focuses only on the problem of uncertainty's inconsistent treatment and what this tells us about the role and limits of knowledge in policy making. I am not attempting to uncover or explain instances of duplicity; doing so would not only be methodologically impractical (how could such duplicity be unequivocally demonstrated without some form of admission by policy makers?)[7] but would also begin to resemble the unproblematic rationalist approach to knowledge and the accompanying argument that it is only political expediency and competition that prevents policy making from becoming an entirely rational and knowledge-based enterprise. Thus, for my purposes, 'policy' is a publicly expressed decision of government claimed, and defended, by policy makers as being in the public or national interest.[8]

Abandoning politics: Rationalist notions of legitimacy and knowledge

The questions my argument addresses, such as how decision makers determine the best advice without knowing – as opposed to *believing* – which advice is correct, and what the 'best advice' means, arise from a level of analysis that mostly has been ignored due to the positivist paradigm within which most of the work on policy and controversy analysis has, until recently,[9] been located. My intention then is to provide an alternative conceptual framework aimed at helping to reveal what is omitted by existing explanations of decision making and the positivist expectations of knowledge and specialist advice that many, but not all, of them rely on. As Allison and Zelikow argue: 'Alternative conceptual frameworks are important not only for further insights into neglected dimensions of the underlying phenomenon. They are essential as a reminder of the distortions and limitations of whatever conceptual framework one employs.'[10]

The various rationalist approaches that traditionally have characterized the policy and controversy analysis literature[11] all share a common neglect of some basic epistemological problems and issues concerning the perception and treatment of uncertainty in specialist advice. And it is their dismissal of the more fundamental issues at this level – that is, those that raise questions concerning the 'why' rather than only the 'how' – that causes positivist-based explanations of what 'is' and what 'should be' to either miss or ignore as irrelevant the kinds of question I will pursue in the following chapters.

The best known among these approaches is the so-called rational actor (or action) model, characterized by its linear, problem-solving process and fundamental reliance on a positivist epistemology, which still dominates perceptions of what policy making should and can represent, despite the strong criticism its straightforward and commonsensical depiction of the policy process has attracted.[12] The continued mainstream embrace of this model is illustrated not only by the contemporary appeal of 'evidence-based' policy making in government and the ongoing imperative that policy must appear rational in order to be legitimate, but also by the way in which policy makers continue to explain policy failure and bad decision making as the product of poor information or inadequate resources as was the case with Iraq's non-existent weapons of mass destruction (WMD), or, alternatively, imperfect knowledge and uncertainty as justification for policy inaction as is currently the case with climate change. The values and ideas actually driving policy choices and the debates that surround them, however, remain hidden away by both the public's disdain for policy that cannot be rationally justified on the basis of what we know and the recognition of this fact by politicians whose main task is to ensure their decisions always appear to be 'rational' rather than 'political'. According to Nieman and Stambough:

> At the very time that popular disquiet with 'politics' as a means of making governing choices has reached a climax, the infatuation with rational models has grown. Indeed, it is fair to say that the dominant approach to making, implementing, and evaluating public policy is one variation of the rational choice theme or another. Ranging across diverse policy areas, from criminal justice to agricultural subsidies, to housing and medical care, the tools employed by rational choice theorists have come to prevail as the paramount criterion used to judge whether public policies are successful. While there are a variety of reviews and critical assessments of various public/rational choice models of analysis, the conclusion remains that rational models seem ever more dominant in studies of what government does and how and what it should be doing.[13]

The rational actor model's simple conceptualization of an otherwise complex and often opaque political process is largely responsible for its longevity, making it, in effect, the default framework for analysis and judgement that practitioners, analysts, and the public turn to when overwhelmed or unsatisfied by much more complicated alternatives. In this sense, an important advantage of rational actor models and their international relations cousins 'realism' and 'liberalism' becomes clear. Although separated by the level of analysis at which they operate, the basic and intuitively correct assumptions inherent to both support a level of parsimony and theoretical simplicity that makes them particularly 'user-friendly'. Rationalist assumptions about the nature of actors (rational, self-interested, unitary) and the knowledge they use (available, obtainable, verifiable) are shared by a broad range of policy and decision making theories as they allow for the creation of a simple heuristic for describing, explaining and judging policy behaviour or choices at either the domestic or international level. More importantly though, rationalist approaches are informed by a fundamental normative assumption that identifies politics as a form of contagion afflicting the policy process; isolating politics from the patient (policy making) will allow the patient to function normally, that is rationally and objectively. Politics then, according to the rationalists, needs to be minimized so that it does not 'vulgarize decision making'.[14] And the way to achieve such 'rationality' is to assume an uncomplicated, positivist view of knowledge in which the messy business of competing values and interests can always be made subordinate to the 'truth' once it is revealed.

Among the many conceptual issues rationalist-based perspectives overlook in the course of providing this otherwise appealing and straightforward depiction of how and why policy decisions are made is the way they gloss over the problematic nature of knowledge claims and demarcation. Because of their positivist foundations, rationalist perspectives ignore the role values and interests play in how we interpret and understand uncertainty and, as a consequence, they allow for the masking of what are essentially political choices between differing interests and preferences as choices that can be made and justified on the basis of value-neutral 'knowledge' and its demarcation with incorrect or false knowledge claims. This inherent element of self-deception that underpins the rationalist perspective – that is the 'irrational' conviction that knowledge demarcation is *always* achievable and can, therefore, be relied upon to guide and legitimize the decisions we make – blurs the important policy distinction between what *should* as opposed to what *can* be achieved. Moreover, ignoring the existence and influence of competing values and interests – that is, politics – is to deny what sets democratic societies, in particular *liberal* democracies, apart from other forms of government and social organization.[15]

Rationalist approaches deny the unavoidable influence of 'politics' in the policy decision making of liberal democracies; moreover, they condemn any intrusion of competing values and interests into the decision making process. In the rationalist schema, decision making should be a neat, orderly, and above all, rational process in which the best (read correct) advice is found and then acted upon as the basis for policy. The ultimate goal is to know one is making the right decision, or at least the best possible decision, and the only way to do so is to remove uncertainty and risk through the creation of and reference to more and better knowledge. However, there is nothing 'rational' about denying the quite obvious competition that occurs between differing values and interests when big decisions need to be made, particularly for no better reason than the desire to craft uncomplicated, 'user friendly' explanations of how policy and decision making works; nor is it 'rational' in the normative sense of arguing how policy decisions should be made, which is the main goal of rationalist perspectives, particularly if at the same time accompanying arguments about the superiority of the liberal democratic model of government are also made or assumed.

Science and expert advice should and can play a major part in determining choices, but they can offer little towards the resolution of the essentially values-based disputes that define the political realm and the issues it seeks to manage. Thus, the major problem of rationalist models for the purposes of this study is not that they fail to adequately explain/describe the policy process, since no one model does, but rather that the rationalist approach itself introduces 'irrationality' into how we understand policy making by encouraging unfounded expectations of what policy can be expected to represent and how it should be judged. My argument is not about rejecting the notion of rational behaviour or even rationalist assumptions of self-interest. On the contrary, the influence of interests *and* values on our perceptions of uncertainty, and also, therefore, our perceptions of knowledge – in addition to the need for a more 'rational' understanding of the limited role expert advice can play in policy decisions – are central to both the descriptive and normative arguments I am making.

An alternative perspective on uncertainty and the treatment of specialist advice

My descriptive argument contends the treatment of uncertainty in specialist advice is best characterized by what I refer to as a 'utilitarian' approach – that is, one dominated by the pre-existing political and ideological interests that provide the context within which specialist advice is received – which, in addition to causing significant policy making inconsistencies and often undesirable/unintended policy outcomes, inverts the traditional rationalist perception of the relationship between knowledge and choice. And since the notion of utility proposed by this approach is entirely a subjective one, different people, groups, societies and cultures will perceive the utility of a given choice or preference differently in relation to the values and cultural preferences they subscribe to.[16] The model's theoretical framework identifies the perceived *utility* of a piece of research or specialist advice (i.e. the extent to which it either complements or contradicts the policy goals being pursued and also the extent to which it contradicts or complements existing priorities and values) as a major factor in determining its acceptance or rejection by policy makers. It is, I propose, these perceptions of utility by policy makers, and society in general, that represent the real benchmark for what constitutes good science and knowledge rather than the commonly held notion that *knowledge*, scientific or otherwise, represents *truth* and is defined as such by its *proven* ability to accurately describe the *real world*.[17]

When looking at decisions and judgements concerning science or other specialist knowledge in this way, knowledge itself becomes only part of the story. Indeed, according to the essentially instrumentalist view of science and expert advice I am presenting here, scientific knowledge is simply unable to play the idealized role of a value-neutral judge guiding policy makers towards the best possible decision. The inability of experts to predict, with any confidence, outcomes or consequence in all but the most familiar (and limited) circumstances and situations (i.e. the domain of what Thomas Kuhn referred to as 'normal science')[18] means that their evidence is always open to various interpretations with no particular interpretation or conclusion able to be privileged above at least several others.

Thus, the story I am proposing is not about how politics gets in the way of good policy making, distorting what should otherwise be a rational and entirely knowledge-based enterprise. In this story, knowledge demarcation claims over the 'best' advice are unavoidable and invariably coloured by normative values and preferences, since no expert or decision maker – at any level – confronts any situation of importance without some prior expectations and notion of a preferred course of action or outcome. Knowledge then clearly is an important part of the story but not in its own right; it is rather the interpretation of 'knowledge' that plays the lead in explaining why expert advice often is treated so inconsistently by policy makers in their justification of Policy A over Policy B, especially when both uncertainties and the political stakes are high. This approach, I believe, can reveal a great deal about why scientists and other specialists, governments, and groups citing the same methods and data so often arrive at different conclusions in addition to explaining the often inconsistent application of the precautionary principle by governments. Such controversies, I propose, are more about the values and predilections of policy makers and the experts themselves in terms of how they perceive the available evidence than they are about any objective process capable of revealing 'the truth' and, therefore, the correct policy option. Why? Because in the absence of compelling empirical evidence in support of a particular proposition or potential threat – the kind of evidence normally only available after the fact – there is no way of knowing what may or may not happen in any meaningful sense.

The case studies

As the comparative focus of the two case studies demonstrates – strong US, UK and Australian government support for military action against Iraq juxtaposed against equally strong US and Australian opposition to the Kyoto Protocol accompanied by a lack of policy commitment to major greenhouse gas reductions by all three governments – policy makers and the public at large interpret and manage uncertainty in a variety of markedly different, and often inconsistent, ways. In each of the relevant policy decisions and debates discussed here, the relationship between decision making and knowledge has been far from straightforward with uncertainty issues having a major impact on both the framing of each debate and also the ways in which governments and other actors have sought to legitimize their positions, both domestically and within the relevant international regime. This *ad hoc* treatment of uncertainty by policy makers, however, cannot be explained by positivist approaches to notions of knowledge and policy making, which locate knowledge and 'truth' as the ultimate source of legitimacy for political decision making, particularly in liberal democratic states.

The ongoing, and often acrimonious disagreement over global warming and also the ways in which science is often employed to obscure underlying values begs comparison with the much longer running, and arguably even more values driven, dispute over the future of commercial whaling as has been played out in the International Whaling Commission (IWC).[19] Indeed, environmental debates and public health controversies have been a major focus of numerous investigations into the important role played by values in shaping perceptions of science and uncertainty, potential risks, and, in particular, precautionary responses to such potential risks in issue areas where uncertainty is 'high' and the associated risks and policy responses are very much 'in dispute'. Sharing important similarities with how expert advice and values have shaped and framed these two high profile environmental debates, however, is the debate and controversy that surrounded the Bush administration's claims of Iraq's ongoing development and possession of WMD. In addition to further illustrating the important role underlying values and interests play in shaping the interpretation of expert advice and empirical evidence, the controversy over Iraq's WMD also illustrates how the problem of masking values behind unrealistic expectations of science and expert advice is not unique to environmental issues and debate.

Moreover, the case for invading Iraq also illustrates the inherently value-based nature of the precautionary principle's implementation as a 'risk management' tool. By arguing the possibility of Iraqi WMD attacks against the US or its allies, and also the potential for Iraq's WMD falling into the hands of terrorist groups like al Qaeda, the Bush administration effectively based its argument on the need for military action against Iraq on a 'precautionary principle' approach to managing Saddam Hussein's possible but unproven possession of WMD. In other words, the absence of evidence that Saddam still retained WMD was not itself sufficient evidence that they did not exist, given the huge risks the Bush administration and its allies argued an ongoing Iraqi WMD capability would pose. The 'precautionary approach' to uncertainty over Iraq's WMD adopted by the Bush administration is well illustrated by Vice-President Dick Cheney's 'One Percent Doctrine' – that is, the perception of even only a 1 per cent chance of a threat existing must be treated as a certainty.[20]

My analysis of these two policy issues is based on the proposition that uncertainty issues and their interpretation, by experts and policy makers alike, are critical to understanding the issues policy debates focus on and the justifications employed by governments and other actors for the positions they adopt. Knowledge, as the positivists tell us, is indeed the fulcrum upon which policy making turns, but not in the naïve, rationalist sense that portrays policy priorities and decisions as mostly the result of decision makers carefully canvassing and considering the 'relevant facts' and available alternatives in the context of an overarching set of well defined policy objectives (defined by the so-called 'national interest'). As I have noted elsewhere,[21] E. H. Carr's description of 'truth' as 'a word which straddles both the world of fact and the world of value, and is made up of both'[22] cuts to the very heart of why rational, knowledge-based depictions of decision making are far too superficial in their knowledge-driven depictions of policy and decision making, ignoring as they do the inescapable presence and influence of uncertainty issues when decisions are made. The conventional portrayal of the policy/knowledge nexus, then, is becoming increasingly irrelevant in either explaining or justifying policy decisions. As Frewer and Salter argue:

> *The use of scientific advice as an aid to regulatory policy making and decision making is based on two assumptions: first, that the advice and, in particular, its predictive content is accurate and, second, that the public sees the advice as authoritative and the decisions and policy flowing from that advice as legitimate. Both assumptions are now questionable.*[23]

The intelligence assessments used to justify the US-led invasion of Iraq suffered from very high levels of uncertainty over key issues and remained highly controversial in the lead up to the US-led attack. The debate over the need for military action against the government of Saddam Hussein, for example, was reduced to competing interpretations of what was little more than circumstantial evidence concerning both Saddam's alleged possession of WMD and, in particular, his willingness and capability to use them; the evidence supporting US claims of his alleged links with al Qaeda, and Iraq's relevance to the War on Terror (WOT) was even more tenuous. But in spite of the absence of any strong evidence of either Saddam's possession of WMD or any significant threat posed by Iraq, the US administration and its allies, most notably the Howard government and also the Blair government in the UK, nevertheless chose to argue that a large enough threat existed to justify military action.

Numerous and significant uncertainties stemming from the quantity and quality of the data allowed a variety of interpretations of what the available evidence could reasonably be taken to mean, making agreement impossible so long as one has an interest in disputing one or another set of conclusions drawn. Moreover, the broadly held view that Iraq had maintained some WMD capability – shared even by some of the invasion's biggest opponents, France and Germany – illustrates the dangers of confusing 'consensus' with certainty and the influence ideological predispositions can have on the treatment and perception of uncertainty in specialist advice. Of particular interest is the way in which uncertainty was understood in relation to the policy responses Iraq attracted when compared with the Australian and US governments' responses to another major policy debate equally shrouded in uncertainty: global warming and its potential effects.

The US and Australian approach (in addition to several other governments, most notably the UK) to the myriad uncertainties surrounding Saddam's possible WMD and terrorism threat was to downplay uncertainty issues that undermined or conflicted with the evidence used to justify the policy position taken by these governments. In contrast, the Australian and US positions on global warming (unlike the UK and other 'coalition of the willing' partners) were justified not through downplaying uncertainty issues but rather by emphasizing them, even though the global warming debate has been characterized by a good deal more 'consensus' among experts on the existence and related dangers of global warming than was available on the question of Iraqi WMD and the threat they posed.[24]

So what explains this apparent switch in perception and what can explain the differences in interpretation of the same empirical data among experts with similar professional backgrounds and training? Why is uncertainty presented as a reason for cautious reaction – or a 'precautionary' reaction, depending on the specific risks precaution is being used against – in one case (global warming) but not in the other (Iraq's WMD and terrorism links)? And why is the debate in which uncertainty concerns are presented as reason for requiring more certainty before action can be justified also characterized by a much higher level of agreement within the relevant community of experts than in the other case where uncertainty was not deemed to be an obstacle to policy action?

Rationalist-based explanations, underpinned as they are by positivist notions of epistemology, are unable to answer these questions (or perhaps even raise them!). If we are to conceptualize and better understand the inherently political and values-driven context in which interpretations and judgements concerning policy – and the knowledge used to inform and justify it – are developed, Enlightenment-inspired claims to some direct and unfettered relationship with the *real* can no longer be accepted as the ultimate benchmarks for policy design and justification. The alternative, I contend, is to develop a perspective on knowledge that explicitly accepts as its departure point both the value-laden nature of knowledge demarcation, and the problems this presents for knowledge claims, and also the limits of what knowledge – in the form of expert advice – can realistically be expected to contribute given our remote prospects of ever 'knowing that we know' as compared to '*believing* that we know'.

The post-positivist alternative to 'great expectations'

The normative argument I present is a product of my argument concerning uncertainty's treatment outlined earlier. It proposes that policy making move beyond its traditional positivist benchmarks for prioritizing the kinds of knowledge and specialist advice that policy decisions rely upon for justification and legitimacy: a practice that mistakenly relies on naïve expectations for the eventual defeat of uncertainty (we can know, and science can tell us) and inevitably leads to dead end debates over whose experts are right and whose interpretation of the facts is correct. Witness, for example, the political theatre that now passes for debate in the IWC or the ongoing disputes over what global warming impacts may or may not occur or what they might mean in terms of human existence.

The alternative, I suggest, is to further develop and adopt a 'post-normal science' approach to uncertainty and policy making, and the specialist advice that informs decision makers' perspectives on both, as has been pioneered by Silvio Funtowicz and Jerry Ravetz and others.[25] We should accept that the uncertainties surrounding major policy issues, like those selected for this study, are not reducible beyond a certain point for a variety of compelling epistemological reasons (that are certainly not new). Maintaining that certainty, or something resembling it, is attainable provides, as I argue, nothing other than the opportunity for policy protagonists to use uncertainty issues as a disguise for the interests that underlie the policy decisions being taken. But if we accept from the outset that certainty is not available, and that it is competing political agendas rather than simply objective knowledge that set the parameters of policy making and debate, it may be possible to produce debates that, rather than being side-tracked by disputes over who has 'the real science', focus instead on the real political and interest-based obstacles to agreement and compromise.

Put differently, positivist-based ideas of rationality require policy to be based on what we know or assertions that we are at least confident about. The post-positivist approach I am proposing instead requires policy rationality to be judged by recognition in decision making of the limits of what we can claim to know and the accompanying likelihood that policy 'assumptions' may often turn out to be wrong, especially in the kinds of big 'post-normal' policy areas discussed in this book where values and interests clearly do shape knowledge claims and perceptions. This approach, then, rejects the idea that rationality is about 'taking the politics out of policy making'; it instead argues that because uncertainty issues make politics in decision making unavoidable, explicit recognition of the influence of values and interests in policy making is, therefore, essential to any standard for 'rational' policy making and analysis.

Much of what has been done to date in terms of questioning the conventional positivist approach to policy and the role of specialist advice and science has focused on environmental issues and policy. With its daunting complexity, wide and diverse impacts, and often polarizing political effects, it is not surprising that the area of environmental risk has attracted the most interest so far from researchers. Funtowicz and Ravetz's characterization of environmental policy issues as situations 'where facts are uncertain, values in dispute, stakes high and decisions urgent'[26] argues that 'normal science' has little to contribute in such circumstances due to its inability to deal with or reconcile the value-based and ethical dilemmas that define and underpin competing perceptions of 'the problem' and appropriate responses to it. And while the causal complexity of environmental issues does not make science irrelevant, their highly political and often polemic nature do, however, make science and specialist advice captive to competing interests. Even the 'honest broker' type expert, as called for by Roger Pielke Jr,[27] can expect little more than a supporting role in what is largely a form of political theatre where competing interests and issue advocates seek to legitimize their respective positions with the mantles of 'truth' and 'knowledge'.

The political and value-based interests driving disagreement are seldom directly addressed; they are instead obscured by circular disputes over who is 'in charge of the facts' as various expert opinions and interpretations of the data are time and time again presented only to be undermined by other interpretations made equally valid by the many uncertainties involved. Jurgen Habermas, writing in the late 1960s, described this as 'the scientization of politics', a process in which values-based issues and questions (i.e. politics) are redefined as *technical* issues and problems that can be rationally solved or managed by scientific enquiry. Several decades later, Sarewitz linked Habermas's concept of scientization to what Sarewitz called 'an excess of objectivity' in his discussion of how values become lost when debate focuses only on questions of knowing in the mistaken belief that even political problems have scientific answers.[28] The business of politics, in such environments, thus becomes *depoliticized* by the rationality of science and its ambition of a direct correspondence with objective knowledge. According to Habermas: 'The depoliticization of the mass of the population and the decline of the public realm as a political institution are components of a system of domination that tends to exclude practical questions [i.e. questions about morals and values] from public discussion.'[29]

Moreover, this analytical framework's emphasis on the need for competing values and ideological preferences to be recognized and addressed – if uncertainty-driven gridlock is to be avoided – can be more broadly applied to the many policy issues involving specialist advice. Through its identification of a utilitarian approach by policy makers in their interpretation and management of uncertainty issues, the method of analysis I am proposing here can contribute a great deal to our understanding of why government policy is often inconsistent in its management of uncertainty and, in particular, in situations where a 'precautionary approach' is deemed necessary. In the realms of foreign policy and international relations theory, for example, a variety of governments entertain various perceptions of the international environment, the threats and challenges it contains, and also how and why notions of national interest and security should underpin policy decisions. But what informs such perceptions and are they not subject to the same kinds of causal complexity and uncertainty that characterize environmental issues?

States pursuing their respective national interests are constantly engaging in a broad range of policy issues 'where facts are uncertain, values in dispute, stakes high and decisions urgent'. Moreover, they do so in an anarchical environment shaped by perceptions of power and self-interest where intangibles dominate and distinctions between 'reliable knowledge' and 'speculation' seldom exist. Here too, I contend, a post-positivist approach to the role of specialist advice in decision making is required, both domestically at the level of executive government, and in particular at the level of inter-governmental contact in international regimes. As the US intervention in Iraq – and also the declining credibility of the Washington Consensus pro-market style approach to development – demonstrate, failure to recognize the myriad uncertainties and risks of ideologically driven 'grand strategies', or at least hedge against them, can have tragic and often far reaching consequences. And it is precisely because of such consequences that the uncertainties and potential costs involved with implementing such grand strategies, in particular their more irreversible components, be explicitly recognized rather than obscured behind policy justifications based ostensibly 'on the best possible advice'.

Overview

Chapters 2 and 3 further expand both the conceptual issues and the descriptive and normative arguments presented so far in the Introduction. Perspectives on the relationship between decision making, specialist advice and legitimacy, the sources and nature of specialist or expert advice, and the nature and treatment of uncertainty issues and the levels of analysis engaged by the arguments are each discussed in some detail as preparation for the historical analysis of uncertainty's treatment in the two major case studies. Chapter 2 explains how the dominance of rational actor-type perspectives in political science and international relations has created a structuralist bias in our understanding of policy and decision making. Here, the significance of agency is addressed in a discussion of the influence over policy exerted by the executive elite and the important ways in which this influence is shaped by the ideological dispositions and worldviews of these elites. When faced with irresolvable uncertainties and conflicting specialist advice, decision making cannot simply look to the 'evidence' or the 'best advice' for legitimacy and rationality – and so the normative aspirations, values and ideas of the policy elites who must decide what is or isn't policy inevitably shape perceptions of uncertainty within the context of an already established hierarchy of risks and preferred outcomes. Chapter 3 elaborates on the unavoidable, and often irreducible, nature of uncertainty in wicked,[30] post-normal science policy issues, noting also how the absence of certainty, or at least high confidence, creates a legitimacy vacuum for rationalist notions of policy and decision making. Within this vacuum, values become the primary determinant of uncertainty's treatment by decision makers – and, therefore, also what constitutes reliable knowledge – but not explicitly. The salient values underlying policy disputes instead become obscured by conflict over competing knowledge claims, the legacy of rationalist standards of legitimacy, which are used to promote various 'what if', nightmare-like scenarios as evidence for why one policy choice is better than another. Precautionary or pre-emptive approaches to uncertainty and the risks it produces have become the mainstream response to policy problems plagued by high levels of uncertainty. But such approaches also can make our perceptions of uncertainty and risk hostage to the 'power of nightmares', resulting in policy debate becoming narrowed to include only the 'scariest' or most undesirable of outcomes as the Iraq and climate change case studies illustrate.

Chapters 4 and 5 highlight the Bush administration, and Blair and Howard governments' contrasting treatment of uncertainty in the specialist advice available on these two high profile policy issues, paying particular attention to how the values and ideological orientation of the policy elites informed their treatment of the many uncertainties involved. The justifications used for the Iraq invasion and the scepticism and lack of policy commitment displayed towards global warming claims and the Kyoto Protocol illustrate, I argue, the strong influence of pre-existing values, ideals and political interests among policy makers on perceptions of risk and uncertainty. This influence brings into question not only the rationalist view of knowledge and its role in policy making but also the long standing benchmark of rational justification as both the primary source of policy legitimacy and as protection against abuses of government authority and power. I use the example of Iraq to demonstrate the extent to which ideological beliefs and preferences can encourage perceptions of certainty and diminished risk among policy elites, particularly when there is a sudden and significant change in the situational circumstances they face, as occurred, for example, with the unexpected collapse of the Soviet Union and the 9/11 attacks on the US.

Conversely, perceptions of risk and uncertainty over global warming within the US and Australian governments, in particular, were given a very different focus with the policy emphasis placed squarely on material economic imperatives over the potential for environmental damage and security despite the growing 'consensus' among many scientists on global warming's causes and potential effects. Climate change and the notions of environmental security it presented – as opposed to the more traditional and entrenched perceptions of what constituted a threat to state or economic security – sat awkwardly enough within the policy frameworks and priorities of many governments, but nowhere more so than in the US and Australia where both governments actively promoted economic and national security as their primary *raison d'être*. Moreover, the ongoing reluctance shown by many governments to 'securitize' global warming by taking direct and more assertive policy control of the issue in the way, for example, that development became securitized in response to the threat of failing states (see Chapter 6) illustrates the limits of specialist advice on policy even when strong expert consensus is available.

Chapter 6 enlists the commitment of many governments in the developed world, in particular, those in the US, UK and Australia, to neo-liberal economic philosophy to further demonstrate how ideological predilections and normative expectations among policy elites not only shape perceptions of knowledge, but also make such perceptions highly resistant to expert criticism, alternative advice and even mounting evidence of falsification. Neo-liberal economic thinking among policy elites, moreover, exerted influence in a range of policy areas ranging from the threats posed by failing states and the occupation of Iraq, to the market-based emission reduction schemes included under both the Kyoto Protocol and the domestic policies of Annex I governments.

After establishing the descriptive argument's contention that the treatment of uncertainty issues in specialist advice, particularly in the context of major policy issues, is largely determined by how well the advice fits with or contradicts the policy goals and values of the policy elite, the book switches to a normative analysis of how uncertainty issues *should* be managed in policy making, which emphasizes the need to bring politics, and therefore also agency, *back into* policy analysis and debate if we are to avoid the kinds of 'scientization' and 'excess of objectivity' problems discussed by Sarewitz.[31] Chapter 7 uses the long running policy disputes within the IWC to further develop my contention that in situations of high uncertainty (i.e. situations where both time constraints and issue complexity put assessment and advice beyond the capability of normal science), the accompanying knowledge vacuum is filled by competing values and preferences – creating an issue area that while driven by policy preferences and preferred outcomes is still contested under the guise of objective knowledge claims and various invocations of scientific authority. In such post-normal policy issues, uncertainty is selectively emphasized and downplayed by various actors and interests and, as the two major case studies also demonstrate, is presented most often only as something to be overcome rather than as an unavoidable 'fact of life' that should be managed and hedged against. But what the IWC experience also suggests is that acknowledging the need to move beyond positivist ideas of knowledge and policy legitimacy, as the Commission was forced to do by the irresolvable uncertainties that characterize cetacean science, can also 'descientize' debate by forcing the values and the risks they inform into the forefront of policy disputes. Chapter 8 revisits the two main case studies to show how a hedging or 'no regrets' approach to uncertainty could, and should, have been applied in the case of Iraq and what its application might look like in the case of the policy challenges presented by global warming. It summarizes the links between uncertainty, risks and values developed in Chapter 7, before then illustrating alternative hedging scenarios for the decision to invade Iraq and the current debate on climate change policy that focus on uncertainty in the context of competing values rather than objective knowledge.

2
Policy Making and Specialist Advice: Concepts and Approaches

In so far as rationalist policy explanations do acknowledge uncertainty issues, it is only with an implicit expectation that uncertainty is something to be conquered rather than managed. If policy goes wrong, the common response from policy makers is to claim their decisions or actions were justified given the advice they received.[1] Thus, we are invited to assume that had they been given 'accurate' advice, the 'correct' policy decision would have been made. A key rationalist assumption is that 'we can know'; the solution to uncertainty issues then is simply to eliminate them by improving the organization, methods, resources and personnel used in the pursuit of 'knowledge'.[2]

This was the coalition response when US forces in Iraq failed to find the weapons of mass destruction (WMD) upon which the invasion and occupation were originally predicated. Coalition governments quickly turned the finger of blame on the intelligence agencies, the US Central Intelligence Agency (CIA) being the main target, via a flurry of investigations intended to uncover why their analysts had so obviously failed to provide the 'right' advice. Not surprisingly 'intelligence failure' quickly became the stock explanation for why the *raison d'être* of the Iraq invasion was suddenly unravelling. But what this explanation conveniently overlooks is that the advice given to the US government and its allies concerning the threat posed by Iraq's WMD was, in the first instance, never at any point unanimous and, in the second instance, was never provided without caveats explaining the significant and numerous areas of uncertainty it contained.

The main avenues of investigation into how the US and its allies had gotten it so wrong should have focused instead on how and why policy makers in Washington, London, Canberra and elsewhere took the military option with such confidence given the high levels of uncertainty in the available evidence and the dearth of any broad consensus, expert or otherwise, on what it meant. On the one issue where consensus did exist in the Security Council prior to the war – that is, general agreement that Iraq was concealing at least some WMD (thereby demonstrating how consensus also can mislead) – interpretations and perceptions of what it actually meant in terms of an appropriate policy response differed hugely. So how, for example, did policy elites (i.e. those with executive authority) in the 'coalition of the willing' countries interpret the uncertainties they faced, and why was their interpretation of the same evidence and information so markedly different from those who opposed a military solution? Why did they choose to accept some advice over other advice, given the high stakes of military intervention, without *any* reliable means of gauging its accuracy? What role did their respective policy ambitions and ideological persuasions play in their treatment and understanding of the advice on offer? And, most significantly, why did their interpretation and treatment of uncertainty in the case of Iraqi WMD differ so markedly from what has occurred in other issue areas, such as global warming, where both the US and Australian executives chose not to act on the basis of uncertainty, citing instead the need for more evidence before policy action could be justified?

Knowledge and decision making

In 1970, Harold Lasswell famously made a distinction in policy science between knowledge in and for the policy process (policy analysis) and analysis intended to generate knowledge of and about the policy process. Consistent with the positivist paradigm within which Lasswell and other rationalist theorists were working was the straightforward and uncomplicated concept of 'knowledge' that his definitions used.[3] This study, not surprisingly, does not fit neatly within either of these categories; or rather, it simultaneously fits both and neither due to its focus on *knowledge* and what it represents in the eyes of policy elites in particular and society more broadly under conditions of high uncertainty. My analysis is *about* perceptions *of* knowledge and their role *in* decision making with the intention of using the conclusions I draw to then say something *for* policy in the prescriptive sense. It is this important difference in focus that makes this study, like other post-positivist approaches, of a fundamentally different type to those developed within the rationalist school.

The absence of this kind of distinction in mainstream policy analysis, whether *of* or *for*, is illustrated by John Dryzek's 2002 observations about technocratic analysis appearing to be better suited to Australian policy making conditions than those in the US.[4] Dryzek contended that, while the application of technocratic assumptions of rational-comprehensive decision making was ill-suited to explaining policy and decision making in the US – due to what he saw as a politically complex, pluralist system characterized by incrementalism – such rationalist approaches appeared to fare better in Australia where examples of rationalist driven policy making have been claimed.[5] However, as Dryzek also pointed out, a key factor in the apparent fit with Australian policy making was that most of the problems where technocratic policy making was successfully employed were 'quite simple and well-bounded', which brings into question the rationalist model's usefulness when confronting more complex issue areas in which conflicting values and interests make knowledge-based, technocratic approaches much more difficult.

Dryzek stopped short of explicitly making the kind of connection between uncertainty and values on the one hand and decision making on the other that my arguments call for. He also was unclear on the role experts can and should play in decision making, beyond noting the need for 'dissenting professionals' and broader participation. Dryzek did, however, recognize the importance of identifying and communicating across the 'frames at issue' and argued that, because complexity ultimately foils the prospects for rationalist, technocratic models and analysis, post-positivist policy analysis is an approach 'that should work anywhere'.[6] Even more importantly, Dryzek also recognized the need for post-positivist approaches to engage with problem solving and not risk policy irrelevance by offering decision makers little more than criticism of positivist assumptions and methods. And the often neglected task of better 'defining problems' is where post-positivist theories can make perhaps their most important contribution:

> *I should stress that post-positivist policy analysis is not just, or perhaps even mainly, about solving problems. It is also about defining problems, and questioning and destabilizing accepted definitions. A purist critical position here would take us into the critique of political economy and society more generally. While there is nothing wrong in drawing such connections, post-positivist* policy analysis *just has to retain the connection to social problem solving. No apology is necessary in a world that features poverty, inequality, violence, and ecological devastation, none of which are* merely *social constructions.*[7]

Post-positivist thinking then should not avoid policy prescription; nor should it be seen as necessarily antagonistic to rationality as a benchmark for judging choices of action or inaction. And such ideas are not new. In 1985, Douglas Torgerson observed that Lasswell, the scholar most widely identified with rationalist ideals about how policy making and its analysis should proceed, also helped to identify many of the problems and issues that post-positivists now engage with. Torgerson, after describing Lasswell as gaining 'a considerable reputation as a positivist and technocrat', notes that 'there is a certain irony in this, for although Lasswell's work reflects some influence of positivism, he developed an approach clearly at odds with a positivist posture'.[8]

Lasswell's goals, however, remained positivist in so far as his notions of the contextual orientation of policy analysis and exposing the unwanted influence of ideology were underpinned by the belief that a higher order of rationality is possible if we, as Torgerson put it, 'overcome sociopsychological resistances detrimental to the ideal of policy science as a rational collective enterprise'.[9] This study, as I already have indicated, is fundamentally different in its approach and objectives since my intention is firstly to argue that an ongoing presence of values disputes in policy and decision is unavoidable due to the presence of uncertainty and its openness to various interpretations, and secondly to argue that recognition of and open engagement with these values disputes is a far more rational response than clinging on to hopes that a higher form of rationality can be achieved by somehow isolating them from analysis and decision making. Post-positivist approaches to policy in general, and in particular the one I am proposing here, should not be seen as some radical theoretical enterprise aimed simply at deposing rationalism in favour of relativism. The questioning and erosion of positivism's long influence instead should be seen more as a logical progression in the way that we think about knowledge and its role in justifying and legitimizing our actions.

Doing so would help produce more transparent, credible and more consistent policy decisions domestically and, therefore, also better policy coordination and cooperation internationally. As Daniel Sarewitz argues:

> *No longer able to hide behind scientific controversy, politics would have to engage in processes of persuasion, reframing, disaggregation and devolution, to locate areas of value consensus, overlapping interests, or low-stakes operations (e.g. 'no regrets' strategies) that can enable action in the absence of a comprehensive political solution or scientific understanding. In particular, the abandonment of a political quest for definitive, predictable knowledge ought to encourage, or at least be compatible with, more modest, iterative, incremental approaches to decision making that can facilitate consensus and action.*[10]

Sarewitz's call for more 'incremental approaches to decision making' on the basis of consensus being achieved, not on scientific or knowledge disputes but on values and interests, invokes Charles Lindblom's ideas about the need to abandon the quest for 'synoptic' or complete knowledge as the basis of policy and instead to face up to our inability to know very much at all about complex policy issues, or even to reach shared understandings of policy goals. Lindblom's famous description of policy making and analysis as 'a science of muddling through',[11] made necessary by the sheer complexity of policy problems, represents what he later stated 'is and ought to be the usual method of policy making'.[12] But while his portrayal of policy making as incremental steps or 'muddling' is widely recognized as having captured the major shortcomings of rationalist descriptions in terms of how policy *is* made, appeals for incrementalism to become accepted as 'best' policy making practice have been widely criticized[13] often on account of the view that we should at the very least aspire for our most important decisions to be made on more convincing grounds than simply 'muddling through' – a term that seems to not only mock notions of rationality and legitimacy as popularly understood, but one that also sits awkwardly even with Herbert Simon's concepts of 'bounded rationality' and 'satisficing'.[14]

However, in spite of the rationalist rancour incrementalism incited as a policy prescription when Lindblom responded to his critics in 1979, both the first presentation of incrementalism in 1959 and the 1979 revisions remained essentially positivist in the sense that his treatment of knowledge assumed there is a clear divide between what we know, what we can know and what we cannot know. Lindblom also appeared to imply that knowledge of the past is unproblematic (i.e. we know what has been working; it's only the present and future we don't know/aren't sure about). The primary reason, then, for making only incremental policy changes in basically the same direction as before is that we *know* what works and what doesn't from past experience! Even in 1979, when Lindblom made his provocative call for the adoption of incrementalism in policy analysis and cited Thomas Kuhn and Imre Lakatos' work to demonstrate the incrementalist nature of science as further proof of the need to think incrementally, the positivist moorings of muddling through were essentially unchanged, as illustrated by the uncomplicated pluralist view of knowledge (competition over who knows, but 'the truth' eventually emerges) Lindblom employs in describing the importance of 'partisan analysis' in dispute resolution:

> *I should like to suggest that partisan analysis is the most charac-teristic analytical input into politics and also the most productive. It is in a fuller appreciation of how partisan analysis might be improved rather than ... curbed, that policy making can be made more intelligent.*[15]

In response to Lindblom's question about how partisan analysis might be improved instead of curbed, I would argue that there is no point in improving it if persuasion through partisan analysis means disputes over competing knowl-edge claims. What does need improving, however, as Sarewitz argues,[16] is the conditions for consensus on competing values and interests. The best way of doing this is by discouraging the scientization of political debates and allowing such debates instead to remain focused on the actual values and interests that drive them, which, according to Bernard Crick, is the very essence of 'politics':

> *For politics represents at least some tolerance of differing truths, some recognition that government is possible, indeed best conducted, amid the open canvassing of rival interests. Politics are the public actions of free men.*[17]

Partisan analysis, as an instrument of politics, therefore, should be about openly debating values and negotiating interests as a means of persuasion and facilitating compromise, thereby allowing incremental policy responses to be agreed upon and pursued with the size of the policy steps involved being determined by the level of agreement reached. Such cooperation, as Lindblom pointed out in his first article, need not require precise agreement on a policy's ultimate goals, since different actors will often have a different understanding of the goals or benefits the policy is intended to achieve. The point is rather to achieve consensus on the action to be taken rather than requiring or expecting detailed agreement on the outcomes to be expected.

Incrementalism, then, provides a pragmatic policy response to high uncer-tainty issues by shifting the focus to developing consensus on how to proceed, as opposed to holding out for consensus on what we know, as the main criterion for legitimate policy action. Whereas Lindblom saw small incremental policy steps when faced with complexity and knowledge gaps as a source of insurance against getting things completely wrong (George W. Bush should have read Lindblom before invading Iraq!), assuming that past or existing policies were or are to some degree effective, my use of it is more about getting over the problem of competing values and the gridlock uncertainty can create when political debates are scientized. Moreover, my argument on the need for hedging/no regrets strategies in order to manage uncertainty is less about providing confidence that the right decision has been made and more about limiting the damage and costs of being completely wrong.

Levels of analysis

Given the problem and argument I am proposing, some explanation is required of the level of decision making I am focusing on in explaining how uncertainty is dealt with and the influence its treatment has in determining the role and contribution of specialist advice. The focal points of policy discussion today reflect more clearly than perhaps ever before the importance of including perspectives and analyses of both the domestic and international environments when explaining the actions and aspirations of governments, particularly those expressing a strong ideological commitment. Pressing contemporary issues such as transnational threats, environmental values and protection, interventionism, and economic development – which are the stuff of the case studies selected here – demonstrate the extent to which the interface between the domestic and international is driving policy agendas in both spheres. Furthermore, major transnational challenges are clearly beyond the scope of national governments to effectively manage alone and require internationally coordinated responses. Yet it is clear that policy responses at the international level carry with them domestically generated notions of national interest and what is politically acceptable, as perceived by the decision making policy elite of each state; in the post-Cold War era, the interplay between domestic and international policy behaviour, particularly since 9/11, has become too obvious to ignore.

At the international level, the reciprocal policy influence of states and international regimes has been well established by numerous examples and case studies.[18] What is less clear, however, is the extent to which state perceptions of national interest can explain contemporary state behaviour within a regime as opposed to the ability of regime generated influence – stemming from, for example, epistemic communities, social learning, integrative bargaining or contextual factors – to modify state behaviour and interest perceptions. Despite the strong convergence that has developed between neo-realist and neo-liberal institutionalist perspectives over the last two decades, aided in no small part by the rationalist heritage of both schools, they remain divided over the prospects for cooperation and explanations for it when it occurs. Liberal perspectives are relatively optimistic about the potential for increasing international cooperation and the future success of international regimes and other institutions. Structural or neo-realists meanwhile maintain a much more pessimistic outlook informed by what they see as the deterministic influence of an anarchical international system and the perennial occupation of states with their own security in what essentially amounts to a zero-sum game between constantly competing actors. One example of this ongoing divide is the distributional versus integrative bargaining debate between the two camps where realists maintain a strong emphasis on relative gains as an important consideration for states whereas liberal theorists believe they are far less important than the absolute gains for each state that cooperation can produce.[19]

But while both perspectives are undoubtedly able to explain much about the sources and nature of international cooperation and can compensate for each other's shortcomings to some degree if viewed holistically, neither is able, or willing, to usefully engage in analysis at the unit (state) level due to the rationalist foundations they share. Governments and other actors are simply assumed to be 'rational actors', whose interests are given and independent of circumstances, while knowledge is accepted as an unproblematic and objective source of policy and decision making, the usage of which in policy distinguishes the rational from the irrational. Constructivists, for their part, share some of the liberal institutionalist optimism for the possibility of increased international cooperation between states but for very different reasons. Rejecting the rationalist assumptions of realist and liberal international relations theory, constructivists instead argue that interests, ideas and identity are not given but are socially constructed and therefore changeable in the context of social learning or altered perceptions and circumstances. Constructivists, however, generally are ambivalent about the kinds of interests and behaviour that may emerge from this process.

International relations constructivists emphasize the social construction of 'identity' as the main driver of the interests that states and other international actors pursue but say little about how this social construction occurs beyond assertions concerning the collective influence of norms and institutions. Constructivists also generally ignore or are unclear on questions concerning the nature of and obstacles to the shared 'inter-subjective' knowledge and beliefs they posit as underpinning the persuasive capability and influence of such norms and institutions (see Chapter 3). Moreover, the distinction constructivists draw between their key concept of shared understandings of 'social facts' as the malleable material constituting identity and what one can only assume to be 'existential facts' by comparison (the moon, falling pianos, etc) is made highly problematic by situations where uncertainty issues prevent a clear demarcation between the two. Anthropogenic climate change, as opposed to the well accepted reality of a 'changing climate', has remained controversial beyond basic claims of some human influence on climate behaviour. It is, therefore, not yet a 'material reality' but still only a political or social reality or 'fact' since its existence depends entirely on collective belief among the public and in particular among scientific and political elites. The implication here is that existential facts and social or political facts can be easily separated, which, as the debates over climate change and Iraq's alleged possession of WMD have demonstrated, clearly is not always the case.

Constructivism also appears to imply on this basis that existential facts are 'known' and therefore not constructed, thus they persuade on the basis of their status as authoritative knowledge alone. So how do we deal with controversies where, due to uncertainty and competition between competing interests and values, norms are in dispute and institutions divided? How do we encourage the kind of intersubjective beliefs and shared notions of knowledge that constructivists tell us will produce similar identities and therefore similar, and hopefully more complementary, interests? On these questions, constructivism is largely silent.

Powers of perception: world views and ideology

As in the international relations debates of the 1990s, where ideas of structure, identity and interests were contested, policy theorists in the domestic sphere have engaged in similar debates concerning the extent to which government behaviour is autonomous as opposed to a mostly structurally determined enterprise. Here, at the so-called unit or state level, we also need to jointly consider both the internal and external influences on uncertainty perceptions and the treatment of specialist advice. As Peter Hall rightly argues, explanations of policy making need to 'avoid positing too rigid a distinction' between the autonomy of governments and the norms, institutions and structure of society, and recognize that the policy process is a product of various linkages between the two. [20]

Thus, the influence given to societal or international factors needs to be balanced by recognition that levels of state (policy making) autonomy are not *always* dependent on only structural or systemic limits. The roles and significance of interpretation and perception and also the ideas that both shape and are shaped by individual perceptions are now well established in the policy and decision making literature.[21] Shaping these perceptions and ideas are various world views or ideological orientations, and the values and interests they produce, that I argue are the key determinants of how policy makers understand and deal with uncertainty issues. 'Ideas' do play a major, although insufficiently understood, role in the policy making process; the question, however, is whose ideas and under what circumstances are they important?[22] I argue that ideology influences the shaping or rejection of ideas by acting as the lens or medium through which social learning occurs; ideology is itself made up of ideas but they are the foundational ideas against which, as Michael Freeden argues, other or new ideas and concepts are judged and on the basis of which decisions are made:

> *In concrete terms, an ideology will link together a particular conception of human nature, a particular conception of social structure, of liberty, of authority, etc. 'This is what liberty means, and that is what justice means,' it asserts. Ideologies need, after all, to straddle the worlds of political thought and political action, for one of their central functions is to link the two. The political sphere is primarily characterized by decision making and decision making is an important form of decontesting a range of potential alternatives.*[23]

Ideologies, therefore, tell us what concepts mean, which ones are important and how they link together. The result is a construct or world view through which we perceive and understand our environment, the situations we face and the lessons we learn. 'World views are', according to Judith Goldstein and Robert Keohane, 'entwined with people's conceptions of their identities, evoking deep emotions and loyalties. The world's great religions provide world views; but so does the scientific rationality that is emblematic of modernity.'[24] One striking example of how social learning (i.e. the creation of ideas within a particular world view or ideology) is influenced by ideological orientation and its related sets of values and sense of identity is former US Federal Reserve Chairman Alan Greenspan's surprising 2008 admission before the House of Representatives Oversight Committee that his ideologically informed view of the world was flawed and had led to overconfidence in the market's ability to regulate itself on the basis of self-interest:

> (Committee Chairman) Henry Waxman: *The question I had for you is you had an ideology. You had a belief that free, competitive – and this is shown – your statement, 'I do have an ideology. My judgment is that free, competitive markets are by far the unrivalled way to organize economies. We have tried regulation, none meaningfully worked.' That was your quote. You have the authority to prevent irresponsible lending practices that led to the subprime mortgage crisis. You were advised to do so by many others. Now, our whole economy is paying its price. You feel that your ideology pushed you to make decisions that you wish you had not made?*
>
> Alan Greenspan: *Well, remember that what an ideology is, is a conceptual framework with the way people deal with reality. Everyone has one. You have to. To exist, you need an ideology The question is, whether it exists is accurate or not. What I am saying to you is, yes, I found a flaw, I don't know how significant or permanent it is, but I've been very distressed by that fact...*
>
> Henry Waxman: *You found a flaw?*
>
> Alan Greenspan: *I found a flaw in the model that I perceived is the critical functioning structure that defines how the world works, so to speak.*
>
> Henry Waxman: *In other words you found that your view of the world, your ideology, was not right. It was not working.*
>
> Alan Greenspan: *Precisely. That's precisely the reason I was shocked, because I've been going for 40 years or more with very considerable evidence that it was working exceptionally well.*[25]

Alan Greenspan's admission of the role ideology had played in his under-standing and assessment of the US economy, and the world more broadly, is something of a rarity among policy figures, from whom the public expectation is always that they behave as 'rational decision makers' acting on the best possible advice and information. Indeed, in a television and radio debate with Naomi Klein only a little over one year earlier, Greenspan, no doubt aware of the dangers of appearing to be anything less than 'objectively informed', had denied any ideological influence on the policies he had recommended and pursued while Federal Reserve Chairman: 'Well, first of all, ideology is not what I hold. I try to learn what are the facts, and I let my opinions, judged on the facts, not by some preconception, which I regret is what ideology as a notion means.'[26] Greenspan's admission to the House Committee is clearly a devastating blow to rationalist notions of knowledge, the facts it is drawn from and how it informs policy. But it is also an important insight into how world views or ideology do indeed shape both our ideas and the kinds of ideas we find acceptable or plausible.

The dominant policy paradigms or constructs that shape and generate particular sets of policy goals and preferences within governments (e.g. pre-emption/intervention and the export of liberal democracy; neo-liberal economic policy and free trade), as described by Peter Hall[27] and demonstrated by Alan Greenspan's admission of ideological influence, are the result of policy makers at the highest level of government engaging in a process of social learning through the prism of their individual world views as constituted by ideologi-cally informed values and interests. Interests and values then, as understood either individually or collectively, are derived from perceptions of material and non-material circumstances, both past and present, as mediated by one's ideo-logical disposition. Thus, for essentially the same reasons that all observation is recognized as 'theory-dependent' within the natural sciences, so too are our perceptions of the world influenced by what we already believe to be true as per our beliefs about what is and what should be.

Robert McCalla distinguishes between the 'situational' and 'dispositional' perceptions of decision makers.[28] Situational perceptions are, according to McCalla, shaped primarily by the facts of a particular situation whereas dispo-sitional perceptions are influenced much more broadly by experience, ideology and notions of interest. Dispositional perceptions must, therefore, be the more fundamental of the two since one would expect situational perceptions to also be influenced by the broader dispositional perceptions. McCalla's categories reflect George Kelly's notion of 'personal construction systems', which 'are ways of construing the world' based on experience. According to Kelly, 'man creates his own ways of seeing the world in which he lives; the world does not create them for him. He builds constructs and tries them on for size'.[29]

Thus the kinds of facts one would recognize as relevant and the priority given to them in terms of causal explanations, for example, would be largely determined by the preconceived or preformed dispositional perceptions used to observe and interpret a given situation. The kinds of 'evidence' and 'facts' Greenspan mentioned as the basis of his strong free market orientation in policy, according to this view, were selected on the basis of their fit with his understanding of how economies do and should work, while other badly fitting or contradictory facts were given less weight or dismissed out of hand. As Robert Jervis has noted, 'Not being aware of the inevitable influence of beliefs upon perceptions often has unfortunate consequences'.[30]

> *If a decision maker thinks that an event yields self-evident and unambiguous inferences when in fact these inferences are drawn because of his pre-existing views, he will grow too confident of his views and will prematurely exclude alternatives because he will conclude that the event provides independent support for his beliefs.*[31]

Greenspan's confession to being something other than a perfectly rational actor making objective decisions based only on the facts also helps explain why dissenting voices that doubted the market's ability to responsibly regulate itself were not heeded by Greenspan or other subscribers to the neo-liberal brand of economic thinking that had become orthodoxy by the late 20th century, a point not lost on Chairman Waxman:

> *For too long the prevailing attitude in Washington has been that the market always knows best. The Federal Reserve had the authority to stop the irresponsible lending practices that fuelled the subprime mortgage market, but its long time chairman Alan Greenspan rejected pleas that he intervene.*[32]

Greenspan's testimony also indicates that dispositional perceptions or personal constructs could be fundamentally changed by dramatic conflict arising between the two categories. That is, if a situational perception were sufficiently convincing yet at complete odds with one's dispositional perception, then a major change in the latter would likely occur. But such paradigm shifts in policy, in the Kuhnian sense discussed by Hall, seem unlikely without a change of government or a major policy crisis within government, since policy shifts on this scale will be publicly viewed as an admission that the previous policy position was either wrong, a failure, or both, thereby inflicting major political damage on the incumbent government's credibilty.[33] Subsequently, the capacity of even compelling specialist advice to alter established government policy objectives also is severely limited by the electoral damage that governments fear its acceptance and implementation would necessarily bring.[34] The usual reaction of policy elites in such circumstances is to alter the policy justification and the policy settings and/or instruments employed to match the new justification rather than abandon the policy itself (See Chapter 6's discussion of the ideological commitment among many Western governments to the so-called Washington Consensus on economic development).[35]

Agency and decision making: The influence of policy elites

Rationalist explanations, including state-centric theories, credit bureaucratic or state-linked 'experts' as the major drivers of ideas and social learning. More systemic or pluralist orientated explanations, in contrast, only discuss the impact of ideas as reactions to and competition within the social and political structures that inevitably influence and shape the actions and identities of political actors, groups and individuals (collectively referred to as 'the state' in traditional international relations parlance). At the international level, this means that to understand state behaviour, one need only look at the system; patterns of rational behaviour, therefore, can be deduced from particular kinds of systems (states that ignore the limits and constraints of the system do so at their own peril and are 'irrational').[36] The major problem with such structural/systemic approaches of course is the accompanying conclusion that governments (or states) will behave largely the same way regardless of who is running them, which clearly is not the case.[37]

Both the policy ideas of decision makers – shaped by what McCalla refers to as their dispositional and situational perceptions, or, according to Kelly, their 'templets' or 'construction systems' (world views) – and social learning processes need to be addressed if we are to avoid the kinds of deterministic explanations of policy behaviour offered by structural realists and some constructivists (Alexander Wendt, for example, has accused neo-realists of not being 'structural enough')[38] at the international level and pluralist theory in the domestic sphere. Such approaches may be more 'user friendly' due to their parsimonious ontological and epistemological content and aspirations (in order to be 'analytically useful' in terms of its 'explanatory predictive powers' according to Kenneth Waltz),[39] but they also gloss over and ignore the problematic 'human' element for no better reason than it being considered too analytically awkward to deal with. Thus, human decision makers are represented and explained as simply 'rational' or obscured altogether under labels such as 'the state'. And, although constructivists examining decision making controversies at the unit level take a strong anti-positivist position on the nature and role of knowledge in controversies, contructivism in international relations is divided on the question of epistemology, with so-called 'modernist' scholars like Wendt supporting a positivist concept and post-modernist scholars and critical theorists adopting a strong anti-positivist position.[40] Both approaches, however, mostly ignore the individual in so far that their structural bias focuses much more on collective beliefs and behaviour than on the individual ideas and actions of the policy elite.

Where constructivists concentrate on and build from the assertion that identity shapes interests, my analysis requires some thought to be given to the question of how identities are formed in the first instance. This is not to say I have any problem with the proposition that identity and interests are causatively linked as the constructivists claim (although I do not agree that interests are exclusively shaped by identity, since there are many interests shared by very different identities); it simply means that I am unconvinced by the *ad hoc* and somewhat opaque constructivist explanations for how identities come about in the first place. The standard explanation that norms and institutions, like international law, shape identity and behaviour remains very structuralist,[41] despite the caveat that agency and structure are 'mutually constitutive'. On the interaction between agency and structure I am in full agreement, but constructivist accounts of how it comes about are underdone, relying as they do on awkward, underspecified terms such as 'structurationists' to differentiate themselves from structuralists.[42] The basis of this distinction, 'structurationists' argue, is the importance not only of how norms and institutions shape identity and accepted behaviour but also the way that the practice of such norms by states and individuals perpetuates the norms and institutions themselves. Outside of international relations theorizing, this is hardly a new perspective. It is, for example, very similar to Peter Hall's 1993 observations on the impacts of human agency and structural forces on policy making, and also resembles Thomas Kuhn's description of the way in which scientists engage in 'puzzle solving' under the direction of the dominant paradigm.

Existing controversy analysis models, with the exception of controversy focused constructivist approaches, reflect both the state-centric versus structure divide and also traditional rationalist depictions of knowledge and decision making. The state-centric positivist view depicts policy controversies as situations where the scientists or experts who actually 'know' will eventually win out on the strength of their evidence, which is then accepted and used as the basis of policy by 'rational' decision makers. Policy debates, meanwhile, mostly exclude those outside of the domain of state recognized 'experts' in the bureaucracy and academia.[43] The pluralist group politics approach promotes an equally positivist account but instead is a group focused portrayal of competition over 'who knows' within a broader market place of ideas setting that includes non-governmental organizations (NGOs), academia, experts and lobby groups. Again, the assumption here is that the 'truth' will eventually emerge. Social structuralist approaches differ in their focus on the nature of groups within society, as opposed to the group politics model's emphasis on the activities of the groups and the sets of social relations that determine their identity and behaviour. This kind of analysis is distinctly Marxist with its focus on dominant forms of class and gender relations and notions of structural power and influence as exercised by the state and dominant/privileged groups.[44]

As a critique on rationalist assumptions about 'who does what and why', the constructivist emphasis on the need to see interests as something more than pre-determined (by material factors and rational choice) is effective. But as an attempt to explain what those applying rationalist models have never cared to think about, constructivism falls short of the mark with its less than convincing attempt at distinguishing itself from what is not hugely different to a 'garden variety' structuralist account of *why*, as opposed to *how*, we think and do what we do. As Martha Finnemore and Kathryn Sikkink note,[45] both constructivism and rationalism provide a framework or method for conceptualizing social life and interaction between actors, but neither can tell us anything about the nature of the actors themselves or the kind of variance that may occur between actors and the differing outcomes such variance may produce. There is no substantive political content to either, which makes them more methodology than theory:

> In a constructivist analysis, agents and structures are mutually constituted in ways that explain why the political world is so and not otherwise, but the substantive specification of agents and structures must come from some other source. Neither constructivism nor rational choice provides substantive explanations or predictions of political behaviour until coupled with a more specific understanding of who the relevant actors are, what they want and what the content of social structures might be.[46]

Moreover, simply relating behaviour to identity as shaped by broadly shared norms, values and ideas, so defined and explained, implies an understated form of determinism that, as Jeffrey T. Checkel argued, 'overemphasizes the role of social structures and norms at the expense of the agents who help create and change them in the first place'.[47] Doing so also makes it difficult to understand the kinds of big and sudden paradigmatic shifts in thinking described by Kuhn and Hall and reflected in the case studies covered in this book.

Focusing on specific actors, then – in this case policy elites in the executive – is one way of attempting to reintroduce agency to what largely has become a structurally dominated exercise in policy analysis. Concepts of ideology, like Clifford Geertz's cultural framing of the term,[48] support the idea of ideology as a cognitive and normative mechanism promoting a 'collective consciousness' among actors that in turn provides them with ways of making sense of the world and their engagement in it. But what Yves Surel describes as 'the privileged role of certain actors in public policy making' also draws our attention to particular individuals within groups sharing such an ideological bond and their ability to both shape and be shaped by the ideological constructs or frames they subscribe to:

> [C]ognitive and normative frames are fundamentally constituted and modified by the interplay of actors. Far from being simple 'revelations', paradigms are, on the contrary, the product as well as the determinant of exchanges between individuals, groups, and the state in a given society. From this point of view, Sabatier, as well as Jobert and Muller, underline the privileged role of certain actors in public policy making, both in producing and diffusing cognitive and normative frames… For Jobert and Muller, these mediators … 'hold a strategic decision-making position insofar as they construct the intellectual context in which negotiations and conflicts take place, and alliances are created, which lead to the taking of decisions'.[49]

My analysis attempts to integrate the abovementioned approaches by recognizing the interplay between, on the one hand, the social imperatives and influences democratically elected governments are exposed to (constitutional and electoral constraints; the influence of NGOs, think tanks, academics and public opinion) and, on the other hand, the degree to which policy makers, as opposed to the abstract of 'the state', exercise autonomy over the broader policy agenda and the policy instruments and settings they choose to pursue it. Policy makers are of course, in democracies at least, constrained by external factors in both the domestic and international realms and also by the bureaucratic structure and practice upon which they rely for both the creation and implementation of policy. They are as Robert Putnam has argued, engaged in a 'two-level game' in which decision making must balance the pressures and political limits of the domestic sphere against those of the international sphere.[50] But they also are able to affect a significant level of individual agency in choosing and shaping their policy preferences, and it is these policy elites who bear ultimate responsibility for 'rationally' explaining why Policy A is better than other options; it is their perceptions that count most in the final decision on how to act or whether to take any action at all. Robert Jervis believes, 'it is often impossible to explain crucial decisions and policies without reference to the decision makers' beliefs about the world and their images of others'.[51] Gideon Rose makes a similar point in his discussion of how neoclassical realism emphasizes the significance of *perceptions* of relative power and resources held by foreign policy decision makers in order to explain instances of states 'irrationally' ignoring the relative power structures of the international system:

> *Foreign policy choices are made by actual political leaders and elites, and so it is their perceptions of relative power that matter, not simply relative quantities of physical resources or forces in being.*[52]

The argument I am mounting, concerning how individual or more broadly shared perceptions of utility determine knowledge demarcation and decisions to either downplay or emphasize uncertainty issues, could also be applied at the bureaucratic level. The bureaucrats and experts who assemble and deliver the kinds of specialist advice used by policy elites regularly apply their own judgements, influenced in no small part by their respective locations and positions within the bureaucracy, in the course of understanding and implementing standard operating procedures and the policy directives they receive. But there is little point in focusing on the bureaucratic level at the expense of the policy elite unless one assumes, and I do not, that bureaucratic loyalties, bargaining, and competition explain more about why Policy A was chosen than do the values, beliefs and policy goals of the executive. Furthermore, and as Hall also has pointed out, bureaucratic competition and political explanations of decision making 'imports a rather underspecified model of pluralism back into the state itself'.[53] Jervis makes a similar observation on the limits of bureaucratic analysis and its tendency to 'feedback' into other perspectives, arguing that:

> *If … there is a good deal of disagreement within the organization about the goals to be sought or the means that are appropriate,*

then we would have to apply decision-making analysis to the bureaucratic level, and so this approach would lose much of its distinctiveness.[54]

In addition to the numerous compelling arguments that reject bureaucratic explanations of policy behaviour,[55] analysis at the bureaucratic level is not warranted by the executive dominated style of government that characterized the Howard, Blair and Bush tenures in office. And while I argue in my analysis that the differing perceptions, values and priorities of those in the bureaucracy and elsewhere (e.g. academia, think tanks, NGOs) can and do shape the kinds of advice on offer (and the uncertainties it contains), this explains much more about the pervasive nature of uncertainty issues and their effects than it does about the advice policy makers are inclined to accept. Indeed, the Howard and Blair governments and the Bush administration each demonstrated a particularly centralized and executive dominated approach to policy making. Prime Ministers Howard and Blair were widely recognized for their 'hands on' approach to all major policy issues, particularly in the realms of foreign and economic policy, while the Bush administration's foreign and security-related policy decisions have frequently been attributed to the strong influence of particular actors within the executive.[56] Moreover, each of these governments has been accused of politicizing their respective bureaucracies and, in the case of intelligence on Iraqi WMD in particular, attempting to shape the content and nature of the specialist advice received. Thus, because the central problem of this study is the inconsistent interpretation by *policy makers* of uncertainty in specialist advice, the level of decision making I focus on is that of the policy elites – that is those at the executive level who assume public and legal responsibility for policy and its justification. These individuals are the key decision makers who ultimately decide, regardless of the bureaucratic influence and filtering specialist advice may be subject to, not only the policy itself but also the specialist advice it is based upon.

3
Empowering Nightmares:
Uncertainty and the Precautionary Principle

Uncertainty and risk

The explanation I am proposing for the inconsistent treatment of uncertainty issues directly addresses the influence of already established policy goals and political preferences on the interpretation and treatment of uncertainty issues in policy making. Moreover, while my analysis of uncertainty's treatment in policy making broadly defines uncertainty as 'any departure from the unachievable ideal of complete determinism',[1] I also distinguish between two essential kinds of uncertainty that reside within that definition: the more policy relevant uncertainty produced by complex, open systems (causation, potential outcomes and attempts through modelling to represent and predict them); and the comparatively limited (and therefore more manageable) kinds of existential and causative uncertainty found within the more limited systems normal science traditionally has focused on.

Within highly closed, or limited, systems, such as games of chance (coin tosses, card games), probabilities can be calculated and used to predict the frequency of future outcomes or events with a level of reliability dependent on the parameters of the system and our understanding of how it works and is constituted. In closed systems, epistemic uncertainty – gaps in our knowledge of the system – is reducible through research and experimentation at least to the point where our understanding of the system's boundaries and how it works will allow for probability to be calculated, or what Walker et al describe as the ability to be 'certain about uncertainty' (we know what we don't know). However, in such systems, aleatory or variability uncertainty, that is uncertainty over which of the known possible outcomes will turn up next (uncertainty over inherent variability), will always remain and is irreducible. The uncertainty posed by closed systems then is at the level of statistical uncertainty where, although all possible future outcomes can be known and predicted in terms of frequency, the next specific outcome (heads or tails; king of hearts or ace of spades) cannot be known.[2]

In open systems, we are far less confident, not only about what we know but also about what we don't know; we are in effect, uncertain about uncertainty. Both epistemic uncertainties, some of which may be resolvable, and uncertainties over variability (aleatory) underpin a lack of knowledge over both the range of possible outcomes and the mechanisms/factors involved, thereby preventing any reliable calculation of which outcomes may be more or less likely than others. Depending on the nature of the epistemic uncertainties involved and their resistance to further research, some open systems may become well enough understood to the point where they become 'closed' and statistical uncertainty becomes the main obstacle to more reliable prediction. Others may remain in a kind of grey area between quantifiable statistical uncertainty issues and the kinds of scenario level uncertainties that characterize our attempts to understand what kinds of behaviours or outcomes within more open systems are *possible*. According to Walker et al:

> *A scenario is a plausible description of how the system and/or its driving forces may develop in the future. To be plausible, it should be based on a coherent and internally consistent set of assumptions about key relationships and driving forces (e.g. technology changes, prices). Scenarios do not forecast what will happen in the future; rather they indicate what might happen (i.e. they are plausible futures). Because the use of scenarios implies making assumptions that in most cases are not verifiable, the use of scenarios is associated with uncertainty at a level beyond statistical uncertainty.*[3]

It is because of exactly such system uncertainty that the Intergovernmental Panel on Climate Change (IPCC) characterizes climate modelling outcomes as 'scenarios' rather than predictions. Due to the inherent complexity of global climate systems and the many gaps in our understanding of them, the general circulation models used in IPCC reports to gauge future climate change impacts are forced to rely on many assumptions that are, while plausible, often highly speculative.[4] As the IPCC itself made clear in its Special Report on Emission Scenarios (SRES), 'Future greenhouse gas (GHG) emissions are the product of very complex dynamic systems, determined by driving forces such as demographic development, socio-economic development and technological change. Their future evolution is highly uncertain.'[5] This distinction, however, is sometimes left unclear in the presentation and reporting of research findings, particularly in policy debate, allowing the subtle yet important difference in confidence between scenarios and predictions to become obscured:

> *Even though – and we are going back to the late 1980s – the IPCC scientists stressed that the 'predictions' from the climate*

*models were nothing more than 'what if?' assessments to indi-
cate how the real climate system might be expected to respond to
enhanced greenhouse forcing, and that the estimates of warming
must always be linked to the input scenarios, the media and those
who sought to make the case for greenhouse gas emission reduction, almost invariably quoted the highest values of warming,
avoided any reference to the input scenarios and presented them
as IPCC forecasts of actual future global climate.[6]*

Open, complex systems also pose the problem of identifying and understanding their constituent parts. Provided everyone is prepared to agree what
'x' is, and its temporal and spatial limits and scope are very narrowly defined
(i.e. do these particular buildings contain WMD at this time?), it is clearly
possible to demonstrate and quantify x's existence if it can be found (i.e. by
inspecting the suspected buildings). The converse proposition, however, 'x
does not exist' is far more problematic since there is no way of conclusively
demonstrating something does not exist (e.g. I cannot prove that there are no
hobbits living in your garden; Saddam could not prove beyond any doubt that
Iraq no longer possessed WMD). Once we go beyond these very narrow limits
by asking other questions involving more open and therefore complex systems
and definitions (Had Saddam maintained WMD or a WMD capability? What
constitutes evidence of anthropogenic climate change versus naturally occurring climate change? What does 'dangerous' climate change mean?), the uncertainties quickly grow in relation to the level of specificity sought in attempting
to answer the question at hand.

Moreover, even existential assertions made with high confidence can
become clouded by uncertainty once we attempt to interpret what they mean
or represent (e.g. what weapons qualify as WMD? Are Iraqi WMD, if they
exist, a threat? And if so, to whom and on what scale?) within a specific
context as determined by the framing of the issue or problem at hand. The
presentation of Iraq's possible possession of WMD as a serious existential
threat within the context of transnational terrorism effectively reframed the
issue of Iraqi WMD by emphasizing some of the potential costs (i.e. risks – in
this case risks that added to the case for war) of being uncertain about their
existence. Similarly, uncertainties over the scope and nature of climate change
are given significance by attempts to frame climate change as either a man-
made phenomenon with apocalyptic consequences or a naturally occurring
phenomenon largely beyond our control. As Michael Smithson has observed:
'Uncertainty does not simply impose itself on us from the natural world; it is
socially constructed.'[7] According to Carol Silva and Hank Jenkins-Smith:

*A substantial body of research suggests that scientists, no less than
lay individuals, employ normative dispositions and broad beliefs
in reaching conclusions about risks. In its most general form, the
argument is that the concept of risk is concerned with values (the
things that may be lost or gained) that, in turn, are grounded in*

larger normative frames of reference such as culture, ideology, and social experience as collared by gender, race and social status.[8]

The French and German governments' framing of Iraq's likely but unconfirmed possession of some chemical and biological capability as a problem confined within Iraq's borders and of little consequence outside of Iraq's obligations under international law to disarm meant that the uncertainties expressed by the United Nations Special Commission (UNSCOM) and later the United Nations Monitoring, Verification and Inspection Commission (UNMOVIC) over Iraqi WMD were limited largely to the question of whether they did or did not exist and in what quantities. Framed in this way, the uncertainties posed by Saddam's patchy record of United Nations (UN) cooperation mixed with occasional outright defiance appeared as issues best managed by further containment and UN inspections, at least until stronger evidence of the existence/non-existence of Iraqi WMD became available. The Bush, Blair and Howard governments, by contrast, sought to frame the issue in a much broader and more complex context, which greatly increased not only the uncertainties involved but also the potential risks. Why? Because uncertainty is a prerequisite of risk; no perception of uncertainty equals no perception of risk since we know (or believe we know) what will happen or, conversely, are unaware of what may happen. In this sense, as Roger Pielke Jr has noted, ignorance is bliss.[9]

> *The state of uncertainty is a fundamentally human quality because it refers to how we associate our perceptions of the world with our expectations of how we find the world to be. In the absence of perception, there is no uncertainty. When our perceptions suggest that only one outcome is possible, there is no uncertainty and we are sure.*[10]

Perceptions of risk are essentially expressions of the values we attach to 'not knowing' the outcomes of doing either something or nothing (i.e. uncertainty). Thus, the context or framing of a particular policy issue, as defined by the relevant values and interests, represents the boundaries of the system the issue is located within, and also therefore the kinds of uncertainties and risks involved. Separating uncertainty and risk, as statistical/economic definitions of risk do, encourages the removal of values from how we think about them, since, according to this view, risk is little more than an expression of our ability to calculate probability based on experience – 'an ordered application of knowledge to the unknown'.[11] But attempting to 'objectify' risk in this way tells us nothing about how people actually perceive and prioritize risks, which is, as I have argued here, a direct function of our values, beliefs and social experience. This is why, in terms of risk perception, it is possible to be uncertain without risk but never possible to have risk without uncertainty. Uncertainty, then, is unavoidable, and 'risk' an expression of how we understand it.

The limits of specialist advice: Post-normal science

The vast causative complexity of major policy issues, in addition to the huge numbers of variables known *and* unknown, leaves experts and decision makers alike mired in uncertainty over what will happen, when it will happen and what to do about it assuming it does happen. The enormity of the challenge and the limits to what expert advice can actually contribute become even clearer if we add to this already formidable task additional uncertainty over the potential opportunity costs of responding in a particular way to what may happen (the precautionary principle dilemma – acting to avoid potential risks does not eliminate them, it merely changes the kinds of threats that may arise),[12] and also the question of whether those costs are worth the expected, but not guaranteed, benefits of achieving one's original objective, assuming that it was clearly understood in the first place (e.g. what constitutes a 'stable and secure' Iraq and what are the criteria for such a judgement?).

Disagreements over environmental policy, for example, often illustrate the core characteristics of a 'post-normal science' scenario, defined by Silvio Funtowicz and Jerome R. Ravetz as a situation where 'typically facts are uncertain, values in dispute, stakes high, and decisions urgent'.[13] The central problem facing scientific expertise in the realm of post-normal science is the inability of scientists and other experts to reconcile unresolvable uncertainties in the advice that they give with political demands for unequivocal advice on the best (read most rational) policy response. In such a scenario, 'normal' scientific method[14] is out of its depth. Its reliance on reductionist methodologies, testable assumptions and 'hard' empirical evidence becomes highly problematic in issue areas characterized by high levels of uncertainty mixed with perceptions of high risk. The resulting knowledge gaps in highly complex policy challenges, such as the possible causes and impacts of climate change, create dilemmas within which scientific authority often becomes a pawn that is either supported or attacked as the various protagonists selectively choose the bits of scientific advice that best support their positions. In such situations, the appropriate answers are still demanded of scientific expertise, even though the relevant questions and problems that define the parameters of debate are inherently political and, therefore, beyond the scope of science's 'normal' reductionist approach.

As a consequence, the regular order of play in which values have traditionally been believed to be subordinate to objective scientific knowledge becomes inverted; research becomes issue-driven and its worth largely determined by the values it is seen to support. Such post-normal pressures not only limit the analytical and predictive authority of normal scientific method but also increase its exposure to counterclaims and conjecture. Thus, the key to managing post-normal challenges – where scale and complexity make for myriad uncertainties and knowledge gaps – is to develop a more nuanced understanding of science's limits and its unavoidable linkages with values and interests. Where uncertainty and risk are high and values disputed, the first goal is to decrease unrealistic expectations for 'scientific' solutions by attempting to explicitly manage (as opposed to eliminate) both the uncertainties involved and the various risks uncertainty necessarily generates when competition over values intensifies. Ravetz refers to such an approach as 'post-normal science' and defines its method and circumstances as:

> Going beyond the traditional assumptions that science is both certain and value-free, [post-normal science] makes 'system uncertainties' and 'decision stakes' the essential elements of its analysis. It distinguishes between 'applied science' where both dimensions are low, 'professional consultancy' where at least one is salient, and post-normal science where at least one is severe.[15]

The notion of 'normal science', or what Kuhn unflatteringly called 'puzzle solving', has its roots in an earlier time, when the role of science was unquestioningly seen as an unfailingly positive contribution to the equally unquestioned process of human 'progress'. The authority and credibility of science was developed through the many successful outcomes of 'applied' or normal scientific method, where the methodologies used are tried and tested, the uncertainties low and the predictability of outcomes very high. Indeed, it was on the strength of these successes, which came to both define and legitimize the concept of 'modern progress', that the distinction between 'real knowledge' and conjecture or belief was made independent of any theological basis. In this view of science, values have no role (and are in any case subservient to the objectivity of scientific inquiry) and uncertainty is to be conquered or ignored rather than accepted and managed.

But as science began to move beyond the relatively closed systems that previously had been the subject of most research (and many of its great achievements), all the while continuing to question and disprove its own past assumptions and findings, the shortcomings and potential dangers of implementing modern scientific findings became of increasing concern in modern societies. Beginning with the Manhattan Project's creation of atomic weapons and intensifying more recently with the advent of genetic engineering, genetically modified food, the unknown side-effects of some drugs, and, more broadly, the negative impacts that human progress is generally seen to have on the natural environment, public perceptions have increasingly focused on the many things that science does not know and cannot foresee, particularly in terms of the unintended outcomes that sometimes accompany its achievements.

And it is these unintended and unforseen outcomes that characterize both the need for additional ways of viewing the contribution science makes and also the kinds of situation that require them. According to Funtowicz and Ravetz,[16] applied science – practised on the basis of normal science's straightforward assumptions about evidence, observation and verification – then gives way to 'professional consultancy' in situations where, although the system uncertainties may remain relatively low, they nevertheless exist and are made significant by the risks that they pose, which are considered to be very high. The engineering required for a nuclear power station, for example, is well understood and the uncertainties involved may also be relatively well understood, at least to the point where engineers and governments are prepared to build and operate them, more or less in the same way that most people are prepared to fly on commercial aircraft or submit to the surgeon's knife. The problems arise, however, with the inability of the applied science used to build nuclear power stations to account for all of the uncertainties and therefore the cataclysmic risks that accompany something going wrong. On this question, that is whether the potential benefits of nuclear power are worth the small but nevertheless real risks of a Chernobyl-like catastrophe, applied science is of no use since its methods cannot guarantee a disaster won't occur or predict with any accuracy the scale and impacts of any such disaster. The question is a political one, steeped in values and questions of priority and myriad interests, for which scientific methods and knowledge have no answers.

At the professional consultancy level, normal science's predictive capabilities and causative understanding are already being stretched to the limit, forcing often critical decisions and estimates to be made more on the basis of 'professional opinion' and educated guesswork than any tried and tested series of verifiable observations and causative explanations. At the post-normal level, where both uncertainties and potential consequences escalate with at least one becoming 'severe', scientific authority decreases in line with the decreasing ability of specialists to confidently rule out (or at least consign to a very low order of probability) various negative impacts and threats. Rather ironically, it is the enormous potential consequences of getting policy wrong on major policy issues, particularly of the kind dealt with in this study, that force policy makers to increasingly demand what they cannot have: demonstrably accurate assessments based on indisputable evidence for why Policy Option A is better than Policy Options B, C or D – assessments that require more and more specificity in their approach to understanding and identifying patterns of causation.

But doing so, as Stephen Kern argues, introduces only greater levels of uncertainty as attempts at increasing specificity produce only greater complexity and multiplicity of possible variables and factors, thereby further exposing even the most carefully formulated argument to doubt and conjecture over the selection and interpretation of the evidence and data its conclusions are based on. Thus, expert advice is undermined by what Kern calls the 'specificity-uncertainty dialectic' and is, therefore, unable to provide the kind of unequivocal certainty needed to prevent demarcation disputes over the 'best advice' from ultimately being settled on the basis of decidedly 'unscientific' criteria such as political expediency, ideology and perceptions of relative power:[17]

> *[The] argument is a variant of the epistemological cliché that the more we know, the more we realize how little we know; or, specifically applied to causality, the more causes we understand, the more we realize how many more causes there are to discover and how little we actually know about the causes we think we know. I refer to this argument as the specificity-uncertainty dialectic… Thus, as researchers sharpened their understanding of causal factors in the physical, biological and social sciences,*

*they also disclosed new areas of ignorance about what they did
not know, and those areas of ignorance and uncertainty suggested
new projects for more specific inquiry.*[18]

On the one hand, from a policy making or advocacy point of view, the need for
one's position to appear 'rational' requires invocation of empirical evidence
and the assertion of causative links. On the other hand, however, such
evidence and assertions are never uncontestable when dealing with the hugely
complex systems that define the post-normal arena (e.g. global and regional
climate systems and ecosystems), therefore allowing a variety of no less valid
interpretations of what the data should be taken to mean. Moreover, in addition to this problem of specific theoretical interpretations and propositions
being 'underdetermined' by the available data, scientific knowledge and claims
cannot be seen as objective in terms of how individual researchers or experts
choose and understand the facts upon which their conclusions ultimately rest.
Indeed, the once uncontested positivist assertion that science is 'value-free'
because its methods and conclusions remain unadulterated by the specific
circumstances, inclinations and experiences of the scientists themselves has
been widely rejected; our treatment and selection of facts are instead unavoid-
ably 'theory-laden' and, as a result, coloured by a variety of assumptions and
beliefs about the world as we see it.

Recognition of these two obstacles to the idealized positivist notion of
what science represents and can be expected to provide is the direct result
of the growing gap between the predictive capabilities of expert knowledge
and the size and complexities of the policy issues it is expected to assess and
provide answers to. Put simply, science is increasingly called upon but decreas-
ingly able to judge what is safe.[19] Moreover, science has never been able to
independently determine what is good, bad or desirable, since it deals exclusively with the 'how' in terms of achieving particular ends. The ends themselves – or put another way the 'what' – are the stuff of values and interests
and therefore reside in the political realm of ideas, ethics and power. These are
subjects on which science has little to say. Thus, the goals of scientific enterprise and endeavour are set in the political realm and it is the task of scientists
to pursue and achieve them; how they go about it is the business of science and
its methods, but what they set out to achieve is the business of politics.

I am not suggesting that the advice of scientists and other experts is of no
significance in the formulation of policy. I am, however, proposing that it is the
nature of science and the question of how specialist advice is understood and
judged by policy makers that should be focused on in order to better understand how it contributes to decision making. This approach is more useful, I
believe, than simply contending that consensus among scientists or other groups
of experts (however such groups might be defined) can (and does) produce
rational policies and intended outcomes. When looked at in this way, studying
what knowledge represents and how it is used is likely to reveal that the concept
of knowledge and its use as a policy making tool is more about people and their
perceived needs than it is about truth and the reality of the world.

In the policy debates presented here, in so far as *genuine* debate actually occurred,[20] uncertainty issues have been or were prominent in the policy making process with decisions to either emphasize or downplay uncertainties, depending on the political goals being pursued, playing a major role in the justifications made by governments and other advocates (e.g. NGOs, think tanks) in defence of their respective policies and positions. The very nature of knowledge, and the many unresolved epistemological problems it involves, means that uncertainty is unavoidable in any advice or research. Uncertainty, therefore, is a factor that always must be dealt with. The unavoidable nature of uncertainty also means that scientific or specialist advice is always open to attack by either: (a) invocation of uncertainty to argue that the evidence is insufficient to conclude harm will not occur (i.e. the precautionary principle approach to managing uncertainty, which holds that an absence of evidence of harm should not be regarded as evidence of an absence of harm); (b) invocation of uncertainty on the grounds of a lack of scientific evidence to say harm will occur (i.e. the traditional scientific approach to managing uncertainty).

Precaution: How much, when and at what cost?

The precautionary principle (PP) is certainly not a new idea and has been in use, in various guises, for some time. Describing the PP as 'merely old wine in a new green bottle', Alston Chase argues that the precautionary concept has been around much longer than its popularly cited debut during the mid-1970s in German environmental law as *vorsorgeprinzip* (the foresight principle).[21] Moreover, when looked at as essentially a recasting of familiar proverbs such as 'look before you leap' and 'an ounce of prevention is worth a pound of cure', it becomes difficult to argue that the PP is an entirely new idea. What is new about the PP is not so much its straightforward (but unclear) prescription for dealing with uncertainty but rather its focus on who or what should receive the benefit of the doubt.

The basic feature of the PP, through its prescription of a 'look before you leap' approach to managing uncertainty, is its shifting of the burden of proof away from those opposing some activity, policy or substance to those who support it. This forces supporters of the activity or substance in question to demonstrate that it is not harmful while also decreasing or eliminating the need for opponents to show why and how it might be considered dangerous: a switch that represents not only an important reversal of roles in terms of responsibility but also a major change in people's expectations of how uncertainty should be understood and managed. Where the requirement once was to show why, and the extent to which, something was harmful before taking preventative action, it is now necessary, under many interpretations of the PP, to demonstrate why and the extent to which something is *harmless* in order to avoid preventative action – a proposition that, in effect, requires us to know what cannot be known.

Scientific method, according to John Lemons,[22] traditionally has preferred minimizing acceptance of Type I errors (false positive results, e.g. mistaken predictions that an activity or substance is harmful) over acceptance of Type II errors (false negative results, e.g. mistaken predictions that an activity or substance is harmless) when evaluating a testable hypothesis, since Type I errors are assumed to lead to 'speculative thinking' and more likely, therefore, to contain a higher likelihood of error.[23] In other words, it is possible to demonstrate, through inductive reasoning, that something is harmful, but it is impossible to demonstrate that something is harmless due to the finite nature of experience.[24] Thus, if a given activity or substance cannot be shown to be harmful, the traditional view has been to attribute a lower likelihood of error to the conclusion that it is, therefore, harmless (Type II) than to the alternative conclusion that it may nevertheless be harmful (Type I) even though we cannot demonstrate it.

In contrast, the PP – by shifting the burden of proof and requiring those supporting an activity to demonstrate it will not cause harm – forces scientists to conduct and test research in a way that minimizes Type II errors by accounting for a indefinite number of potentially harmful, but less likely, Type I effects. In the case of the International Whaling Commission (IWC) this approach has resulted from the altered political priorities of cetacean management and fisheries more generally and, as a consequence, it has fundamentally changed the nature of cetacean research by turning the role of scientific uncertainty in policy making on its head. Taking extra precautions of the kind built into the IWC's agreed upon but yet to be implemented Revised Management Procedure (RMP),[25] for example, is a practical way of interpreting the PP because it recognizes worst-case scenarios that are not entirely unknown (e.g. unsustainable levels of hunting) and puts in place safeguards against their occurrence (e.g. very conservative population and sustainable yield estimates). But, as Julian Morris argues,[26] requiring 'guarantees' that something will not happen, particularly if there is little or no clear evidence of its eventual occurrence, is unreasonable:

> *The demand that a technology should not be admitted until it has been proved to be harmless means an infinitely high standard of proof. Obviously such a standard can never be achieved. It is epistemologically absurd; it demands a level of knowledge that simply cannot be reached. It is not possible to prove something is harmless, anymore than it is possible to prove there are no faeries at the bottom of one's garden.*[27]

As others have noted, many definitions of the PP exist.[28] All, however, promote this fundamental shift concerning where the 'burden of proof' should lie either explicitly or implicitly. The most widely cited PP interpretation, broadly regarded as the current 'international standard definition',[29] comes from the 1992 Rio Declaration. This version is generally regarded as a *weaker* form of the principle, as opposed to other definitions supported by some environmental NGOs, due to its requirement that protective measures be 'cost-effective' and the absence of any *explicit* repositioning of the burden of proof:

Where there are threats of serious or irreversible damage, lack of full scientific certainty shall not be used as a reason for postponing cost-effective measures to prevent environmental degradation.[30]

In contrast to the Rio definition, which is generally favoured by governments, environmentalists take a much *stronger* line by dispensing with economic considerations and stating very clearly the responsibility of proponents of an activity to demonstrate its benign character:

When an activity raises threats of harm to human health or the environment, precautionary measures should be taken even if some cause and effect relationships are not fully established scientifically. In this context the proponent of an activity, rather than the public, should bear the burden of proof.[31]

But despite their differences, both of these definitions also serve to illustrate one of the most common criticisms made of the PP: its lack of clarity. In all of its manifestations, ambiguity regarding what might constitute a threat worthy of invoking the PP and the extent to which cause and effect relationships need to be established in support of such threats, if at all, diminish the PP's utility as a regulatory tool and also have resulted in it meaning many different things to many different people. The Rio definition, for example, tells us that a lack of 'full scientific certainty' is no reason for not taking action against a possible threat. This is unhelpful in that it seems to presume that: (a) full scientific certainty is achievable – an expectation that cannot be realized; and (b) that the task of distinguishing between serious and 'trivial' threats is straightforward; while providing (c) no indication or guide as to the extent to which or how 'some' certainty need/could be acquired before invoking the PP in the first instance.

Other 'weak' definitions or interpretations of the PP display similar shortcomings, such as the European Commission's requirement for 'preliminary objective scientific evaluation' indicating 'that there are reasonable grounds for concern'.[32] Terms such as 'objective scientific evaluation' are of no use when dealing with conflicting scientific advice on a particular issue or problem, since equally 'objective' (whatever that might mean) analyses of the data at hand more often than not arrive at markedly different conclusions and recommendations. The usefulness of stipulating 'reasonable grounds' is equally dubious for similar reasons. Indeed, as the often acrimonious nature of many policy debates, in particular environmental policy debates, has shown, securing any kind of consensus on what is or is not 'reasonable' is seldom an easy task.

The stronger of the two definitions, supplied by the Wingspread meeting of environmentalists, uses vague wording such as 'When an activity raises threats of harm to human health or the environment…' to make it sound as if we can expect the nature and extent of such threats to be self-evident, which contributes nothing to solving the problem of how threats can be identified, defined and prioritized. Furthermore, this definition's open insistence on the burden of proof being switched to the activity/substance's proponent suggests that the opponents of the activity/substance in question need do little more than flag the potential threats before then waiting to be proven wrong. This is unreasonable both in the epistemological sense, as I have already noted, and in terms of how already limited and over-extended research resources could be expected to deal with testing potentially myriad threats and dangers. Initiatives like the European Commission's requirement for 'preliminary objective scientific evaluation' obviously are intended to make such testing more manageable, but, in the absence of unanimous expert advice, such an approach is likely to raise more problems than it solves.

Another closely related problem that arises from the PP's lack of clarity on these issues is how trade-offs between potential costs and benefits can be managed: a question that highlights the double-edged nature of adopting a precautionary approach to research and technology. Preventing an activity or the use of a particular substance or technology on the grounds of precaution does not eliminate uncertainty (or its potential costs); it merely changes the nature and focus of the uncertainty at hand. What, for example, are the opportunity costs incurred by banning a new, potentially life-saving drug on the basis of unclear evidence that suggests but cannot demonstrate possibly life-threatening side-effects? Without actually using it, no one can ever know. Indeed, as Aaron Wildavsky notes:

> *One could well ask whether any technology, including the most benign, would ever have been established if it had first been forced to demonstrate that it would do no harm.*[33]

One way of illustrating the huge potential cost of being subjected to precaution based on little more than what might happen is to look at how a retrospective application of reversing the burden of proof would affect the technological and medical innovations that have occurred so far. Sandy Starr, for example, cites a survey of 40 internationally recognized scientists[34] in which respondents listed innovations ranging from aspirin, chlorine and the measles vaccine to pasteurization, penicillin, pesticides and even the aeroplane as advancements that all 'would have been thwarted by the precautionary principle'. Furthermore, how does one gauge the consequences of taking a precautionary approach in relation to the outcomes it is likely to provide? Ironically, we probably know less about the negative consequences of banning a given activity than we do about the consequences that applying the PP was initially intended to avoid. Chase uses the examples of the National Park Service's 'Natural Regulation' approach in Yellowstone National Park – which resulted in unsustainable numbers of elk and bison, habitat destruction and widespread erosion – and the spotted owl controversy in the US Pacific North-West during the late 1980s, where logging was banned at considerable economic and social cost on the basis of conclusions drawn from one empirical study that were later shown to be false.[35] Pesticides, according to Ronald Bailey (1999), provide yet another example of the kinds of costs that precaution can incur:

Take the use of pesticides. Humanity has used them to better control disease-carrying insects like flies, mosquitoes, and cockroaches, and to protect crops. Clearly, pesticide use has significantly improved the health of scores of millions of people. But some pesticides have had side effects on the environment, such as harming non-targeted species. The precautionary principle gives no guidance on how to make this trade-off between human health and the protection of non-pest species.[36]

Thus, as Daniel Bodansky also has noted, application of the precautionary principle is not a simple matter of choosing between 'risk and caution'; it is more often a choice 'between one risk and another'.[37] And, as the following chapters will demonstrate, the manner in which potential risks are judged or even recognized is shaped largely by political decisions that can be influenced by any number of factors aside from scientific evidence and advice.

Epistemic communities: Speaking truth to power?

On the question of how specialist or expert advice can contribute to policy making within both national governments and international regimes, the epistemic community approach, developed by scholars such as Peter M. Haas, has had the most to say about how communities of recognized experts influence policy and also the obstacles that can prevent them from doing so.[38] This essentially rationalist approach, however, suffers from its heavy reliance on consensus being reached among experts and failure to address questions such as when consensus should be judged to have occurred; what 'consensus knowledge' represents as a basis for decision making when uncertainty issues remain unresolved; and also the more fundamental question of how 'consensual knowledge' on deeply controversial issues could be arrived at and then broadly accepted. The problematic nature of these problems and questions for epistemic community explanations of cooperation is also shared by constructivist approaches, which despite the anti-rationalist orientation of most, but not all constructivists, has much in common with Haas' concept of epistemic communities.

As the IWC experience[39] and also the case studies presented here indicate, consensus advice from experts on the detail of big policy questions is rare – particularly when the political stakes and uncertainty are high. The specialists and experts making up an epistemic community may very well share the same 'causal beliefs' and 'notions of validity', which Haas describes as central to the concept's definition,[40] but this often does not prevent them from disagreeing over what the same empirical data should be taken to mean. Moreover, specialist or expert advice seldom comes without caveats and almost never is unanimously supported or unquestioned. Haas, for example, contends, in spite of his anti-positivist posturing, that such disputes will eventually give way to consensus because 'correct beliefs' will evolve over time,[41] but here we come to the same dead end that Karl Popper's idea of 'rational criticism' led to when he attempted to resolve the problem of how falsification could lead us closer to the truth. On this point the issue is less about our capacity to uncover or find the true nature of reality than it is about our capacity to distinguish it from other assertions and interpretations when the actual truth finally emerges. Thus, in what sense can a belief or assertion be qualified as 'correct' given the problems involved with recognizing one as such should it ever emerge?

Furthermore, when consensus has occurred before the fact (i.e. without the support of any compelling or unequivocal empirical evidence) it is often confused with or misleadingly presented as 'certainty' (as has been the case with the IPCC climate change projections and as occurred with claims of Iraq's possession of WMD), or has only been arrived at after previously disputed predictions of a particular result or threat have been borne out by it actually taking place (as was the case with the collapse of Antarctic whale stocks in the early 1960s; warnings that the Iraq occupation required much higher troop levels than those deemed adequate by US Defence Secretary Donald Rumsfeld; and the failure of deregulated financial markets to prevent the high risk lending and speculation that led to the 2008 global financial crisis). In this sense, the ability of epistemic communities to 'rationalize' policy making and help avoid undesirable policy outcomes remains unclear.

The other big problem concerning consensus claims is the question of how much consensus is required before uncertainty issues can or should be considered sufficiently resolved for policy decisions to confidently be made. Presenting the existence of a 'consensus' as grounds for ignoring or downplaying dissenting advice or opinion introduces the early mentioned danger of confusing consensus with 'certainty', particularly in the public domain, and may also encourage the assumption that expert generated consensus is unsullied by interests and values and therefore is reliable. This problem largely has been left unanswered, and is further complicated by instances – such as the IWC, climate change and the status of Iraq's nuclear weapons programme – where even a clear majority opinion from experts is unable to compel those with strong ideological preferences or important interests at stake to refrain from using any lingering uncertainties to their political advantage.[42]

With his development of the epistemic communities approach to understanding the impact of specialist advice on policy making and the formation and relevance of international regimes, Haas attempted to bridge the realist/liberal institutionalist divide that has characterized much of the literature dealing with international relations and the potential for (or limits to) intergovernmental cooperation.[43] His studies on the role of epistemic communities in the establishment of regulatory regimes for Mediterranean pollution and chlorofluorocarbon induced ozone depletion,[44] for example, created considerable interest and debate among scholars, but so far there has been little attention paid to the political dimensions of uncertainty and the problems they pose for a central tenet of the epistemic community thesis: the need for 'consensus' among experts in order for their advice to have influence and the unwarranted assumptions that expert consensus is: (a) readily available; (b) recognizable when it occurs; and (c) sufficiently authoritative to override the influence of conflicting values and interests.[45] Put simply, while the epistemic community approach accounts for the epistemological problems inhibiting specialist advice by framing the work of specialists in post-positivist terms (Haas even goes so far as to use Thomas Kuhn's notion of a paradigm to help define epistemic communities),[46] it fails to address the problems that doing so create for notions of what epistemic communities represent and the influence they exert. If we accept, as Haas does, that uncertainty is unavoidable, since knowledge perceptions are socially constructed and therefore inherently political, how, for example, is it possible to avoid situations where uncertainty can be used to undermine consensus when people have an interest in doing so?[47]

The uneven influence of epistemic communities at both the international and domestic levels illustrates the kinds of problems that uncertainty issues and the strong influence of competing interests and ideological predilections can create for knowledge-based approaches to policy making and its analysis. On some issues, such as ozone depletion and, to a lesser degree, climate change, there is strong evidence to support knowledge-based explanations attributing a major role to the ability of epistemic communities to promote shared awareness of a policy issue and provide an accepted knowledge base on which policy can be agreed and implemented. In both these issue areas, epistemic communities were instrumental in regime formation although their ability to influence bargaining between state actors has varied; negotiations on a post-Kyoto Protocol regulatory framework are proving far more complicated than was the case with the Montreal Protocol and its many subsequent, and mostly successful modifications.[48]

However, in the decision to invade Iraq, there is little to indicate that epistemic communities contributing to international security policy – such as the transnational intelligence community operating between the US, UK, Australia and Canada at the inter-state level and the UN's UNSCOM and UNMOVIC – were able to significantly influence policy decisions at either the state or regime level (the Security Council) in the face of high levels of uncertainty and strongly conflicting interests between state actors, which largely went beyond the issue of Iraq's possible possession of WMD. The applications of the so-called Washington Consensus principles to economic development as reflected by the policies of the World Bank and the International Monetary Fund (IMF) and Alan Greenspan's earlier noted commitment to financial deregulation, meanwhile, demonstrate that, although professional consensus within a broad international epistemic community can be achieved, the importance of such consensus can be easily misrepresented or at the very least overstated as a basis for policy and become, as a consequence, impervious to legitimate criticism and dissent.

On this point, expert consensus over the causes and potential impacts of climate change has truncated debate and marginalized professional dissent in ways not dissimilar to what occurred in the late-1990s when criticism of the Washington Consensus as a universal development model began to build.[49] Nobel laureate Joseph E. Stiglitz, whose recent work is essentially a robust critique of the Washington Consensus, became a leading member of this informal group of dissident economists. Other dissenting voices included Dani Rodrik at Harvard, Ravi Kanbur at Cornell and Jeffrey Sachs at Columbia. Even 'pro-globalization' economists such as Jagdish Bhagwati also at Columbia, Bill Easterly (formerly at the World Bank and now at New York University) and Paul Krugman (*New York Times* columnist and Princeton economist) became increasingly critical of the results the Washington Consensus was producing. Bhagwati, for example, stated that an IMF-Treasury-Wall Street cabal had sabotaged any meaningful discourse on the benefits and costs of globalization. Easterly, meanwhile, concluded that, despite the enormous intellectual capital invested in econometric and statistical studies, one really cannot assert that a particular combination of policies will engender sustained growth. Krugman demonstrated that decades of conservative economic ascendancy had not been able to undermine the validity of Keynesian economics and proclaimed that we should all be Keynesians now![50]

Like all positivist models seeking to tie rationality and therefore also legitimacy to the prospect of 'the truth' emerging through a mixture of open debate and objective enquiry and research, epistemic community and other knowledge-based explanations of and prescriptions for decision making and policy are incapable of either recognizing or managing the enormous challenges uncertainty can present in issue areas where knowledge gaps are the norm and causative complexity defies the best efforts of 'normal' scientific method. In these policy scenarios, expert advice and conflicting knowledge claims compete against each other, stripping themselves of the kind of authority that 'speaking truth to power' requires in the traditional rationalist schema. Rather than rationally guiding policy on the basis of what is objectively known, knowledge claims instead become employed in the service of competing interests and the values that underpin them. Policy debate, as a consequence, becomes little more than a quest for a positivist ideal of policy legitimacy that remains politically powerful in spite of its untenable claim to what is little more than an idealized form of rationality.

4
Legitimizing the Iraq Intervention: Threat Inflation Versus Precaution

In his 1978 article 'Analysis, war, and decision: Why intelligence failures are inevitable',[1] Richard K. Betts argued: 'Observers who see notorious intelligence failures as egregious often infer that disasters can be avoided by perfecting norms and procedures for analysis and argumentation. This belief is illusory.'[2] Nearly three decades on, in the wake of the 9/11 attacks and the failed policy rationale for the Iraq invasion, Betts' warning remains equally valid following the various US, UK and Australian investigations into the intelligence on Iraq's so-called weapons of mass destruction (WMD) programmes, which largely have explained the Iraq invasion's erroneous basis as an 'intelligence' rather than 'policy' failure.

Indeed, the many uncertainties over both the continued existence of and, in particular, the threat posed by Iraq's possession and production of chemical, biological and nuclear weapons – and the extent to which the intelligence advice differed on these two questions – were ignored by US, UK and Australian leaders in public statements they made in support of the case for war shortly before the invasion began. On 4 February 2003, for example, Prime Minister John Howard told the Australian Parliament that his government *knew* of the existence of chemical and biological weapons in Iraq (and also the regime's future intentions) despite the absence of any clear, direct evidence to that effect and on the basis of what could only have been, therefore, circumstantial speculation:

> *The Australian government* knows *that Iraq still has chemical and biological weapons and that Iraq wants to develop nuclear weapons. [my emphasis]*[3]

British Prime Minister Tony Blair similarly informed the House of Commons on 18 March 2003 that:

> *We are asked now seriously to accept that in the last few years – contrary to all history,* contrary to all intelligence – *Saddam*

decided unilaterally to destroy those weapons. I say that such a claim is palpably absurd. [my emphasis][4]

One day earlier in the US, on 17 March 2003, President George W. Bush told the American public in his 'Address to the Nation' that:

Intelligence gathered by this and other governments leaves no doubt *that the Iraq regime continues to possess and conceal some of the most lethal weapons ever devised. [my emphasis]*[5]

Betts argued that 'the most crucial mistakes' are most often made by decision makers rather than analysts,[6] yet efforts to explain why the Bush administration was caught off guard by both 9/11 and the absence of Iraqi WMD mostly have targeted 'the usual suspects' – the intelligence agencies – rather than also examining the key issue of how policy makers dealt with the often conflicting assessments on key issues that were on offer. Paramount among these issues were Iraq's intended use of a large number of aluminium tubes; Saddam's alleged plans to import African uranium and claimed links with al Qaeda; and the status of Iraq's chemical, biological and nuclear capability and programmes, and the threat posed by any such capability.

This chapter will apply Betts' observations to the case for war presented in the US, UK and Australia during 2002 and early 2003, focusing in particular on how the dominance of pre-existing policy priorities and goals encouraged the blurring of strategic and tactical capabilities in intelligence assessment as a mechanism for legitimizing the Iraq invasion. By 'scientizing' the debate over Iraq's alleged possession of WMD through the selective use and interpretation of sometimes vague or unsubstantiated tactical intelligence, proponents of the war were able to introduce a range of difficult to dismiss existential threats as justification for military action while also obscuring the partisan values and policy priorities that actually informed the decision to go to war. Investigations into the intelligence assessments and evidence used to justify the US-led invasion of Iraq in the US, the UK and Australia – in addition to the failure of coalition forces and the Iraq Survey Group (ISG) to uncover any evidence of chemical, biological or nuclear weapons in Iraq – indicate that the coalition case for going to war was based mostly on speculative thinking in an environment where, as a joint Australian parliamentary investigation concluded in 2004, 'policy was running strong'.[7] Moreover, the largely speculative conclusions drawn concerning Iraq's threat capability and potential often reflected only some of the many intelligence assessments available during the lead up to the Iraq invasion – much of which was based on dubious sources and occurred largely in isolation from the strategic assessments on offer. *Jane's Intelligence Digest*, for example, noted that much of 'the often flawed intelligence cited' by both the US and UK came from 'outside the usual channels', in particular, the US State Department-funded Iraqi National Congress.[8]

Indeed, the Australian, US and UK governments' approach to the myriad uncertainties that surrounded not only the existence of Iraqi WMD but also the threat they posed contrasts sharply with the much more cautious policy position each government adopted in response to potential climate change threats, where a dearth of clear, uncontested evidence in support of possible impacts was cited as good reason for *not* immediately reducing emissions, or – in the case of Australia and the US – questioning whether emission cuts were even necessary. The high levels of uncertainty in the policy advice given on the threat posed by Iraq instead created a very different policy reaction from these governments, one in which considerable uncertainty over not only the nature but also the existence of the perceived threat was not an impediment to acting against it. And, unlike the position adopted on global warming, the rationale used for interpreting the available evidence on the Iraqi threat was in effect precautionary due to its clear employment of the 'absence of evidence of harm should not be regarded as evidence of an absence of harm' approach to interpreting uncertainty.

Intelligence and the limits of expert analysis and assessment

Within both the policy making and intelligence communities, there is a basic assumption that intelligence analysis and advice are fundamentally different to scientific research and advice because the latter can be tested, demonstrated and repeated as proof of its conclusions while the former cannot. But this distinction is unwarranted in the policy sense since once we enter the 'post-normal'[9] world of science, which is what policy relevant scientific advice usually involves, the normal business of observable and repeatable experimentation and falsification is no longer possible due to the hugely complex systems and myriad variables that policy issues normally involve (one obvious example here is climate change, but even smaller scales such as regional wildlife management still involve very complex systems producing major system uncertainties, particularly over cause and effect). Disagreements on environmental policy often illustrate the core characteristics of a 'post-normal science' scenario, as discussed in Chapter 3, and introduce the problem of how unresolvable uncertainties in the specialist advice on offer can be reconciled with demands from policy makers for clear and reliable advice upon which to base, and legitimize, their policies.

Intelligence, as Paul R. Pillar has argued, is primarily about strategic assessment with the possibilities for tactical assessment and warning being far more limited, particularly in the realm of transnational, non-state-based threats such as al Qaeda, due to the system complexities involved; general trends and intentions can be identified but individual attacks or actions are too specific in terms of the information required and therefore defy prediction unless one gets lucky. Based on the distinctions drawn by both Pillar and Mark Lowenthal, my working definitions of tactical versus strategic intelligence assessment are as follows: Tactical assessment involves specific assertions about what exists (the existential) where (spatial) and is *temporally* limited to the current or short term. It allows only limited interpretive assessment (as opposed to claims) of meaning and significance by necessity of the short time horizons it operates within. In contrast, strategic assessment interprets what is believed to exist, re: the tactical, in the context of an existing logic and accepted set of assumptions and long(er) term goals. Strategic assessment is also distinct from the tactical in that its indefinite time horizons allow for broader use of sources and much more in depth research and analysis, and as a consequence much greater contestability.[10]

Thus, one could argue (as Pillar does) that the 9/11 attacks were a policy rather than intelligence failure because intelligence cannot reasonably be expected to predict a particular terrorist attack for the reasons above.[11] There had been plenty of 'strategic' assessment prior to 9/11 warning of an attack on the US mainland, which policy makers failed to act upon.[12] So 9/11 was, as Lowenthal also notes,[13] a tactical rather than strategic surprise. But the fact that intelligence cannot reasonably be expected to avoid such tactical 'surprises' has been ignored, and this is why the intelligence communities have been left to 'carry the can' for what should have been understood as a policy failure to act on available strategic assessments, rather than a case of policy makers being let down by a lack of specific tactical intelligence, which they cannot realistically expect to have had anyway given the open and complex nature of the system they were dealing with (covert, non-state actors operating transnationally). When we shift forward from the 9/11 attacks to the intelligence on Iraq WMD and the threat their alleged existence posed, it is ironic that again the strategic consensus was ignored, but on this occasion it was undermined by policy makers selectively emphasizing the uncertainties in some tactical and technical assessments while downplaying often higher levels of uncertainty in others. The various post-mortems into why no action was taken to prevent the 9/11 attacks and why the stated policy rationale for invading Iraq proved false have predictably, as Betts observed nearly 30 years earlier, focused almost exclusively on why the intelligence communities rather than the policy makers got it wrong.

Two notable exceptions here are the Parliamentary Joint Committee (PJC) on the Australian Security Intelligence Organisation (ASIO), Australian Secret Intelligence Service (ASIS) and Defence Signals Directorate (DSD) held in Australia during late 2003, and the more recently released (June 2008) US Senate Intelligence Committee investigation into whether the public statements by Bush administration officials, including the president, were supported by the available intelligence. Both reports found numerous instances where government statements in Australia and the US respectively had exaggerated or misrepresented the strength of the available intelligence. The two investigations also found many instances where policy statements were supported by intelligence available at the time but, in doing so, neither report properly addressed the question of why some assessments were chosen over other equally, perhaps more, plausible but dissenting assessments. The Senate Intelligence Committee report also ignored the information available from the UN inspections in assessing the accuracy of the Bush administration's statements given the available evidence and findings at the time. In some cases, the sources of dissenting judgements possessed recognized technical expertise on the issue at hand, as occurred, for example, with the International Atomic Energy Agency (IAEA) and US Energy Department's views on Iraq's acquisition of aluminium tubes and the opinions of unmanned aerial vehicle (UAV) experts from the US Air Force on Iraq's development of UAVs as delivery systems for biological and chemical agents.[14]

Drawing the above distinctions indicates that not only do important differences exist but also that the apparent absence of a commonly understood distinction between the strategic and the tactical can affect our understanding and treatment of uncertainty in the following ways:

1   blurring the strategic/tactical distinction muddies the distinction between intelligence and policy failure by distorting our understanding of what intelligence analysis can reasonably be expected to provide (i.e. it encourages a positivist bias; more specificity equals more certainty); and
2   as a consequence, the need for reform and restructuring of the intelligence community is overemphasized, obscuring the critical role played by policy makers' interpretations of the uncertainties within the analysis and assessments they receive.

According to Heidenrich, confusion of the two terms is common: '[I]n official circles and beyond, too many people attribute meanings to "strategic" and "strategic intelligence" that no dictionary supports. Ignorance of the meaning of these words has bred ignorance of the strategic product, with, in my view, enormous consequences'.[15] Confusing what strategic versus tactical intelligence assessments can realistically be expected to represent and achieve – in addition to an increasing post-Cold War emphasis on current intelligence at the expense of longer term intelligence assessment (broadly understood by some as 'tactical' versus 'strategic')[16] – encourages policy makers and analysts to see uncertainty issues as something to be eliminated rather than managed: 'We can find out what is happening if our intelligence is current enough and specific enough; if we're still not sure (or not getting the answers we want) we need more!'. The Kerr Group in its third report to the US Director of Central Intelligence George Tenet noted a decline in resources provided to the US intelligence community in the post-Cold War period and an accompanying deterioration of its analytical capabilities:

> In response to changed priorities, and decreased resources, the Intelligence Community's analytic cadre underwent changes in both its organization and its methodological orientation. Perhaps the most significant change was the shift away from long-term, in-depth analysis in favour of more short-term products intended to provide direct support to policy.[17]

Moreover, inflated expectations of tactical intelligence and assessment capabilities – sometimes encouraged by some members of the intelligence community in an attempt to appear 'relevant' – also increase the likelihood that uncertainties in assessments will be selectively emphasized or downplayed depending on the advice one is looking for.[18] Why? Because positivist perceptions of knowledge (i.e. 'the truth is out there and it can be known'), once exposed to the enormous system complexities of a 'post-normal' environment, lead to policy issues becoming dominated by often unresolvable knowledge claim disputes, which obscure the competing values and preferences actually driving debate and disagreement. Thus it was possible to interpret the available, and often inconclusive, evidence on Iraq's capabilities and intentions in a variety of ways, depending on either what one believed or wanted to *be believed*. As a consequence, a lack of evidence for a particular assertion could be construed as further proof of, rather than against, that assertion (e.g. inability of UN inspections to find WMD demonstrated the existence of an effective Iraqi concealment programme). In November 2002, for example, the National Intelligence Council prepared a report on Iraq's underground facilities (UGFs) for Secretary of Defense Donald Rumsfeld, which stated that: 'We assess that Iraq has some large, deeply buried UGFs, but, because of the Iraqi denial and deception (D&D) programme, we have not been able to locate any of these...'[19]

In some instances, policy makers went beyond selectively downplaying the relevant uncertainties and knowledge gaps in the available intelligence; they simply ignored them altogether as John Howard did with his February 2003 claim that he knew Iraq still had chemical and biological weapons Even the Office of National Assessments (ONA), which had become – as the Australian Joint Parliamentary Committee (AJPC) inquiry found – more 'definitive' and 'assertive' in its assessments from mid-September[20] would only go as far as saying Iraq was 'highly likely' to still possess chemical and biological weapons. Unlike ONA, the Defence Intelligence Organization (DIO) had remained cautious in its assessments, advising, for example, that Iraq 'probably' retained a small amount of chemical weapons but also warning that such weapons may have degraded over time since there was no evidence of any recent chemical weapon production.[21] Given the conflicting assessments within the broader intelligence community over Iraq's chemical and biological weapon status and the total absence of any hard empirical evidence capable of demonstrating their existence, it is indeed hard to understand how the prime minister came to the conclusion that he *knew* Iraq still had them.

Tactical intelligence and Iraqi WMD: 'Ye can not see the wood for trees'

It remains unclear – without reference to some form of at least indirect policy pressure having been exerted as Paul Pillar and others have asserted[22] – as to why some in the intelligence community in the US, UK and Australia were willing to uncritically accept assertions based on various bits and pieces of often unverified evidence that chemical, biological and even nuclear programmes remained active and in place *despite* a large body of well known contextual information that, at the very least, should have cast doubts over many of the assertions being made in Washington, London and Canberra. Information and assertions that matched established positions and assumptions, which were clearly defined by the 'policy-heavy process' within which analysis and collection occurred,[23] were instead viewed independently of the broader strategic context, particularly in relation to assessments of the actual threat posed by Iraq. Pillar, who served as National Intelligence Officer for the Near East and South Asia from 2002 to 2005, believes that the emphasis and caveats used in assessments, particularly the 2002 National Intelligence Estimate (NIE), were a problem and that there was insufficient alternative analysis, but he largely attributes this to the policy environment in which intelligence was operating. In Pillar's view, policy makers 'bent' intelligence judgements to suit their policies but not in an obvious way; some administration officials, such as John Bolton, however, were far more 'crass' in their attempts to influence intelligence assessments.[24]

As Mark Phythian has argued, it is indeed difficult to conclude that, given the close interface and frequent visits between intelligence staff/senior managers and policy makers, analysts felt no pressure to conform to the policy goals plainly being expressed by the executive in Washington, contrary to the findings of the Senate Select Committee on Intelligence and the Silberman-Robb Commission.[25] Similar findings were presented by the Flood Report in Australia and the UK's Butler Report. But the conclusions of these reports, like those in the US, were based on the absence of any obvious or direct policy pressure to change assessments (i.e. interference that could be demonstrated with 'a smoking gun'). However, the form that policy pressure occurred in was likely to have been much more contextual, creating an environment where it became obvious to analysts not only what policy makers wanted to hear but also what they were willing to accept. As a consequence, it is hard to imagine that analysis was not on at least some occasions shaped to suit such expectations, particularly if analysts or senior officials wanted their work recognized. Frank Lewincamp, former Director of the Australian DIO, has said, for example, that the day after US Secretary of State Colin Powell's speech to the UN, DIO informed the Australian executive that many of his claims were not supported by the available intelligence, but, according to Lewincamp, 'DIO was sceptical that its assessments were getting through to the PM himself'.[26]

Another example of how the 'policy running strong' environment marginalized alternative views and influenced perceptions within the intelligence community of what policy makers expected is the treatment of a Department of Defense (DOD) analyst's concerns over the use of evidence from an Iraqi defector code-named Curveball in Colin Powell's UN speech in early 2003. The DOD 'detailee' – the only US intelligence official to have met Curveball prior to the Iraq invasion – had read Powell's draft speech the day before the Secretary of State's presentation to the Security Council on 4 February and, recognizing Curveball as one of the speech's main sources on Iraq's alleged biological weapons programme, sent an email to the Central Intelligence Agency (CIA) Iraqi Task Force Deputy Chief expressing his doubts over Curveball's reliability (Curveball's information on Iraq's biological weapons underpinned many of the assertions used in building the US case for war, despite various warnings that he was an unproven source *and* a possible fabricator).[27] The deputy chief had already received numerous warnings about Curveball from the same analyst but chose to downplay the relevance of the detailee's mounting concerns. In his email reply to the analyst, the deputy chief wrote:

> As I said last night, let's keep in mind the fact that this war's going to happen regardless of what Curve Ball [sic] said or didn't say, and that the Powers That Be probably aren't terribly interested in whether Curve Ball knows what he's talking about. However, in the interests of Truth, we owe somebody a sentence or two of warning, if you honestly have reservations.[28]

Among the 'big picture' intelligence and information overlooked in this policy dominated process were the findings of UNSCOM, UNMOVIC and IAEA[29] in addition to the lack of *any* material evidence (which was oddly interpreted only as evidence that the Iraqis were hiding WMD programmes rather than evidence that there weren't any); Saddam's son-in-law's testimony in the mid-1990s that Iraq's weapon's programmes had been discontinued; and the rather obvious question of how Iraq could have continued such programmes on any significant scale (some policy statements suggested an even larger scale than before the 1991 Gulf War)[30] without *any* detection over so long a period (1992–2003), especially during a time when intrusive inspections occurred for all but four years (1998–2002) and the country was crippled by economic sanctions and regular US and UK air strikes on its infrastructure. As Hans Blix observed while commenting on the steadfast belief that Iraqi WMD/programmes existed even though no trace of them could be found: 'It is very odd that [the Bush administration] can be 100 per cent certain that WMD exist, but have zero knowledge of where they are'.[31] Former UNSCOM, UNMOVIC and ISG weapons inspector Rod Barton recalls that the 'general feeling' within UNSCOM by late 1998 was that '95 per cent of the weapons had been accounted for'. Furthermore, Barton believes that the material balance assessments of Iraq's prohibited programmes and assessments, which tallied what Iraq was known to have had against what the regime declared or had been found by inspectors, was 'further improved' under UNMOVIC: 'By early 2003 it was already clear that they [the Iraqis] had not reactivated their weapons programmes; it was possible that some capability had been retained... Anthrax, which was likely to have existed in only very small amounts, was the only real problem in 2003 along with mustard gas in terms of chemical weapons.'[32]

In addition to dismissing the consensus from the UN inspection teams that Iraq likely possessed only a small stockpile of chemical weapons and that there was no evidence of any chemical, biological or nuclear programmes having been recommenced, the US, UK and, to a lesser extent, Australian governments uncritically accepted information from unverified or suspect sources, the most notorious of which was Curveball, who provided information on Iraq's non-existent weapons programmes and mobile laboratories. In contrast to the credibility given to these Iraqi sources, however, the information provided by

Saddam's son-in-law, General Hussein Kamel, following his 1995 defection, in particular, his claim that he had ordered all Iraqi WMD be destroyed in 1991, was deemed unreliable. But in spite of such evidence, policy makers were steadfast in their conviction that not only had Saddam Hussein retained a large amount of chemical and biological weapons, but that he remained intent on acquiring more at the peril of Western interests and security. One such example concerns Prime Minister Howard's statement in Parliament on 4 February 2003 that:

> *On the basis of the intelligence available, the British Joint Intelligence Committee judged that: 'Iraq continues to work on developing nuclear weapons – uranium has been sought from Africa that has no civil nuclear application in Iraq…'*[33]

The prime minister made this statement supporting military action against Iraq even though:

1 US Secretary of State Colin Powell had decided to omit reference to the African (Niger) uranium claim in his address to the UN on 5 February;
2 both Australia's DIO and ONA had expressed caution over claims that Iraq was attempting to buy uranium; and
3 the CIA and the US State Department Bureau of Intelligence and Research assessments, which had been made available to the Australian Office of National Assessments prior to Mr Howard's statement,[34] had expressed serious doubts over the reliability of the intelligence and sources used.

One month after the prime minister's statement on 4 February, the IAEA revealed on 7 March that the documents used to support the claim had been forged.[35] Moreover, both John Howard and George W. Bush, who had included the Niger claim one week earlier in his State of the Union address, chose to ignore the doubts over the claim expressed by their own intelligence communities and instead cite undisclosed sources used by British intelligence. According to George Tenet, then CIA Director, he had personally vetoed a previous attempt to include the Niger claim in President Bush's Cincinnati speech in October 2002 due to a lack of evidence supporting the claim. It reappeared, however, three months later in the president's January State of the Union address despite a continuing lack of corroborating evidence and no change in the CIA's assessment of the British claim, which Tenet had described to Congress as 'exaggerated'. The White House also had attempted, according to Tenet, to include the Niger claim in a presidential speech in the Rose Garden one month before the Cincinnati speech, but had been persuaded by the CIA at that time not to include it.[36]

Leaving aside the many problems and uncertainties over the intelligence and analysis used to assert the ongoing existence/production of Iraqi WMD, the main issue of contention in the decision to invade or continue containment – as debated in the Security Council and elsewhere – was the level and kind of threat that Saddam posed if he did in fact have WMD. Of importance here, and also to the question of whether WMD actually existed, is the way in which the three very different kinds of weapons Saddam was alleged to possess or be pursuing – chemical, biological and nuclear – were misleadingly grouped together as WMD even though only a nuclear capability is broadly agreed by experts to qualify as a weapon of *mass* destruction.[37] Grouping the three weapons together while building the case for war allowed the evidence for one set of supporting judgements (e.g. evidence of past possession and usage of chemical weapons) to bleed over into support for claims about other weapons (capabilities and intentions for biological and nuclear weapons and vice-versa). Arguments supporting the Saddam as threat thesis could, therefore, appear to increase the body of evidence they relied upon by simply referring to the existence and threat of WMD as opposed to discussing them as three very different forms of weapon.[38] Intelligence judgements for the most part only referred to these weapons by their individual names and avoided the term WMD, whereas government officials and the media more often referred to them jointly as WMD.

Outside of analysts such as Kenneth Pollack[39] and the material coming out of the Office of Special Plans and the Secret Intelligence Unit within the US Department of Defense and Vice-President's Office (and Whitehall's so-called Iraq Dossier), for example, the bulk of analysis on offer did not see a WMD-armed Saddam as a direct or immediate threat to the US or any of its allies. On the contrary, there was agreement that military action would increase rather than decrease the chances of Saddam actually using any of the proscribed weaponry he was alleged to possess. Bush, Howard and Blair argued that Saddam Hussein, due to his possession of (and intention to secure more) WMD, represented an existential threat to the US and its allies that justified the use of military force even though the 2002 NIE, ONA, DIO and the UK's Defence Intelligence Staff had concluded otherwise. The US Senate Select Committee, for example, judged in its June 2008 report on the Bush administration's use of intelligence in public statements (Phase II) that both Bush and Cheney's statements on Hussein's willingness to provide WMD to terrorist groups for attacks on the US 'were contradicted by available intelligence information'.[40] The report also stated that:

> *The October 2002 National Intelligence Estimate assessed that Saddam Hussein did not have nuclear weapons, and was unwilling to conduct terrorist attacks on the US [sic] using conventional, chemical, or biological weapons at that time, in part because he feared that doing so would give the US a stronger case for war with Iraq. This judgment was echoed by both earlier and later intelligence community assessments. All of these assessments noted that gauging Saddam's intentions was quite difficult, and most suggested that* he would be more likely to initiate hostilities if he felt that a US invasion was imminent.[41] *[my emphasis]*

The strategic assessments that did dissent from or did not support the claims being made by the US, UK and, to a (slightly) lesser degree, Australian governments on Iraq and its threat capability were given short shrift on the basis of essentially 'what if' suppositions that were, as John Morrison argues, being piled on top of each other with little or no supporting evidence.[42] This occurred, for example, with the claims of an al Qaeda link to Saddam from within the Bush administration, statements using Iraq's attempt to import aluminium tubes as evidence of a clandestine nuclear programme, and the Blair government's vague and misleading claim in the now discredited 2002 'September Dossier' concerning Iraq's ability to deploy 'some' of its chemical and biological weapons 'within 45 minutes of an order to use them'.[43] In the case of the aluminium tubes and the issue of Iraq's UAVs, the conclusion of recognized technical experts was insufficient grounds for doubting alternative sets of conclusions that supported the policy position that Saddam's ambitions represented an existential threat. The Bush administration continued to use Iraq's attempted acquisition of approximately 60,000 aluminium tubes as evidence of an active nuclear programme from early September 2002 until March 2003 despite numerous contrary opinions – from the State Department, Department of Energy, US centrifuge experts and the IAEA – stating they were more likely intended for reverse engineering conventional rockets. Secretary of State Colin Powell officially accepted the dissenting UNMOVIC/IAEA opinion on 7 March 2003 at a Security Council meeting. Powell, however, indicated that the issue was not yet fully resolved by adding that the US was 'aware of further technical information regarding the tubes'.[44]

According to the then WMD branch head in the UK's Defence Intelligence Staff (DIS), Dr Brian Jones, dissent from DIS analysts over many of the claims made in the Blair government's 'September Dossier' were discounted on the basis of a mysterious report, often referred to as 'Report X', provided to the Joint Intelligence Committee by Secret Intelligence (MI6). Neither Jones nor his staff were allowed to see the report, but were told that it nevertheless resolved the issues they had with the dossier's claims. Report X was later discredited, but is yet to be released.[45] As the AJPC observed, from September 2002 'there was a ten-fold increase in intelligence reports' but 'most of it untested or uncertain'. As noted earlier, the UK dossier's public release on 24 September occurred only shortly before the public release of the US NIE the following month, and it was from this time onwards – when the policy executive in Washington, London and Canberra stepped up its public campaign on Iraq's WMD and the threat they posed – that some intelligence assessment and reporting became firmer and less cautious, despite the untested and secretive nature of the 'new' intelligence, such as Report X, these assessments were based on. The assessments from Australia's ONA, for example, became markedly less cautious from late 2002 onwards, in contrast with DIO assessments that had remained sceptical of the policy assertions being made in the US concerning Iraq's 'known' possession and development of proscribed weapons. Commenting on the performance of the Australian intelligence community during the lead up to the invasion, the AJPC asserted that:

A large number of the assessments commented on patterns of behaviour within the ambiguous area of dual use. The assessments that were less accurate, from the vantage point of hindsight, were those that assumed the worst, that extrapolated too much from efforts at concealment and that dropped the caveats of uncertainty. This appeared to happen more often and more strongly as the war came closer, and mostly within ONA assessments, certainly after September 2002.[46]

A fine line: precaution or threat inflation?

The majority view across the US, UK and Australian intelligence communities was that no tangible or immediate threat from Iraq existed – even if some WMD capability were assumed, an assumption broadly held at the time[47] – and that containment appeared to be working. The tactical intelligence used to discredit this assessment has since been demonstrated to be totally wrong. But what was motivating senior officials in the US, UK and Australia to interpret the uncertainties involved in the ways they did and what does it suggest about not only the role of intelligence assessment (and specialist advice more broadly) in the policy process, but also the grey area in which assessment and policy meet (or collide)?

Debate over the respective policy motivations within the Bush administration and Blair and Howard governments continues and is unlikely to be conclusively resolved one way or another any time soon. However, the fact that the US was already committed to invading Iraq as early as mid-2002 is now generally accepted, as is the UK and probably also Australian governments' awareness of the Bush administration's intentions by this time.[48] Indeed, by the close of 2002, it was well understood that 'policy was running strong' in the lead-up to the Iraq War and playing a key role in the interpretation and treatment of the intelligence on offer. In short, the US decision was most likely based on a combination of ideological assumptions about the world, what it should look like, and the US role in shaping its future, alongside genuine security concerns over the *future* potential for increased WMD proliferation among 'rogue' states and trans-national terrorism. Blair and Howard, however, were most likely less concerned with the threat potential of Iraqi WMD than they were with the impact that an unsupported US invasion of Iraq would have on US power, and also no doubt what the costs of not supporting the Bush administration might be for their own bilateral relations with the US.

The major challenge confronting the Bush administration's conviction that Saddam would always be a problem and that even if he wasn't currently a threat, he would be in the future,[49] was the difficulty of finding political support to act now against something that did not yet exist. In short, strategic assessments on Saddam, without evidence of a genuine WMD capability (i.e. nuclear weapons) in the short term, would not support the kind of threat potential to the US and its allies that would be needed if an invasion of Iraq was to be successfully sold to voters and, in particular, the Security Council.

Bush – with Blair and Howard's support – in effect applied a 'precautionary principle' approach to dealing with the uncertainties surrounding Saddam and his potential for posing future WMD threats (i.e. 'absence of evidence of harm does not equal evidence of absence of harm') as the rationale for efforts aimed at finding enough tactical intelligence and evidence to undermine the strategic consensus that Saddam was being 'kept in his box' and that inspections, therefore, should continue at least until more compelling evidence of Iraq's capabilities and intentions (i.e. the two defining criteria of a threat) could be found. This approach to managing uncertainty in post-normal policy issues where 'knowing' is unlikely or impossible now informs, to varying degrees, the environmental policies of many governments; it was also the underlying logic of the 2002 US National Security Strategy's pre-emption strategy (and also Vice-President Cheney's 'One Percent Doctrine').

But as noted in Chapter 3, the precautionary principle is highly problematic. Its application is primarily driven by 'beliefs' – argued often on the basis of whatever 'tactical' intelligence or empirical evidence that can be found to support such beliefs – about what might happen, which are themselves informed by perceptions of how likely and how catastrophic or undesirable such outcomes might be (e.g. 'the smoking gun – that could come in the form of a mushroom cloud').[50] The basic feature of the precautionary principle is its shifting of the burden of proof away from those opposing some activity or substance to those who support it. This forces supporters of the activity or substance in question to demonstrate that it is not harmful while also decreasing or eliminating the need for opponents to show why and how it might be considered dangerous: a switch that represents not only an important reversal of roles in terms of responsibility but also a major change in people's expectations of how uncertainty should be understood and managed. Where the requirement once was to show why, and the extent to which, something was harmful before taking preventative action, it is now necessary, under many interpretations of the precautionary principle, to demonstrate why and the extent to which something is *harmless* in order to avoid preventative action – a proposition that, in effect, requires us to know what cannot be known.

Moreover, for some in the Bush administration, the practice of extrapolating 'what if' scenarios from inconclusive tactical intelligence and supposition dates back as far as Gerald Ford's presidency during the mid-1970s when, following a cabinet reshuffle, Donald Rumsfeld became Ford's Secretary of Defense and Dick Cheney his Chief of Staff. Ford also appointed George H. W. Bush as Director of Central Intelligence. Known as 'competitive intelligence analysis exercises' or 'Team B experiments', then CIA Director Bush approved in 1976 an exercise in which CIA and Defense Intelligence Agency (DIA) analysts prepared assessments on Soviet military strategy that would then be compared and debated against assessments from an independent team of 'outside' analysts, which included Paul Wolfowitz.[51] The Team B assessment emphasized the Soviet threat, and in particular the view that Soviet military capability was much greater than what Team A type analysis had been producing in contemporary NIEs. This particular experiment in competitive analysis, intended to improve the quality of NIEs, ended with some disgruntled Team B members leaking their conclusions to the media, which caused significant public controversy and an effective end to the use of competitive analysis for the time being at least. The Team B assessments, selectively leaked to the public and aimed at building support for new weapon systems, were later found to have greatly exaggerated Soviet military and economic capability at the time.[52] Two decades later, however, the Team B approach re-emerged, this time as an attempt to make a case for the Republican Party's advocacy of the ballistic missile defence programme (BMD). On this occasion, Rumsfeld chaired a collection of Team B analysts, which again included Wolfowitz, charged with providing an alternative assessment of the threat posed by the development of ballistic missile technology in countries such as Iran, Iraq and North Korea.

Convened in early 1998 as the 'Commission to Assess the Ballistic Missile Threat to the United States', but better known as the 'Rumsfeld Commission', this Team B assessment adopted the same 'hypothesis-based' *modus operandi* as its 1976 predecessor and again exaggerated the capabilities of potential foreign aggressors.[53] In what appeared as an unmistakably partisan report released in July 1998, in which Republican BMD policy was 'running strong', the Team B analysts attacked the intelligence community's far more conservative strategic outlook, as set out in the 1995 NIE, claiming that emerging missile states such as Iran and North Korea *could* develop an intercontinental ballistic missile (ICBM) capability within the next five years and be able to directly threaten the US mainland, possibly with WMD (the 1995 NIE had stated a time frame of at least 15 years).[54] Writing in 2003, former senior analyst in the US State Department's Bureau of Intelligence and Research Greg Thielmann[55] noted that 'since the [Rumsfeld Commission] report's release, none of the emerging missile states have flight tested a missile with even half the range of an ICBM', and that all of its predictions had been proven 'dead wrong'.[56] Thielmann, in addition to detailing how the Rumsfeld Commission pressured intelligence analysts to emphasize what 'could' happen over what was 'likely to' happen, also noted how the Team B approach yet again had been implemented in 2002 by many of the same identities from 1976 and 1998. This time, however, the policy objective being pursued was war and foreign occupation:

> *Defense Secretary Donald Rumsfeld has come under fire for his part in the Bush administration's misuse of US intelligence to justify the US invasion of Iraq. But Rumsfeld's tendency to hype selective portions of intelligence that support his policy goals was already familiar to intelligence professionals. They remember his chairmanship of a 1998 congressionally chartered commission charged with evaluating the nature and magnitude of the ballistic missile threat to the United States. As with Iraq, Rumsfeld's work on ballistic missiles often ignored the carefully considered views of such professionals in favour of highly unlikely worst-case scenarios that posited an imminent threat to the United States and prompted a military, rather than diplomatic, response.[57]*

Conclusion

So evidence has little role to play in such precautionary calculations about the future where uncertainties abound, except in so far as it can be found to support various propositions about what *might* happen, which are by their very nature often impossible to disprove in the short term environment of policy making and decision. It also, therefore, allows wide scope for the proposal of 'what if' scenarios and the 'piling of supposition upon supposition' in order to undermine alternative perspectives and arguments, which is precisely what the many thinly corroborated tactical intelligence claims about WMD build-ups, al Qaeda links, and a recommenced nuclear weapons programme were intended to do. What occurred then, in the context of a blurred and poorly understood relationship between the tactical and strategic assessments on offer in 2002 and early 2003, was too much significance being given to what was believed, but not known, to exist on the one hand, at the expense of attention to the broader context and the many uncertainties involved on the other. Put another way, tactical evidence was accepted on the basis of assertions about what it *could* mean in terms of threat potential and consequences with little or no attention given to its veracity while strategic assessments of the potential threats and policy alternatives to invasion based only on assumptions about what was known, knowable, or likely (on the basis of the more reliable evidence available) were given short shrift.

The events and circumstances surrounding the treatment of intelligence assessments on Iraq by policy makers in the US, UK and Australia, alongside the choice of evidence and arguments chosen to support the case for war, are clearly at odds with the idea that policy making is an entirely rational process that proceeds in an orderly fashion only upon the basis of what we 'know'. This clearly is not an adequate explanation of how and why policy choices are made or the influence of specialist advice in the policy process, yet rationalist models of policy behaviour and decision making continue to be put forward both as the basis for understanding how governments develop and implement policies and also as the benchmark against which their legitimacy is gauged. The reaction to the 9/11 and Iraq policy failures illustrates this perfectly, I think, since almost every inquiry/commission has focused on the question of why the intelligence was wrong, rather than the question of why the policy makers chose some information/analysis over others as justification for the decisions they made.

The UK Iraq Inquiry, also known as the Chilcot Inquiry, began in mid-2009 with the intention of establishing 'a reliable account of the United Kingdom's involvement in Iraq, based on all the evidence, and identify[ing] lessons for governments facing similar circumstances in future'. At the time of writing, the inquiry was only halfway through its investigation (a full report is scheduled for release by the end of 2010) and had focused initially on the 'major decision makers', most notably former Prime Minister Tony Blair. As a result, the inquiry is yet to release any formal conclusions or findings, but the early indications are that its focus, as with its predecessors, will be on why an otherwise 'rational' policy process broke down due to political interference and how this can be prevented from happening again. Any serious questioning of whether such expectations are even warranted given the role that values and preferences among the policy elite inevitably plays in the interpretation of intelligence uncertainties currently looks unlikely.[58]

The basic assumption being peddled here by the policy makers (and some like Howard said as much)[59] is: 'We made the right decision on the basis of the information we were given; had we received the right information, we would have made the right decision!'.

It is, therefore, the policy decisions that also need to be examined and questioned, particularly in terms of how they are justified/legitimized, rather than only the intelligence/specialist advice that is/was on offer. Reforming the interface between policy and intelligence is the area in which potential reforms should be located, with a particular focus on what intelligence assessment can reasonably be expected to provide, the influence of values and preferences on the treatment of uncertainty, and the responsibility of policy makers to be aware of both these issues in their use of intelligence as justification for the policies they pursue. These examples clearly illustrate the problem of policy makers and advisors being confronted with conflicting specialist advice in addition to the important role their particular interpretations of the uncertainties involved plays in 'knowledge demarcation' at the policy making level. It also illustrates the need for a better understanding of why policy makers often inconsistently interpret and represent uncertainty issues when explaining and justifying their policy decisions – an understanding encompassing more than only the kinds of 'politics distorting rationality' or 'provide more and better information' responses that positivist-based approaches are necessarily limited to by their adherence to idealized forms of rationality and knowledge.

5
Climate Change and the Politics of Precaution

As noted in Chapter 4's discussion of how some intelligence was interpreted in ways meant to undermine conflicting intelligence and assessments and provide a legitimate rationale for the use of force against Iraq, the policy goal of toppling Saddam Hussein's regime had already been well established in US foreign policy and also had strong bipartisan support. And although the removal of the Iraqi dictator was no doubt seen as a positive development by both sides of politics in London and Canberra, it was not a foreign policy priority for these governments. What was a priority for these governments and governments before them, however, was the health of their security and economic relationship with the US, and the longstanding view that their national interests were best served by remaining close to the undisputed global hegemon. Moreover, the practice of finding alternative sources of expert advice and reinterpreting available evidence on the basis of various hypotheticals also had been well established, and was used to great effect by the Rumsfeld Commission to argue the need for US development of a missile defence system. These two developments, in the context of 9/11 and the threat of transnational terrorism, helped create a political environment where a case for invading Iraq could be built on the basis of little more than circumstantial evidence and speculation.

In understanding the Bush and Howard governments' opposition to the Kyoto Protocol and the Blair government's contrary support for it, it is necessary to look again at the already existing policy priorities, political circumstances and values base from which the executive policy elite (i.e. those with the executive authority to publicly state what is or is not government policy)[1] in each government made calculations of the 'national interest' and the Kyoto Protocol's potential for either helping or hindering the pursuit of established policy goals. Among all three governments, policy was again 'running strong' in the treatment of specialist advice, and again the policy debate became dominated by competing knowledge claims and assertions as protagonists arguing for and against the implementation of the Kyoto Protocol looked to specialist advice and uncertainty for evidence and arguments that would 'legitimize' their policy preference. When comparing the treatment of uncertainty issues in the global warming/climate change debate with their role in the arguments and specialist advice used by Bush, Blair and Howard to justify military action in Iraq, the most obvious difference is that uncertainty was used as a basis *for* acting, or as insufficient reason for *not* acting, in one case (Iraq) but then interpreted as a basis *for not* acting, or as insufficient reason for immediate action *beyond* existing policy, in the other (the Kyoto Protocol). A less apparent distinction concerns changes in policy settings and instruments versus a more fundamental paradigm shift in policy goals and priorities as per Peter Hall's often cited analysis of the UK government's shift from a Keynesian economic philosophy to what has since become known as neo-liberalism under Margaret Thatcher in the early 1980s.[2]

The decision to invade Iraq essentially represented a change first in policy settings (more frequent UN inspections and stronger warnings of 'dire consequences' for Iraqi non-compliance) and then a shift in the policy instruments used (military force and occupation rather than containment). The use of military force to topple Saddam Hussein from power was a change in the choice of policy instruments rather than a paradigm shift in policy thinking since the need to remove Saddam from power had been part of publicly stated US policy since at least 1997.[3] And although this particular outcome did not become 'policy' in the UK or Australia until after 9/11, when the Bush administration made their intention to remove Saddam sooner rather than later clear, their respective commitments to US foreign policy and goals – upheld in the interests of strengthening their security and economic relations with the US – were longstanding, bipartisan pillars of nationalist interest perceptions in both countries. The Iraq debate then was not over the question of whether Saddam should go, but rather the question of by what means and how quickly he should go and, in particular, whether the alleged risks his regime posed justified the kind of change in policy instrument advocated by the US and its allies (i.e. from containment to invasion). In contrast, the climate change debate quickly became polarized over more than simply questions of the appropriate settings and instruments. The response mandated by the Kyoto agreement effectively required, in the eyes of the US and Australian governments at least, a paradigm shift in policy priorities and goals within an area of policy where policy makers are highly risk averse: the economy.

Because the policy elite within the US, UK and Australian governments saw military action against Iraq as fitting within their existing policy paradigm – either in terms of Saddam's removal or the importance of security relations with the US – they downplayed uncertainties over the need for, and outcomes of, using military force. In the case of the Kyoto Protocol, however, only the Blair government regarded this agreement's mandatory carbon emission reductions, and the changes they would require in fossil fuel usage and cost, as being compatible enough with existing policy to allow their implementation through further adjustment of policy settings and instruments. For George W. Bush and John Howard, no such accommodation within existing policy and calculations of the national interest was possible – even under Australia's entitlement under Kyoto to a limited increase in emissions until 2012[4] – and a policy shift in economic and energy thinking of the scale required by the Kyoto agreement was unacceptable. For Bush and Howard, it was the implementation of the Kyoto Protocol's emission reductions and the paradigmatic shift in policy priorities and thinking required, rather than the unknown potential for long term climate change consequences cited by the protocol's supporters, that represented the clearest and most immediate threat to the security of their countries. This perception continued despite efforts by some scientists, economists, non-governmental organizations (NGOs) and governments to 'securitize'[5] anthropogenic global warming by arguing that its potential impacts make it at least as compelling a security issue as traditional state-centric notions of threats to the economy or the integrity of the state.

As a *bona fide* threat to the security of states, global warming should, according to this argument, become a policy priority and be given the same level of government attention and resources as other national security issues, such as transnational terrorism and weapons of mass destruction (WMD) proliferation. However, support for the Kyoto Protocol among even its most vocal government supporters like the Blair government ultimately proved to be dependent on the extent to which emission reductions could be reconciled within established policy priorities and security perceptions. Indeed, in terms of government responses to climate change, a significant gap has developed between, on the one hand, policy rhetoric seemingly promoting the securitization of global warming and, on the other hand, an absence of any clear policy commitment or response from governments. As a consequence, global warming has been *securitized* only in so far as the political and scientific debates have become less tolerant of dissent against the orthodoxy of anthropogenic global warming; the implementation of an unambiguous, government resourced and directed policy response – the hallmark of a truly 'securitized' issue – is yet to occur.[6]

Scientizing politics: Climate change and the power of nightmares

By the time of the Intergovernmental Panel on Climate Change's (IPCC) Third Report in 2001, international scientific opinion was largely in agreement that anthropogenic generated greenhouse gas emissions were exerting a warming influence and causing climates around the world to change. But despite claims of a growing consensus around the IPCC's findings, debate and controversy continued to grow, especially over the scale, nature and likelihood of future climate change impacts. Numerous disagreements over the reliability of the global warming scenarios produced by Global Circulation Models (GCMs), and in particular the data and assumptions fed into these models, have continued to rage, allowing differing interpretations of the available evidence and the many uncertainties it involves to be used by governments and various groups to substantiate either their support for or opposition to calls for immediate emission reductions. The Howard government and Bush administration, and various industry groups, initially chose to amplify the uncertainties in climate change science and its predictions as a means of justifying their opposition to emission reductions while also arguing that the levels of uncertainty – over future emission levels, their environmental impact and the effectiveness of the Kyoto Protocol approach – did not warrant the significant economic costs that they believed implementation of the Kyoto agreement would 'certainly' incur.

Indeed, for the governments of highly fossil fuel dependent and energy intensive economies like those of Australia and the US, the potential political costs of emission reductions, whether through cap and trade schemes or direct government regulation and taxation, are likely to be high thanks to the domestic price increases that would inevitably follow from such reductions. Moreover, a global commitment to reducing emissions could also lead to a decline in demand for coal, Australia's biggest export. In the absence of clear and incontrovertible evidence that high social and economic costs are a lesser evil than future global warming impacts, the high social and political value placed upon economic growth, low inflation and low unemployment, and standard of living expectations more generally, will unsurprisingly trump the spectre of global warming disasters many years into the future. Put another way, 'clear and present dangers' to current levels of wealth and security, as represented by the economic costs of emission reductions, are always going to receive higher priority than more distant and poorly known threats looming decades into the future, particularly when the benefits of bearing such costs are distant and unclear.

Shortly before taking office in 2001, then Governor George W. Bush already had made his doubts over the conclusions of global warming science, and the need for more certainty, clear during his presidential campaign: 'I – of course there's a lot – look, global warming needs to be taken very seriously, and I take it seriously. But science, there's a lot – there's differing opinions. And before we react, I think it's best to have the full accounting, full understanding of what's taking place'.[7] Then in 2001, in a letter to Republican senators, President Bush highlighted both energy security and the economy in explaining his rejection of mandatory emission reductions: 'At a time when California has already experienced energy shortages, and other Western states are worried about price and availability of energy this summer, we must be very careful not to take actions that could harm consumers. This is especially true given the incomplete state of scientific knowledge of the causes of, and solutions to, global climate change…'[8] Still focused on energy and the economy, Bush later informed reporters that:

> We are now in an energy crisis. And that's why I decided to not have mandatory caps on CO_2, because in order to meet those caps, our nation would have had to have had a lot of natural gas immediately flow into the system, which is impossible… We'll be working with our allies to reduce greenhouse gases, but I will not accept a plan that will harm our economy and hurt American workers.[9]

In December 2003, Prime Minister John Howard explained his ongoing opposition to the Kyoto Protocol, since informing the Australian Parliament in

2002 of his government's intention not to ratify the Kyoto Protocol, by saying, 'I'm not going to be a party to something that destroys jobs and destroys the competitiveness of Australian industry'.[10] Three years later, in August 2006, Howard continued to downplay the risks of climate change relative to the economic risks of reducing emissions. In an interview with the Australian Broadcasting Corporation's (ABC) *Four Corners* programme, the Prime Minister stated that:

> *I accept that climate change is a challenge. I accept the broad theory about global warming. I am sceptical about a lot of the more gloomy predictions. I also recognize that a country like Australia has got to balance a concern for greenhouse gas emissions with a concern for the enormous burden to be carried by consumers through much higher electricity prices, higher petrol prices, falls in GDP [gross domestic product] of too dramatic an imposition of what you might call an anti-greenhouse policy. It's a question of balance.*[11]

The prudent response, therefore, according to President Bush and Prime Minister Howard, was to resolve the uncertainties through more research before committing to any particular policy response, especially one likely to affect economic and energy security. Underpinning such a course of action, or in this case non-action, is the rationalist policy model and its faith in science's ability to inform policy decisions by producing reliable knowledge, which in turn will be used to arrive at a legitimate policy decision based on science. This approach to uncertainty has remained bipartisan, with the only real difference being disagreement over various policy issues on how much certainty is needed (or how much uncertainty can be tolerated) before acting on the specialist advice and evidence at hand. As Roger Pielke Jr and Daniel Sarewitz have noted,[12] the US Global Change Research Program, for example, has spent billions in government funding since 1989 on research, which, according to then US Senator Al Gore, has been aimed at building political consensus on environmental challenges through the reduction of uncertainty. According to Senator Gore, the solution to complex policy problems was obvious: 'More research and better research and better targeted research is absolutely essential if we are to eliminate the remaining areas of uncertainty and build the broader and stronger political consensus.'[13]

But as already indicated, the rationalist model can also legitimize decisions *not* to act, to wait and see until the evidence is in, which is precisely what the Bush and Howard governments were advocating despite their acknowledgement of global warming as an important policy issue. For those wanting a policy response sooner rather than later, the obvious strategy is to downplay the uncertainties involved by arguing that failing to act introduces unacceptable risk; rising oceans, increasingly frequent and extreme weather events, and depleted biodiversity are, after all, more fundamental challenges to human societies and their economies than price increases, unemployment and energy shortages even if they are in the distant future. Global warming's credentials as a major security issue deserving of the same kinds of policy action taken to protect against terrorism, external military threats and economic recession thus are imbued with a sense of urgency – *vis-à-vis* the logic of the precautionary principle (PP) – that makes taking a 'wait and see' approach more difficult to justify. Such a precautionary approach, however, suffers from the same challenge faced by proponents of the Iraq invasion, that is how to demonstrate that currently imagined future threats will, or are at least likely, to occur? Policy debates, framed in these terms, become dominated by competing perceptions of future outcomes and the nightmares invoked to illustrate them, and provide only a choice between either a 'look before you leap' (wait until we *know* more) or a 'he who hesitates is lost' (take preventative action before it is too late) approach to managing uncertainty and its associated risks.

The executive elites of governments elected to three or four year terms before facing re-election are necessarily more focused on the short term, as are the majority of voters striving to manage today's financial and family related pressures and concerns. Thus, it is hardly surprising for national governments and societies to be less concerned with speculation over threats in the distant future than with those they feel are much more likely to occur in the shorter term. This point has been supported by a 2009 Gallup poll in the US showing higher levels of concern for the economy than the environment in the wake of the so-called global financial crisis. For the first time since the 1980s, levels of environmental concern fell below a sharply increased level of concern for the economy in the US and elsewhere, indicating the extent to which environmental priorities may be a product of economic good times.[14] In the case of global warming, adopting a strong precautionary approach today as protection against future (and unknown) warming impacts will not guarantee a safer future but will guarantee a politically difficult, perhaps even fatal, set of problems for governments that must be addressed in the short term. From a policy point of view, such calculations are unavoidable, but they are seldom, if ever, made explicit in contemporary policy discourse where values prioritizing the importance of maintaining biological diversity and an unchanged natural environment often compete against human-centric priorities such as development and economic growth. As Sarewitz argues, governments seeking to justify or delay policy in the public sphere choose to avoid the politics of competing values and interests where possible, preferring instead to rely on the credibility of 'scientific authority' and invoking it as the source of objective rationality behind the decision taken:

> *If you were a policy maker, would you rather participate in a debate about the scientific aspects of a controversy, or about the interests and values that underlie the controversy? Arguing about science is a relatively risk free business; in fact one can simply mobilize the appropriate expert to do the talking, and hide behind the assertion of objectivity. But talking openly about values is much more dangerous, because it reveals what is truly at stake.*[15]

On the other side of the political equation, we see alternative policy positions supported by groups with very different interests who in turn derive and put forward very different scientific interpretations of the data and evidence in order to objectify and rationalize their own particular policy preference. Environmental groups, alternative fuel lobbies (including the nuclear lobby),[16] and segments of the media, for example, are unrestrained by electoral accountability and view global warming through an entirely different prism of values and interests. For these players, the short-term political and economic consequences of taking action today are of little concern in comparison to the long-term risks they invoke as justification for a PP response. Moreover, the debate over competing knowledge claims has spilled over from climate-related science into the realm of economics where very different arguments have been made over both the current cost of acting against climate change and the future cost of not acting. The Bush and Howard governments cited sometimes sparse or incomplete economic analysis[17] warning of the high costs emission reductions will impose on their respective economies while other analyses, most notably the Stern Report, advised us that the potentially high future costs of not reducing emissions can be avoided if we accept the relatively small cost of reductions now. Stern's approach, which controversially values future benefits and consumption equally with the present as a means of undermining the economic dangers of action today, clearly illustrates the normative dimension of climate change debate. As one economist noted, 'the strong, immediate action on climate change advocated by the authors [of the Stern Report] is an implication of their views on intergenerational equity; it isn't driven so much by the new climatic facts the authors have stressed'.[18] The kinds of risks cited both by Nicholas Stern and the IPCC were indeed extreme enough to capture the public imagination, despite their place in the more distant future, and to compete for priority against the short-term social and economic costs of emission reductions that governments and other groups (e.g. business and industry) have advocated avoiding. Climate science and its many associated uncertainties then, as Stephen Bocking argues, have become 'deeply embedded in political debates',[19] and are regularly invoked in the service of specific interests:

> [T]hose opposed to action on climate view it as more effective to question the science than to defend their interests directly. On the other hand, those advocating climate action tend to minimize scientific uncertainties... In effect science serves as a surrogate for political and economic conflict, imparting authority to positions on either side, but at the expense of becoming fully embroiled in these conflicts.[20]

The interpretation of uncertainty in political debate then is mostly about values, particularly in big issues like climate change where uncertainty is high (preventing science from providing the kinds of specific information policy requires) and values are hotly disputed (which is more important, jobs or polar bears?).[21] But because the rationalist model still survives, despite the sustained scholarly criticism it has received over the years as noted in Chapter 1,[22] many people still think in terms of good policy simply being based on the best knowledge, as demonstrated by the ongoing faith of politicians in so-called 'evidence-based' policy making,[23] which of course means 'scientifically derived' knowledge. So what happens when science can't give us definitive, testable answers? Policy elites and people in general nevertheless claim that the science is on their side in order to make their values and priorities seem more legitimate than other people's (who are using different scientific opinion to do the same thing), which causes what Sarewitz calls the 'scientization of politics'[24] (an inversion of what rationalists call the 'politicization of science'): dead-end debates over who has the 'real' science that obscure the values actually in dispute.

The fundamental conflict in values underpinning the distinction between short-term economic and energy security and long-term 'climate security' becomes, as a consequence, obscured as protagonists use competing scientific claims to gain advantage in what are actually political disputes over competing values (what Sarewitz also has referred to as 'an excess of objectivity').[25] And as the scientific disputes intensify, fuelled by uncertainties, political debate is subsumed into what soon becomes a zero-sum contest for the mantle of scientific objectivity and the policy legitimacy it provides. The result is highly polarized debate that:

1 excludes all but the more extreme policy options (future risk warrants drastically reducing emissions versus economic consequences of reductions and uncertainties over future impacts too great to justify any significant short term reductions); and
2 employs scientific advice and uncertainty as a smoke screen to hide the core values and interests actually driving disagreement between the various actors.

In contrast to the rationalist complaint of politics distorting what otherwise could be rational policy making informed by science – popularly referred to as the 'politicization of science' – highly complex, or 'wicked', policy problems like climate change most often create debates where the 'scientization of politics' becomes the main obstacle not only to the development of any broadly supported policy, but also to policy responses made *rational* by their attempt to manage rather than vanquish uncertainty issues.

The United Nations Framework Convention on Climate Change (UNFCCC), for example, frames climate change in the positivist, human-centric language of anthropogenic global warming and betrays an ongoing subscription to the linear good science equals good policy orthodoxy of the rationalist model. By doing so, the convention has effectively encouraged the scientization of policy debate from the outset. The UNFCCC, unlike the much broader IPCC definition, defines climate change as an issue of policy and decision making *only* in terms of human activity having a 'dangerous' influence on climate and by doing so automatically excludes natural climate change or variation as irrelevant in addition to causing confusion over what is or is not conclusively known about current climate change's causes.[26] Making such a distinction, however, assumes that not only is the distinction between human and naturally caused climate change knowable on the basis of science, but also that the question of what constitutes 'dangerous climate change' can be resolved scientifically.[27] Thus, according to the UNFCCC, climate change can only qualify as a policy issue if it can be shown to be both human induced and dangerous. As a consequence, the climate change debate has become extremely narrow in its scope, limited to unresolvable disagreement over one set of potential causes and outcomes (greenhouse gases or GHG, in particular, carbon emissions, are the primary cause of future climate change threats), and one set of unimplementable policy proposals in response to those highly uncertain outcomes and causes (global reduction of carbon emissions is necessary to mitigate future climate change threats).

This narrow framing of the climate debate to date is well illustrated by the 2009 announcement of a conference convened by the University of Oxford, the Tyndall Centre for Climate Change Research and the UK Met Office entitled: '4 Degrees and Beyond: Implications for People, Ecosystems and the Earth System'. Ignoring ongoing uncertainties over climate sensitivity, feedback mechanisms and future human behaviour that so far have prevented the IPCC from asserting anything more than a *possible* temperature range over this century, adjusted in 2007 to between 1.1°C and 6.4°C, the conference's call for participants asserts that global temperature will increase 'well beyond' 4°C and limits its focus only to the consequences and policy options relevant to such a major increase:

> *Despite 17 years of political negotiations since the Rio Earth Summit, global greenhouse gas emissions have continued to rise, which presents the global community with a stark challenge: Either instigate an immediate and radical reversal in existing emission trends or accept global temperature rises well beyond 4°C.*[28]

Thus, according to the conference organizers, societies and policy makers alike are confronted only with a simple choice between accepting the costs of radical action to dramatically reduce emissions immediately or accepting the implied catastrophic consequences of an extreme increase in global temperatures somewhere beyond 4°C. Such framings of the climate change/global warming issue, relying as they do on a misrepresentation of the complexities and uncertainties involved in order to invoke future nightmare scenarios as the cost of not following one particular course of action (and indeed with no regard for the costs of following that course of action), serve only to further delay policy responses and cooperation. The choice presented here is for the vast majority of people, and no doubt all governments, completely unacceptable without a good deal more certainty that such a 'stark' proposition is what we must now face, which is of course not available. So, rather than discussing what kind of policies may be adopted and implemented, given the different values, interests and unknowns, debate remains locked within an all or nothing conflict driven by political competition over values but fought in the language of science.

Consensus science versus consensus politics

Contrary to many media claims – such as those inspired by Al Gore's controversial documentary *An Inconvenient Truth*[29] – and the public assertions of some scientists, uncertainties over the causes and especially the potential impacts of climate change have remained plentiful and cannot be dismissed in any serious treatment of the contemporary global climate change debate. Supporters of the mainstream, human-induced global warming view are able to cite climate change facts that are largely uncontested, such as increased GHG levels in the atmosphere and a general warming trend in global temperatures over the last 150 years – a period of warming weather some scientists have argued is not surprising since it begins at the end of a mini-ice age period that began in the 1300s. Furthermore, there is broad agreement and very strong evidence to support both the observed warming trend and the assertion that carbon dioxide levels in the atmosphere are now higher than pre-industrial levels.

There is, however, a minority view that, with some exceptions, dissents from the IPCC assessment less on the broader issue of a global temperature increase and the thesis that human activity has contributed to this increase than on more specific and detailed questions and problems about the extent to which human activity is responsible for the current global – as opposed to regional – warming trend and the many uncertainties that undermine attempts to model the global climate system and 'predict' how it will behave in the long term. The myriad scientific uncertainties plaguing the assumptions used in these models, GCMs, range from issues of climate sensitivity and different forcings, both human-induced and naturally occurring, to unresolved questions about the nature and behaviour of the forcings themselves (e.g. do clouds and aerosols produce negative or positive feedbacks?). The reliability of the future climate 'scenarios' produced by the various GCMs the IPCC relies on is further undermined by their use of economic modelling aiming to foresee global economic growth trends as an indicator of carbon emission trends among both developed and developing economies. The difficulties of doing so, however, have been made plainly evident by the sudden and mostly unexpected onset of the 2008 financial crisis.

It is then the *extent* to which these facts are causally related and the specifics of the assumptions involved, as opposed to *whether* they are related, that is in dispute as is, therefore, the IPCC assertion that it is 'very likely' that increasing global temperatures are the result of human activity.[30] Controversies such as the long running and increasingly acrimonious 'hockey stick' graph debate[31] (a graph used to great effect by the IPCC in its 2001 report to support its finding that higher GHG levels are the cause of higher temperatures), for example, serve to demonstrate that claims of a so-called 'scientific consensus' on even global warming's current causes are problematic at best.[32] Doubts over the current warming trend's exact causes pale in contrast to the inscrutability of what the future impacts of a warming climate actually will be. Even if we do accept the current consensus on global warming, there is little agreement among those who otherwise generally concur with the human-induced global warming theory regarding the kinds of carbon emission reductions needed to reduce future increases in temperature; some warming and GHG retention rate estimates and impact assessments indicate that nothing short of major short-term reductions will be effective. One such study was reported in the *New Scientist* in February 2007,[33] with the report adding that the European Union's (EU) target of limiting global warming to 2°C 'now appears wildly optimistic'. The study claimed that if GHGs are to reach 'safe levels', current global emissions need to fall to between 30–50 per cent of 1990 levels by 2050 (the Kyoto Protocol aimed to reduce the collective GHG emissions of industrialized countries by 5.2 per cent compared to 1990 levels by 2012). If such studies are reliable, the economic and political costs of trying to avoid the worst of global warming are looking more and more likely to be so great as to be unacceptable to all but the most devout environmentalists; many people, particularly in developing societies, quite simply could not or would not tolerate the serious economic effects that such major, short-term emission reductions are likely to involve.

Moreover, research published in *Nature* illustrates the likelihood of *knowledge* suddenly morphing into questionable assumptions. Four European-based scientists concluded in 2006 that, contrary to conventional scientific wisdom, large amounts of methane (an important GHG) are produced by living – instead of decaying as had previously been assumed – terrestrial vegetation, such as trees. As all good research should, this study both questioned what we think we already know and raises new questions that we haven't previously thought about. One of the questions it raises in the context of global warming is the usefulness of mitigating carbon emissions by using forests and reforestation projects as 'carbon sinks', one of the Kyoto Protocol's major initiatives, since it is now possible that forests are contributing to rather than only absorbing GHGs.[34]

Due to the uncertainties involved, many of which may be unresolvable, the extent to which climate-related impacts on human society are entirely, or even mostly, the result of GHG increases caused by human activity may, therefore, never be entirely clear. The role of natural climate variation, the impact of aerosols, water vapour, clouds and sun spots, in addition to the causes and effects of naturally generated methane, to name but a few areas of concern, all have raised questions that scientists and their climate models remain unable to unequivocally answer or account for. The scientific basis of anthropogenic climate change indeed has reached a point where some level of broad consensus is accepted among many scientists, governments and the public as to the existence, cause and possible future effects of global warming – as opposed to naturally occurring climate change. But the actual science underpinning this consensus is really of little use to policy makers working within and limited by, for the purposes of legitimacy, the rational actor paradigm, since the justification of major policy changes requires what normal science is unable to provide in 'post-normal' situations: certainty or near certainty about not only present causes but also future effects.

What has become apparent since the Kyoto Protocol, and its attempt to compel societies and their governments to prioritize 'climate security' over economic and energy security, is that the 'scientific' consensus, plagued as it is by untestable assumptions, knowledge gaps, and the reliability of peer review,[35] is not on its own a sufficient basis for 'political' consensus when important or entrenched values and interests are at stake. The 'science informing policy and making it [a] rational depiction' of how policy should be made relies on science being able to provide certainty, or something very close to it, in its explanations of phenomena and cause and effect – at least to the point where all are sufficiently compelled by logic and reason to choose only the 'right' response as illuminated by science. But science is seldom able to provide such guarantees and guidance in issues of policy where complexity and uncertainty abound and the making of one decision rather than another can result in heavy losses and consequences, both known and unknown. In post-normal policy issues, rationalist expectations of science encourage political disagreements to be played out under the guise of scientific debate (since in post-normal issue areas no one can claim a decisive victory on the basis of science) until one set of values finally becomes dominant and further debate becomes untenable. The scientific advice aligned with the most widely embraced values (save the whale, anti-smoking, anti-genetically modified food) subsequently becomes the 'consensus view' (read 'only scientific' view), while all remaining dissenting scientists become contrarians and are tainted by suspicion (e.g. self-interested links with industry, government). Thus, the process becomes self-perpetuating since all the while the values that actually drive the debate remain out of the spotlight and are therefore never explicitly debated outside the realm of competing knowledge claims. And because a scientific consensus is ultimately declared in support of those values (even though the values are likely to be informing the science rather than vice-versa), science is seen to have won the day by producing the rational policy.

It is also worth noting that, while it is often regular, normal scientific endeavour that identifies the potential problem or risk (as with climate change or ozone depletion, for example), the issue then becomes open to being more or less hijacked by whoever has an interest in pursuing it. Pressure for scientific consensus begins to build, depending on how well the issue bites politically, causing the normal practice of science, particularly when it is forced to operate in the post-normal realm, to produce ongoing controversy rather than 'consensus'. So there exist fundamental tensions and incompatibilities between what science can actually do and what policy makers, interest groups and the general public want it to do (i.e. prove to everyone else that the policy response that supports and reflects their values is the appropriate one). And therein lies the rub: *policy making is necessarily about the future whereas science is restricted to the present and the past for the evidence it relies on to theorize and test knowledge claims.* The business of determining policy responses to climate change impacts, for mitigation and adaptation strategies alike, is an entirely political process that must manage competing values, choices and preferences. And although some scientists appear to think otherwise (i.e. those who try and present their preferences as *more scientific* than others), policy advocacy is beyond the realm of scientific expertise. While most physical scientists no doubt believe their task to be about uncovering the realities of the natural world, policy is about the reality of what is acceptable and therefore achievable in the political world. Even if, for example, everyone accepted the consensus on human-induced 'global warming' as the most compelling explanation for what is happening today, as most governments now have, we would be no closer to understanding either what global warming means in terms of what will happen tomorrow or reaching agreement on how best to respond to it.

So what should acceptance or rejection of one or another of the various global warming scenarios (the IPCC has produced some 40 'scenarios', not 'predictions'), which range from minor to catastrophic climate change consequences, be based upon? Hard evidence, guesswork, ideology, faith or all of the above? And, most importantly, how does our confidence in such scenarios actually occurring stack up against the costs of taking precautions today against the possible (but unknown) costs of global warming tomorrow? Given the numerous uncertainties that characterize our understanding of the global climate and the effects of our interaction with it,[36] it is not surprising that many governments, especially those in developing countries, are unwilling to accept a high risk of significant economic cost and hardship today – despite the Stern Report's relatively optimist assessment on this point[37] – in order to limit only one of the many variables that may or may not cause future global warming catastrophes. The central policy question then should not be all about who has got it right; we should also be thinking about how we can develop a strategy that best manages the risks involved with getting the causes and potential effects of climate change wrong, at least until we are in a position to more confidently discuss what may or may not happen and adjust our policy responses accordingly.

The climate consensus and policy making: New rhetoric but no paradigm shift

Opposition to the emission reductions called for in Kyoto on the grounds of the harm it would cause to the US economy was made clear in the Republican-dominated US Senate as early as 1997 by the 95–0 vote supporting the Byrd-Hagel Resolution's rejection of US participation in any emissions reduction agreement that excluded developing countries.[38] In addition to concerns expressed by both the Bush administration and Howard government about the uncertainties surrounding claims of anthropogenic climate forcing and its future impacts, the other major reason cited by both governments was that the Kyoto agreement did not require emission reductions or limits from developing economies as well, in particular China and India. This often cited source of opposition to ratifying the Kyoto Protocol's planned emission reductions illustrated the kind of state preoccupation with self-interest and concerns about international cooperation creating the kinds of unequal benefits that realist theorists had long warned of as an obstacle to international agreements. But given the increasing domestic pressure within both countries – encouraged by the IPCC and various media reports and NGOs – for their governments to recognize global warming as a serious threat, it was also becoming clear by late

2005 that if Kyoto was off the list of policy options, then some kind of surrogate response was needed to show that the issue at least had the government's attention. Thus, President Bush and Prime Minister Howard found themselves in the kind of bind described by Robert Putnam's two level game[39] depiction of how policy elites are forced to reconcile tensions between foreign policy ambitions shaped by their own notions of the national interest and the international system on the one hand, and the domestic plurality of competing interests that elected governments are ultimately accountable to on the other hand. The solution Bush and Howard adopted for their two level game dilemma regarding how to appear engaged with global warming as a policy issue while minimizing any risks to their fossil fuel dependent economies was to propose a new international forum with a very different, technology-based strategy for controlling emissions: the Asia Pacific Partnership Group (AP6).

Buttressing the need for an alternative approach to global warming were the numerous critics of the Kyoto Protocol that had emerged by this time. In addition to the now regularly cited issue of the Kyoto agreement's failure to require any emission reductions in the developing world, some argued that the Kyoto strategies were undermined by too many questionable assumptions in relation to the likely costs involved. Meanwhile debate raged – even among those supporting the anthropogenic global warming consensus – regarding how effective, if at all, the protocol's reductions would be even if full international cooperation and implementation were possible, which was by now looking increasingly unlikely. Indeed, by late 2005 even Tony Blair was becoming critical of the approach drawn up in Kyoto, drawing accusations that he was again falling into line with Washington, as he had on Iraq. At a climate change conference convened by former US President Bill Clinton, Blair's criticism of the Kyoto agreement and endorsement of the technology focused response to global warming proposed by his allies in Washington and Canberra attracted a storm of protests and accusations of backtracking on his formerly strong pro-Kyoto rhetoric:

> *I'm changing my mind about this ... no country is going to cut its growth or consumption substantially in the light of a long-term environmental problem. To be honest, I don't think people are going, at least in the short-term, to start negotiating another major treaty like Kyoto... How do we move forward and ensure that, post-Kyoto, we do try to get agreement? I think that can only be done by the major players in this coming together and finding a way for pooling their resources, their information, their science and technology.*[40]

Interestingly, Tony Blair's publicly-stated reluctance to sacrifice economic security in the pursuit of 'climate security' and emphasis on a 'market-based' response prefaced a softening of climate policy in Washington and Canberra the following year in late 2006. The Bush and Howard governments had been gradually toning down their sceptical position on global warming impacts since 2002 as public fears in both countries over climate change intensified, especially in the wake of the release of Al Gore's documentary *An Inconvenient Truth* and *The Stern Review Report on the Economics of Climate Change*. Prime Minister Howard made his new-found enthusiasm for acting against climate change clear at the Asia Pacific Economic Cooperation (APEC) summit in Hanoi in November 2006, where he actively promoted discussions on regional measures against climate change, giving it the same priority as Iraq and global trade.[41] The Howard government, however, continued to reject policy it claimed would harm Australia's economy and fossil fuel interests, but, nonetheless, made global warming a government priority, particularly in relation to the energy debate that was emerging at home over his government's calls to end Australia's long-running ban on nuclear power. President Bush was also undergoing a gestalt switch of sorts on global warming policy that was remarkably similar to the new line of thinking espoused by his Australian ally, as demonstrated by the softening of the Bush administration's position on the need for international policy action on global warming witnessed at both the APEC meeting and later at the 2007 UN Climate Change Conference in Bali. In his 2007 State of the Union speech, President Bush already had indicated a shift in his position on climate change, and, in particular, America's oil dependency, was underway when he said:

> *America's on the verge of technological breakthroughs that will enable us to live our lives less dependent on oil. And these technologies will help us become better stewards of the environment, and they will help us to confront the serious challenge of climate change.*[42]

Howard and Bush's rhetorical shift on global warming was most likely motivated by increasing public concern and the greater weight anthropogenic global warming had acquired as a policy issue, particularly with federal elections looming in both countries, since no new or more compelling evidence on the likelihood of global warming's most serious threats being realized appeared prior to either government adopting a less sceptical position. But despite the greater acknowledgement by both leaders of global warming's importance and potential consequences, their priorities were still very much about avoiding any economic disruption at home.

At the inaugural meeting of the AP6 in January 2006, George W. Bush and John Howard, two of the Kyoto Protocol's biggest critics, talked up the importance of developing renewable energy sources as a way of combating global warming threats without incurring potentially crippling economic penalties; little actually had changed, however, in terms of the policy priority given to short-term economic growth over the longer term and still largely speculative challenges posed by global warming. Prime Minister Howard, for example, also made it quite clear that the Australian government remained committed to fossil fuels with his endorsement of the AP6 view that fossil fuels 'will be an enduring reality for our lifetime and beyond'.[43] According to figures reported in *The Australian*, of the A$100 million dollars the Howard government had dedicated to the partnership over the next five years, only A$5 million dollars per year was for developing renewable energy projects. This, according to a government AP6 press release, was in addition to the A$200 million the Howard government claimed it already had invested in developing renewable energy (A$500 million, meanwhile, had been 'invested' in so-called 'low emission technologies' such as carbon sequestration). For its part, the US government, which spends more than US$350 billion on its military each year, committed a meagre US$52 million from its 2007 budget, subject to approval by Congress ('expected' to grow to US$260 million by 2011).[44] Moreover, both governments essentially used the AP6 as a cover for dodging the global warming issue entirely by announcing their intention to hand the job of developing and implementing new energy technology over to the private sector.

The ongoing focus in climate change policy discussion on often vague and complex market-based responses to climate change, such as the various carbon trading scheme models, is perhaps the clearest indication that it still is not regarded as a 'security' issue by many governments, despite efforts and claims to the contrary within the EU. The UK government in 2007, for example, attempted to promote climate change as a security issue in the UN Security Council[45] while the European Commission has sought to use climate change as a catalyst for new energy security measures and targets for renewable energy among member states.[46] But even among governments supportive of emission reductions and targets, there has been no direct government policy response of the kind normally seen when an area of 'national security' has been at risk. Put simply, the policy rhetoric on climate change and its threat potential has not been matched by the kinds of measures and policy shifts (e.g. the rapid introduction of carbon taxes by governments) one would expect to see if such threats were indeed being taken seriously:

> *Whether someone is serious about tackling the global warming problem can be readily gauged by listening to what he or she says about the carbon price. Suppose you hear a public figure who speaks eloquently of the perils of global warming and proposes that the nation should move urgently to slow climate change. Suppose that person proposes regulating the fuel efficiency of cars, or requiring high-efficiency lightbulbs, or subsidizing ethanol, or providing research support for solar power – but nowhere does the proposal raise the price of carbon. You should conclude that the proposal is not really serious and does not recognize the central economic message about how to slow climate change.*[47]

Unlike the transnational threats posed by terrorism, failing states, epidemics and the ongoing economic fallout from the sub-prime mortgage meltdown in the US, for example, where governments have directly intervened using state resources on the grounds of national security, policy responses to climate change have relied almost entirely on market mechanisms and the private sector for their implementation and funding. And in so far as governments have taken the lead in implementing climate change responses, these measures have focused much more on the issue of energy security than climate security. Moreover, they are motivated and informed primarily by traditional state-centric notions of security and relative gains in contrast to the more multilateral, 'global public good' framing of 'climate security' characterizing both domestic and international policy debates.[48] And for the economies of Australia and the US, and many developing states, the cure may well represent a bigger threat than the disease. Thus, the Janus-like nature of emission reductions as either a threat or threat response, depending on one's circumstances, perceptions and priorities, is the main obstacle to anthropogenic climate change becoming securitized to the extent that its potential threats are directly linked by states to their own national security.

For some governments, such as the Blair government and many of its EU partners, the implications of such a paradigm shift largely had been minimized by already implemented industry and energy reforms that had, rather ironically, been deemed necessary for reasons of economic security and growth. In the UK, the move away from high coal and oil dependency towards cleaner options in the form of natural gas and renewables had been underway since the early 1980s. UK emissions had been falling since the late 1980s thanks largely to the 'dash for gas' and increased emissions regulation that followed Margaret Thatcher's liberalization of the UK's energy industry, at the expense of the country's coal mines, and the discovery of large oil and gas deposits in the North Sea.[49] Moreover, these domestic energy reforms meant that the timing of the UK's reductions meshed nicely with the Kyoto agreement's 1990s baseline for emission reductions. As John Howard remarked in a 2006 interview, 'with very great respect to my good friend Tony Blair, Kyoto was in a sense designed to suit the Europeans because of the starting date and which happened to coincide fairly neatly with some very significant emission-reducing events that took place in Europe'.[50] But for the still coal and oil dependent economies of the US and Australia, where emission levels steadily had been increasing, emission reductions of the scale and nature being called for by the Kyoto Protocol and its supporters represented a shift in policy thinking that not only would be difficult to implement but also would certainly involve significant short-term economic risk and pain with no more than the prospect of highly uncertain long-term benefit in return.

Conclusion

Bush and Howard's change in policy rhetoric indicated their acceptance of global warming as a 'political fact' that no longer could be ignored or downplayed, regardless of the many uncertainties that still surrounded its causes and possible impacts, but only in terms that maintained the economy as the *central* referent of security. Bush and Howard also shared very similar views and values on security and the economy as the fundamentals of the 'national interest', and in particular on the need to avoid sacrificing any aspect of the national interest on the altar of multilateral engagement and commitment.[51] The economic costs that both governments believed major emission cuts would have in their respective societies, despite the public mood towards the potential dangers of global warming, remained the dominant influence on the kind of specialist advice the policy elites in these two governments were prepared to accept as the basis of policy. In contrast, the positions on the need for an international response to global warming, especially on the kind of role their countries should play in that response, taken by Bush and Howard's Democratic and Labor Party predecessors stemmed from a national interest perspective more accepting of the potential for environmental threats and also far more supportive of engagement with international institutions as a response to international issues and threats. It is, however, unlikely that the economic costs of implementing Kyoto would have remained without influence for very long under either side of politics in Australia and the US given the ongoing fossil fuel dependence both economies share.

One conclusion to draw from the apparent about-face on climate change by President Bush and Prime Minister Howard is that a combination of expert consensus, international pressure and domestic public opinion finally proved effective in influencing US and Australian policy, giving some weight to rationalist notions about how knowledge can and does play a significant role in policy decisions and also pluralist claims about the ability of the 'truth' to finally win out in the course of public debate and then, on the basis of its validation in the marketplace of ideas, to become accepted by governments as the legitimate basis of policy. Constructivists and liberal institutionalists interested in the ability of international regimes and emerging norms to influence the policies of member governments and facilitate cooperation among states on international issues also might point to the US and Australian policy shifts as evidence that new norms can evolve and influence state notions of national interest and that cooperation in international politics need not be hamstrung by fears of unequal relative gains and an unwavering commitment to state self-interest. According to these perspectives, the case of Iraq would be an aberration in policy terms, a blatant example of political manipulation or ideology perverting the idealized rationalist policy making schema and further proof of the need, therefore, to get politics *out* of policy making.

The explanation presented here, however, paints a very different picture of the role specialist advice and uncertainty played in the policies adopted by the Bush, Blair and Howard governments, one that looks not only to how established policy priorities and the world views of policy elites shape the interpretation of uncertainties in policy advice, but also to the role such interpretations play in justifying the adoption of some specialist advice over other specialist advice. Moreover, this perspective also questions the extent to which the kinds of explanations outlined above are useful in understanding the pro-Kyoto policies adopted by some governments. In contrast to the Australian and US positions, it also seems clear that those governments that supported the Kyoto Protocol, such as the Blair government, had judged that the political benefits of doing so (e.g. a positive commitment to environment values) could be realized without incurring unacceptable levels of job losses, price increases and GDP impact.[52] In the UK, significant emission reductions had already been achieved during the 1990s due to the phasing out of Britain's coal-fired power plants in favour of cheaper and cleaner natural gas-powered generators. And, in contrast to Australia and the US, climate change already had a history of bipartisan support as a major policy issue – due in no small part to the complementary role climate change threats played within ongoing government plans for privatizing the UK's electrical providers and making the country more energy secure – which dated back to a mix of energy and pro-market reform policies that began with Margaret Thatcher's confrontation with Britain's coal miners and her goal of expanding Britain's supply of nuclear-generated electricity.

6
Uncertainty, Ideology and the Politics of Denial

In contrast to the relative ease with which President Bush and Prime Ministers Blair and Howard were able to elevate the still unknown dangers of an Iraq armed with weapons of mass destruction (WMD) to the level of an immediate and existential threat – despite the absence of any compelling empirical evidence or expert consensus to that effect – arguments made for a similar elevation of climate change to the status of a major security issue in need of *immediate* action were met with caution and at times outright opposition within all three governments. As noted in Chapter 5, the various international and domestic efforts aimed at 'securitizing' climate change were undermined both by the more distant and unconventional nature of the threats it posed, and also by its framing, by both sides, as an issue that required paradigmatic changes in the policy priorities and thinking of most governments. In the absence of a tangible sense of crisis, such as that created by proponents of the Iraq invasion, the advocates of major, short-term emission reductions struggled to convince government leaders, industry and businesses, and sections of the public of the need for the kind of major shift in policy priorities and thinking they were in effect calling for. As a consequence, governments remained uncommitted to any substantial shift outside of the policy assumptions and goals they were already operating with.

Beyond fiddling with existing policy settings and debating the use of various instruments, such as carbon taxes and emissions trading schemes, governments are yet to implement any clear set of policies aimed at achieving major short-term greenhouse gas (GHG) reductions. Moreover, uncertainty over the nature and scope of future climate change impacts has left ample scope for counter arguments invoking the economic risks involved with imposing emission reduction schemes. And, in the absence of an unequivocal demonstration of why the short-term economic dangers of emission reductions are a lesser evil than the long-term dangers of climate change, which is highly unlikely given the range and nature of the uncertainties involved, the scientific advice on climate change and the economic costs of responding to it will continue to be contested at least until either a crisis emerges demonstrating the failure of existing policy, or the prospects for such a crisis diminish over the coming decades.

By arguing for the possibility of Iraqi WMD attacks against the US or its allies, and also the potential for Iraq's WMD falling into the hands of terrorist groups like al Qaeda, the Bush administration effectively added an element of urgency to its argument for a 'precautionary principle' (PP) approach to managing Saddam's possible but unproven possession of WMD. The absence of evidence that Saddam still retained WMD was not itself sufficient evidence that they did not exist, given the huge risks the Bush administration and its allies argued that an ongoing Iraqi WMD capability would pose in the near future. Thus, the US government and its UK and Australian allies sought to legitimize the Iraq invasion by presenting it as a precautionary act made necessary by the threat *potential* of a WMD-armed Iraq, a proposition that itself relied on interpreting the many related uncertainty issues in order to produce various 'what if' threat scenarios involving both traditional and transnational security concerns.

The precautionary argument made for toppling Saddam Hussein's regime was then an extension of both an already stated and bipartisan commitment to his removal from power and also the broader reaction to the threat of transnational terrorism in the post-9/11 era within the foreign policy communities of the US and its allies – a reaction which announced pre-emptive military strikes and regime change as a viable policy option against rogue or recalcitrant states. And unlike the various 'what if' scenarios used by advocates of bigger and faster emission reductions to justify the threat of catastrophic climate change, the nightmare scenarios used in Washington, London and Canberra to justify military action against Iraq – the threat of mushroom clouds, weapons proliferation and a repeat of the 9/11 attacks on the US – were not in the distant future, were not without tangible precedent and, most importantly, did not contradict or undermine the shared notions of national interest and security to which the executive elites in the US, UK and Australian governments all subscribed. The issue of Saddam Hussein's WMD capability had always been a prominent security issue in the eyes of many governments, but it was a security issue that had been broadly believed to be under control *vis-à-vis* the UN's inspection and sanctions regimes. What made the question of Iraqi WMD a compelling security problem in need of *immediate* state action and intervention was the short-term potential for devastating transnational terrorist attacks by groups like al Qaeda, as demonstrated on 11 September 2001, and the further proliferation of WMD among rogue states such as Iraq. Thus, it was this reframing by the Bush administration and its allies of Iraqi WMD in terms of their threat potential that made the argument for war compelling in spite of the many uncertainties and untested assumptions involved.

What made the case for invading Iraq even more compelling for the US, UK and Australian executive elite, however, was not only the neat fit it provided with the state-centric security paradigm policy makers were still operating within, but also a set of ideologically informed policy assumptions they already had adopted about the contemporary international environment, the kinds of states it is made up of, and, in particular, the kind of state that was preferred.[1] Informing many of these assumptions was neo-liberalism (also known as 'economic rationalism' in Australia), a free market-based brand of economic philosophy that had been embraced by both sides of domestic politics in the US, UK and Australia from the early 1980s onwards. The credibility of the market-based theories derived from neo-liberalism was greatly enhanced by the chronic stagflation and unemployment that had plagued Western economies in the 1970s, and they quickly became the next 'big idea'[2] guiding economic policy in the Thatcher and Reagan governments (the Hawke–Keating led-Labor government in Australia was another early adherent to economic rationalist principles).[3] By the late 1990s, the dispositional perceptions or world views of Western policy makers had, with very few exceptions, become heavily influenced by neo-liberal economic thinking, especially at the meta-theoretical level where it provided an ideologically appealing guide to policy ideas about not only what the big picture should look like, but also how it could be achieved:

> *Analytically, neoliberalism presents a problem because in some respects it is everywhere and nowhere at the same time. Its concrete geographical associations with the 'Washington Consensus' and the 'Chicago School' economics give clues to some of the more important spatial anchoring points, but much of the power of neoliberalism stems from the way in which it structures the wider 'policy environment' – of programmatic conventions, (perceived) external constraints, and received understandings of what the World Bank, the credit ratings agencies, or the 'markets' will bear. There is, consequently, a strong sense in which the spaces of the state – those which it makes and those it inhabits – have been neoliberalized in a deep but often implicit way.[4]*

The widespread acceptance among government executives and bureaucrats of its prescriptions for the privatization of state assets and the deregulation of labour and financial markets (sometimes more a case of only 'reregulating' in favour of business interests than genuine deregulation)[5] demonstrated both the strong ideological underpinnings of policy and the influence of the executive elite's own world views in the casting and legitimization of that policy. And, as had been the case with the specialist advice on Iraqi WMD and also the evidence for anthropogenic climate change and its impacts, a level of consensus in the economic advice on offer had become confused with certainty and, as a result, also an obstacle to alternative or dissenting views being recognized as grounds for genuine policy debate. The fundamental faith of neo-liberal theory in the self-correcting ability and rationality of the market also encouraged the market-based responses to global warming contained within the Kyoto Protocol. As with development thinking during the 1980s and 1990s, direct government intervention in the control of emissions, such as taxing emissions, was widely seen as inhibiting such self-correction and rationality. Given the right institutional setting and forms of governance, market mechanisms – in the form of emissions trading schemes – became therefore the foundation of the Kyoto Protocol's strategy, a blueprint for reducing emissions that was adopted at the strong insistence of the US government but initially opposed by the European Union (EU).[6]

Thus the so-called 'Washington Consensus' on economic policy and development provides another contemporary illustration of the important role played by the ideological orientation of policy elites and the extent to which dominant world views can inhibit open policy debate by selectively empha-sizing or downplaying uncertainty in the policy advice on offer. The Wash-ington Consensus, for its part, continued to influence both domestic economic policy in many developed states and the kind of economic development assist-ance they provide to developing countries – either individually or through the International Monetary Fund (IMF) and the World Bank[7] – despite a growing list of economic and development failures and growing criticism in response to those failures, most notably the IMF's much maligned handling of the 1997 Asian financial crisis. In contrast to the dogged adherence by the Bush, Blair and Howard governments to both the Washington Consensus and the intel-ligence consensus on the existence of Iraqi chemical and biological weapons programmes (i.e. that some of this capacity most likely still existed), the Inter-governmental Panel on Climate Change (IPCC) consensus on anthropogenic climate change was (and continues to be) treated much more cautiously as a basis for policy. As justification for this marked difference, uncertainty was invoked to play the role of *deus ex machina* in rationalizing the decision to ignore the consensus advice on offer. And like the dissenting voices on Iraq's alleged WMD programmes and the threat they posed, the growing chorus of professional dissent that had seriously eroded the credibility of a 'Wash-ington Consensus' by the early 2000s also was dismissed due to its incompat-ibility with the already established policy paradigms of executive elites. Robert Jervis attributes the tendency of decision makers to downplay the problems or failures of existing or favoured policy approaches to both the level of ambi-guity in the available evidence (i.e. the level of uncertainty), and also the deci-sion maker's level of commitment to an established world view or ideology. Thus, 'the hypothesis that incoming information tends to be assimilated to pre-existing images'.[8] Jervis then goes on to explain that a corollary of this explanation is that:

> *A person is less apt to reorganize evidence into a new theory or image if he is deeply committed to the established view. Commit-ment here means not only the degree to which the person's power and prestige are involved but also – and more importantly – the degree to which this way of seeing the world has proved satisfac-tory and has become internalized.*[9]

The degree to which international development policy had become impervious to dissenting expert views and opinions by the late 1990s was illustrated by Joseph Stiglitz's 1999 departure from his position as Chief Economist at the

World Bank. According to *The New York Times*, Stiglitz said he had felt under pressure to either resign or stop speaking out against what he believed to be poor policy. Stiglitz had earlier criticized the strong pro-market influence of the Washington Consensus on development policy as excessive and having too much faith in the self-correcting abilities of free markets. Moreover, there existed, according to Stiglitz, 'an intellectual gap between what we know and what is practised' at the US Treasury Department and the IMF.[10] According to media reports, many insiders at the World Bank believed that, as a result of Stiglitz's public comments, World Bank President James Wolfensohn had come under direct pressure from US Treasury Secretary Lawrence Summers to silence Stiglitz. Amid official denials of any executive pressure from the Clinton administration, Stiglitz nevertheless felt that his position at the World Bank was no longer tenable, '… as misguided as I believe these policies were, you have to either speak out or resign'.[11]

Washington Consensus or zombie economics? Killing the undead

The turn away from Keynesian principles to what have since become known as neo-liberal economic policies and thinking, based as they are on neo-classical and Hayekian[12] prescriptions for free markets, free trade, privatization, and an increasingly smaller state role, began in the UK with Margaret Thatcher's election in 1979[13] but was already taking root in the US under the Carter administration. Domestic US policy, however, would not fully embrace the fundamentals of neo-liberalism until after Ronald Reagan's election as President in 1980. By 1982, the increasingly rapid acceptance of neo-liberal economic principles among the Anglo–American economies, regardless of the governments' political persuasion,[14] was also beginning to manifest itself in the thinking of development economists and in foreign policy. Mexico's debt crisis and the apparent failure of the centrally planned economies of Europe and Asia juxtaposed against the rapid growth experienced firstly by Japan and then by East Asia's Dragon economies (Hong Kong, South Korea, Singapore and Taiwan, and later Malaysia, Thailand and Indonesia) each served to reinforce the need for change in development policy thinking.[15] The introduction of loan conditionality by the Bretton Woods institutions for developing countries seeking loans and debt relief at this time, in the form of Structural Adjustment Programs (SAPs) requiring the freeing up of trade and markets, and fiscal restraint, marked a shift in development priorities that John Williamson would later summarize as the Washington Consensus: a blueprint for social and economic development focusing on fiscal restraint, deregulation and free trade. According to Williamson, 'I made a list of ten policies that I thought more or less everyone in Washington would agree were needed more or less everywhere in Latin America, and labelled this the "Washington Consensus"'.[16]

When Williamson summarized and named what he saw as the non-controversial fundamentals of development at the time, he was less than a decade past a major paradigm shift in developmental economics and the role of the state but standing also at the beginning of the end of the Cold War and the ideological battle that had helped sustain it. But while Williamson himself has objected to the strong neo-liberal flavour his term has since assumed, it is nevertheless clear that the professional consensus on economic development he originally described has become an integral part of a much broader ideological agenda pursued by the Bush administration and like-minded governments in the UK, Australia and elsewhere.

For most of the remainder of the 20th century, the development strategies of the Organisation for Economic Co-operation and Development (OECD), the World Bank, the IMF and the US Treasury rested upon a set of policy fundamentals that contradicted the major policy assumptions on development of the preceding 30 years. The policy pendulum had, by the time of Williamson's announcement of a 'Washington Consensus', completed its journey from one extreme to the other. The conventional wisdom of the initial post-war period on development, influenced as it was by decolonization and the geopolitical and ideological confrontation of the Cold War, stood in stark contrast to the new, 'free market good/government intervention bad' thinking of the 1980s and 1990s. In the 1960s, government was the 'driving force' of development. Trade and integration were largely seen as unimportant, while foreign direct investment (FDI) was to be avoided; external government borrowing was judged far more beneficial.[17] By 1989, the 'consensus' perceived by Williamson directly contradicted all but one of these assumptions: the Washington Consensus itself did not explicitly reject state controls on the market but its prescriptions would, in effect, erode state influence and control. The clarion call for the removal of state interference in economic development, and the rent-seeking activities such interference allegedly led to, would come from other, and more ideologically explicit, quarters.

With the election of the Reagan administration came the opportunity for several fast rising political figures in Washington – in particular, Paul Wolfowitz, Francis Fukuyama and Richard Perle – to begin implementing their ideas on how to pull the US out of the malaise they believed it to be in. According to these figures, later to be identified among the vanguard of neo-conservatism, the excessive liberalism of the 1960s combined with defeat in Vietnam and years of appeasing the Soviets under *détente* had led to a weakening of US power with its economy now struggling under stagflation and a general sense of aimlessness pervading Washington. The solution was a reassertion of US power and its projection against communism in order to spread internationally the neo-conservative vision they embraced, based as it was on notions of democracy, marketplace freedoms, the role and nature of the state, and a strongly held belief in US power as a force for good.[18] The views of Wolfowitz and others sympathetic to the neo-conservative position in the administration, such as Richard Armitage and Secretary of State George P. Shultz, were often challenged by the more traditional realist elements within the administration, most notably Secretary of Defense Caspar Weinberger, but they sat well with the strong anti-communist and pro-monetarist policies pursued by the UK under Margaret Thatcher. Indeed, the close relationship that developed between Thatcher and Reagan was in part the product of a general conservative dominance and consensus among the Anglo–American economies during the 1980s.[19] Thus, by the late 1980s, economic analysis and ideological commitment had converged to produce a consensus on development and how it should occur that went beyond only economists to include policy makers and politicians as well.

The pivotal moment in the ascendancy of neo-liberal economic thinking, however, came with the collapse of the Soviet economy. The ensuing dissolution of the Soviet Union in 1991 and the widespread acceptance in the West that the Soviet demise demonstrated once and for all the supremacy of liberal free market economics and democracy not only appeared to reaffirm the policies of the Anglo–American governments, but also opened up a vast set of opportunities for the export of these policies into undeveloped and still developing states. Buoyed by communism's collapse in Europe and its apparent validation of Fukuyama's politically appealing 'End of History' thesis, analysts and senior officials in the US treasury and Bretton Woods institutions felt relieved of any remaining doubts they may have had about the appropriate way forward for development.[20] Furthermore, thanks to the Soviet demise, democracy was increasingly regarded as a defining characteristic of economic and state development.[21]

The Washington Consensus approach to development, with its focus on market liberalization, deregulation and privatization, remained mostly unquestioned in the US and elsewhere until the 1997 Asian financial crisis,[22] which saw some of Asia's economic miracles grind to a halt after the sudden flight of overseas short-term capital from their economies. Hardest hit were South Korea, Indonesia and Thailand. The governments in these countries had, under pressure from the US Treasury and the OECD, liberalized their capital accounts in order to facilitate greater foreign investment, a policy Williamson denies was part of the original set of Washington Consensus recommendations.[23] The ensuing closure of many otherwise profitable companies resulted in huge economic and social disruption and rapidly rising unemployment. These economies were plunged into further hardship by the IMF's insistence on raising interest rates as the best way of attracting foreign capital back into the struggling economies and shoring up their free falling exchange rates. The 1997 Asian financial crises soon triggered a growing wave of criticism of the neo-liberal free market focus that Williamson's 1989 list was now increasingly seen to be prescribing, despite his protests to the contrary. Nevertheless, the US commitment to free markets, trade and democracy as the necessary ingredients for development remained resolute, as demonstrated by the Clinton administration's 1998 National Security Strategy document, which asserted that:

> *The forces necessary for a healthy global economy are also those that deepen democratic liberties: the free flow of ideas and information, open borders and easy travel, the rule of law, fair and even handed enforcement, protection for consumers, a skilled and educated work force. If citizens tire of waiting for democracy and*

free markets to deliver a better life for them, there is a real risk
that they will lose confidence in democracy and free markets.[24]

The institutional response to the financial crisis and the failed IMF advice
was to turn to the nature of the institutions in developing economies and the
state itself for an explanation of what had gone wrong. What emerged was
the so-called 'augmented' Washington Consensus, which added a further ten
points to Williamson's original list that focused on required areas of governance and institutional reform. Proponents of the augmented version, which
was preceded by the World Bank's 1997 World Development Report (WDR)
entitled *The State in a Changing World*, argued that market reforms alone
are unable to generate sustainable economic growth. Without institutional
capacity – providing corporate governance, social safety nets, financial codes
and standards, protection against corruption and targeted poverty reduction
– the original Washington Consensus prescriptions for financial and trade
liberalization, fiscal discipline and privatization and deregulation cannot be
properly implemented. In the case of the Asian Dragons, the failure, therefore,
was not with the economic principles that had, to a greater or lesser degree,
been adopted by each government but rather was the result of their failure to
implement them properly. According to Mark Beeson and Iyanatul Islam:

> *Pundits – most notably the IFIs [international financial institu-*
> *tions] which, on the very eve of the crisis, praised the East Asian*
> *economies for their 'miraculous' achievements – now rushed*
> *to condemn them as 'failed' cases of 'crony capitalism'. What*
> *appeared to be close government-business relations that were,*
> *in the past, argued to facilitate a virtuous process of equitable*
> *growth now became 'corrupt regimes' that encouraged inefficient*
> *state intervention, bred structural deficiencies and brought about*
> *their own downfall. The solution – crafted through the so called*
> *'Letters of Intent' that were negotiated between the IMF and the*
> *crisis-affected economies of Indonesia, Thailand and Korea –*
> *essentially called for a re-imposition of 'augmented' Washington*
> *Consensus policies.*[25]

The augmented version of the Washington Consensus was essentially an
attempt by its advocates, attracted by both the ideological underpinnings of
free market economics and also the neat fit it provided for promoting liberal
democracy, to salvage the original Washington Consensus principles in the
face of growing criticism. But from 1997 onwards, an advancing tide of both
internal and external criticism continued to erode the Bretton Woods institutions' credibility, attacking in particular the strong, pro-market ideological beliefs that many critics believed were driving policy. Within the World
Bank, senior staff members such as Joseph Stiglitz, Ravi Kanbur and Branko
Milanovic, to name but a few, spoke out against the neo-liberal policies of
the Bank and IMF and also the strong political influence exerted by the US

Treasury and executive. Stiglitz and Kanbur, for example, resigned from their positions at the World Bank as a result of political pressure from the US Treasury.[26] Other critics included Harvard economist Dani Rodrik, who, writing in 2002, stated:

> *After more than two decades of application of neo-liberal economic policies in the developing world, we are in a position to pass unequivocal judgment on their record. The picture is not pretty.*[27]

Rodrik went on to point out that levels of growth in most of Latin America in the 1990s were lower than in the 1950–1980 period, while poverty rates and real output in many of the former socialist countries were worse than 1990 levels after more than a decade of Washington Consensus-led development in those countries; development in Sub-Saharan Africa too is 'very disappointing' and in many of these countries the situation is worse today [in 2002] than it was in the 1970s. Moreover, the countries that achieved the best and strongest rates of growth and poverty reduction during the 1990s – China, India and Vietnam – 'violated virtually all the rules in the neoliberal guidebook even while moving in a more market-orientated direction'.[28] By 2006, Rodrik and others proclaimed that the Washington Consensus, as implemented, was dead and buried as a development blueprint, since the evidence of its failure to produce lasting (or in many cases any) economic growth and development had become simply too overwhelming for even its strongest supporters to ignore. 'While the lessons drawn by proponents and skeptics differ,' Rodrik writes, 'it is fair to say that nobody really believes in the Washington Consensus anymore. The question now is not whether the Washington Consensus is dead or alive; it is what will replace it.'[29] And as for the augmented version's remedy to the original's apparent failures, this too offers little hope for escaping the dead end that development policy and thinking in the World Bank and IMF now appears to have reached, since it in effect requires developing or under-developed states to be developed – in terms of the kind of state setting the Washington Consensus principles need to work – in order for them to develop![30]

Given the sustained criticism that the Washington Consensus has suffered, in addition to the poor results obtained from more than two decades of its implementation, what can explain the continued adherence to its principles by many in the developed world, in particular, the Anglo–American governments? And how can we understand the continued emphasis on institution building, in spite of the huge and as yet unmet problems and challenges it presents, that now underpins not only development but also current security strategy thinking in the US and elsewhere? Contrary to Rodrik's 2006 claim that 'nobody really believes in the Washington Consensus anymore',[31] faith in the primacy of privatization, free trade and fiscal discipline (US defence spending is clearly an exception here) remained alive and well from Washington to Canberra and London to Tokyo where it continued to drive not only domestic economic policy but also foreign policy initiatives aimed at managing international security, in particular, transnational threats, as well. Indeed, it was not until the financial meltdown of late 2008, which directly affected Western economies and financial institutions, that any real, policy level criticism of the neo-liberal model began to appear, as was illustrated by Alan Greenspan's surprising comments in late 2008 on the role ideology played in his own thinking (see Chapter 2).

Worldviews, ideology and the power of perceptions

As earlier noted, Williamson presented his notion of a Washington Consensus on the eve of one of the most significant events of the last century: the ending of the Cold War and the bipolar structure it created within the international system. The US, for the first time in its history, was suddenly (and unexpectedly) in a position where its power and international influence were mostly unchallenged. The foreign policy rhetoric from both the George H. W. Bush and later the Clinton administrations, and even George W. Bush when he first took office, appeared to confirm a strong US commitment to maintaining a multilateral international environment, based on international law and cooperation through multilateral institutions such as the United Nations (UN). For a short while at least, it seemed that the ultimate liberal dream of transplanting the key ingredients of domestic society – civil and legal order and civil rights, shared values and institutional arrangements – into the international realm was close enough to no longer qualify as an idealist fantasy. High on the list of features that the 'new world order' would include were a strong commitment to liberal democracy, human rights and, of course, the major tenets of neo-liberal economic thinking: free trade, deregulation, privatization and free markets.

It is not surprising then that the 'Washington Consensus' that Williamson recognized in 1989 was warmly received and generally agreed upon within most developed governments at the time (Japan remained largely unaffected by the neo-liberal bug until Junichiro Koizumi became Prime Minister in 2001),[32] since major economies like the US and UK had already been practising neo-liberal fundamentals for almost a decade while less influential economies, such as Australia's and New Zealand's, followed suit. For Williamson, however, the problem is that he never subscribed to any form of neo-liberal agenda and certainly never intended his Washington Consensus list to contribute to one. He maintains that the policy prescriptions he listed were simply empirically sound economic principles that most economists could agree upon in the context of creating and maintaining economic development.[33] Williamson's basic argument seems to be that had the Washington Consensus principles been implemented differently, which he has indicated to mean a more balanced and case specific approach, the development outcomes of at least the last 20 years could have been different.

But given that Williamson's 'laundry list' of policy prescriptions stopped short of providing any detail or guidance on exactly how the Washington Consensus should be implemented and, importantly, under what circumstances (hence the 'one-size fits all' approach adopted by the World Bank and IMF discussed by Stiglitz),[34] his protestations over it being wrongly labelled as 'neo-liberal' are unreasonable. Indeed, since it was the prevailing neo-liberal political climate surrounding the major economies at the time that provided acceptance of his consensus in the first instance, it is hardly surprising that the same neo-liberal thinking should interpret and implement the Washington principles in ways that were consistent with that mindset. Contrary to what Williamson appears to be arguing here, the 'facts' do not speak for themselves; nor do they exist in any form of theoretical vacuum. As Richard S. Eckaus notes, in his commentary of Lindauer and Pritchett's 2002 overview of how post-war development theory has swung wildly from one set of assumptions to another on the basis of new 'facts' emerging from the development experience:

> *In economics, facts are reflected through the theories we carry around, as if those theories were prisms with different indexes of refraction that separate and display the colours in the light differently. So what Lindauer and Pritchett describe as irrefutable facts of the times were actually readings of events that were generated by the theories with which they were interpreted. Lindauer and Pritchett's list of the influences on each period's perceptions of the problems and policies in developing countries should include the power of the ongoing theories.*[35]

Fast-forward to the post-9/11 international environment in 2002 and we find a fundamentally different ideological and theoretical mindset taking hold among the US and its allies in the aftermath of the 9/11 attacks. The Bush administration responds to transnational terrorism and the security threats posed by failed and failing states by asserting its ability – as the only superpower and in accordance with neo-conservative views on the role of US power – to act unilaterally in pursuit of an open-ended War on Terror (WOT). Unilateral military intervention to overthrow 'rogue' states is clearly stated as a policy option in the 2002 *National Security Strategy* document, which also presents an unequivocal policy statement on the future course of development policy and thinking:

> *We will actively work to bring the hope of democracy, development, free markets, and free trade to every corner of the world. The events of 9/11 taught us that weak states, like Afghanistan, can pose as great a danger to our national interest as strong states. Poverty does not make poor people into terrorists and murderers. Yet poverty, weak institutions, and corruption can make weak states vulnerable to terrorist networks and drug cartels within their borders.*[36]

In addition to the 2002 *National Security Strategy* document's often cited announcement of the Bush administration's plans to pursue a 'post-sovereignty' inspired doctrine of pre-emption, it also reaffirms the relevance of the Washington Consensus in its augmented form – despite its past failures and the mounting criticism it is attracting as a development model – by effectively *securitizing* both the ends and means of international economic development.

Put differently, failed and failing states are no longer regarded only as obstacles to development and the proliferation of human rights. They have become, since 9/11 and the al Qaeda presence in Afghanistan, the key focus of security strategy in the developed world, since failed states like Afghanistan are regarded as potential 'incubators' for terrorist attacks against the West (read free market, liberal democracies).[37] Thus, the solution is to ensure that failed or failing states are reconstructed in a pro-liberal democratic form and are free market orientated so that the finished product will be: (a) pro-Western (read pro-US) in its political orientation; and (b) easily and profitably integrated into a global, neo-liberal orientated global economy. The earlier notion of negative sovereignty that characterized attitudes in the developed world to developing, post-colonial states was driven by the stigma of colonial exploitation and a post-war emphasis on self-determination, as enshrined in the UN Charter, in development and modernization approaches. Widespread popular, rather than government, concern with egregious human rights abuses and development failures in many of these states emerged in the 1970s, particularly in the aftermath of the massacres in Cambodia. This trend was further augmented by South Africa's apartheid rule, the Tiananmen Square violence in China, the perceived human rights victory that accompanied the ending of the Cold War, and then further outbreaks of ethnic cleansing/genocide in the Balkans and later Rwanda. By the late 1990s, it had become clear that political pressure for some standard of 'conditional sovereignty' to be enforced was mounting, both domestically and internationally, but most states still remained reluctant to become directly involved in the internal affairs of other states, particularly in the absence of any clearly defined mission and exit strategy.

Conclusion

Thus, the major impact of the 9/11 attacks was a strengthening of not only the need for state accountability, but also the augmented Washington Consensus argument, formed in the wake of the 1997 Asian financial crisis, that weak or corrupt governance posed serious obstacles to economic development strategies.[38] Completing the rationale for direct intervention post-9/11 was the widely accepted assessment of failed and failing states as 'a clear and present danger' to the security of other states via a host of potential transnational threats, most disturbingly terrorism. In an abruptly altered security paradigm – one where traditional notions of sovereignty no longer apply, transnational threats abound, and the supremacy of liberal democratic societies exists as an article of faith – the US-led 'coalition of the willing' appeared to take the ability to directly implement neo-liberal economics and liberal democratic governance in failed and failing states as a given. As Michael Wesley has noted,[39] Anglo–American states have, until recently at least, largely agreed on the attributes of a properly functioning state, despite the many ambiguities involved, and the actions required for turning failed states around since the late 1990s. This consensus is more broadly reflected in the goals of the various interventions since that time (Kosovo, East Timor, Democratic Republic of Congo, Liberia and the Solomon Islands): a consensus based on the principles mapped out by the augmented version of the Washington Consensus and given added conviction and validity by the 9/11 attacks and subsequent War on Terror. And, despite increasing public and academic opposition to this 'consensus', there remained a strong, bipartisan commitment within the US and among its allies to the neo-liberal interpretation these, and past, governments have given to Williamson's original principles.

The ideological commitment to neo-liberal economics and belief in the manifest destiny of liberal democracy that underpinned the politics of the conservative Anglo–American governments throughout the 1980s and 1990s clearly played a significant role in limiting the so-called 'market place of ideas' to one that was highly 'brand specific'.[40] Indeed, the widespread influence of neo-liberal and neo-conservative policies was such that market-based solutions to policy problems remained virtually unassailable in policy debates despite the increasing criticism they were attracting in the aftermath of the 1997 Asian financial crisis. The integrity and relevance of the Washington Consensus principles were maintained firstly by offering the augmented version as the explanation for why the original Washington Consensus was not working, and then, by implementing it in a concentrated, 'shock therapy'-type form in 'failing states' as the response needed to combat terrorism and other transnational threats. Despite earlier failures of this strategy (rapid privatization of state assets; quick liberalization of trade, prices and capital flows), most notably in post-communist countries, Iraq became the initial test case for an even more radical brand of economic shock therapy implemented by the Bush administration that Joseph Stiglitz described as more extreme and 'brutal' than what had been attempted in the former Soviet Union and contrary to a 'broad consensus' that shock therapy had failed.[41]

So what does this suggest about the role of specialist advice in formulating responses to policy challenges beyond the scope of normal science and the extent to which we can expect policy making to ever be an entirely 'rational process' in the conventional usage of the term? And to what extent do theoretical 'big ideas' and the ideologies/belief systems that underpin them handicap our ability to make judgements about the world in a consistent and logically coherent way? Rather than lamenting the current dearth of 'big ideas' in response to the ongoing challenges posed by the kinds of post-normal policy issues discussed here, we may instead find that their absence is an opportunity for some much needed change. In addition to the two main case studies presented in Chapters 4 and 5, the longevity of the Washington Consensus's influence on economic thinking further demonstrates that the ideologies and values informing differing world views are important determinants of how uncertainty issues in specialist advice are understood, by specialists and policy makers alike, and are also, therefore, an important influence in determining which advice is prioritized over other conflicting advice. The extent and nature of this influence, however, is often hidden or obscured by expectations of and demands for more certainty. As a consequence, policy debate becomes bogged down in unresolvable disputes over 'who knows' when in fact nobody actually does, despite claims to the contrary. The real policy challenge then is not to continue trying to reduce or remove uncertainty as the basis for 'rational' policy, but rather to simply accept its existence and manage it in ways that allow us to hedge against unwanted or unforeseen outcomes. But framing uncertainty issues in this way requires abandoning the still dominant positivist context in which policy making occurs – a context that enhances the ability of both policy elites and the experts themselves to selectively emphasize or downplay uncertainty issues, depending on how well they either complement or detract from existing goals, preferences and values.

7
Revealing Values and Uncertainty in Policy Debate

The increasingly complex and highly polemical character of policy debates reflects a fundamental shift in the expectations of modern, developed societies. Where once people turned to the state and science for protection from the threat of hunger, destitution and disease, many are now far more concerned with threats emanating from both the state and science itself, in particular, those seen to be damaging the natural environment from which we had previously sought protection. This gradual turning away from the ideas and processes that not so long ago defined our concept of 'progress' has led to a popular mindset where even the very notion of progress and its ultimate destination now arouses suspicion, a phenomenon captured by Ulrich Beck's notion of the 'Risk Society' – the product of 'the overlapping of normal and exceptional conditions', which, according to Beck, stem from fears about our increasing ability to initiate our own destruction:

> [S]ince the middle of this century the social institutions of industrial society have been confronted with the historically unprecedented possibility of the destruction through decision-making of all life on this planet. This distinguishes our epoch not only from the early phase of the industrial revolution, but also from all other cultures and social forms, no matter how diverse and contradictory these may have been in detail.[1]

In the developed world, perceptions of threat and risk are inspired less by Hobbesian-type nightmares delivered by the natural world so much as by an ever increasing list of potential threats that are of our own making – the externalities of our previous, and broadly shared, understanding of what progress represented. And it is the increasingly problematic and contentious nature of 'progress' and what it does or doesn't mean and should or shouldn't represent that creates the normally divided and fractured political environment from which equally fractured policies and debates more often than not emerge.

In addition to being portrayed as one of the culprits behind progress's dangerous excesses – the usual suspects can include anything from 'Frankenstein food' to the entire industrial process – science's once unchallenged image as a 'neutral magistrate in the marketplace of ideas' has been further tarnished by its apparent openness to supporting a wide range of conflicting interpretations. The vast causative complexity of major policy issues, not to mention the huge numbers of variables known *and* unknown, leaves experts, decision makers and the public alike mired in uncertainty over what will happen, when it will happen, and what to do about it assuming it does happen. Such inescapable uncertainties over not only the identification of particular threats but also their potential impacts create a 'knowledge vacuum' within which popular but often poorly defined *values* begin to play a dominant role in the debates regarding the nature and existence of various problems and threats and what, if anything, should be done about them.

The relevance and influence of expert knowledge subsequently becomes largely dependent upon how closely it aligns with such broadly held but often differently understood and weighted values. Indeed, the extent to which otherwise commonly shared values are not commonly understood or prioritized is well illustrated by the frequent disagreements between environmental groups over both the nature of the problem at hand and in particular the policy response required. Specialist advice that clashes with one set of values or another (e.g. international security threat responses versus non-aggression and cooperation; economic prosperity versus environmental protection; economic freedoms *to* versus social freedoms *from*) can expect a rough reception in the realm of public debate as opponents seek to undermine both its relevance and reliability. The value-laden character of interpreting and prioritizing 'facts' and the inability of evidence to 'speak for itself' also means that questions about what *should* be done remain unresolved even if claims to objective knowledge are accepted. The existence of Iraq's weapons of mass destruction (WMD), for example, was broadly accepted by most governments but this 'knowledge' was a source of policy dispute rather than policy agreement, since its acceptance only introduced further uncertainty (and, therefore, speculation) over questions of quantity, kind, intention and capability. Moreover, the United Nations Monitoring, Verification and Inspection Commission's (UNMOVIC) attempt at removing the uncertainty by verifying either the existence or non-existence of proscribed weapons in Iraq via its calculation of the 'material balance' (i.e. the process of accounting for the weapons and materials Iraq was believed to have against what the Iraqi government accounted for or declared) was never going to provide a definitive resolution to the Security Council debate over Iraq because, as Robert Gallucci has noted, findings either way by UNMOVIC could be used to support very different policy decisions:

> There was enthusiasm for Hans Blix and UNMOVIC by both those wanting to get involved in Iraq and by those who didn't want to get involved in Iraq. And both of them had it as a win–win, no lose proposition no matter what Hans did.[2]

Finding WMD in Iraq could have been interpreted as evidence that Iraq was indeed an immediate threat to the region and beyond, or it could also have been used as evidence that the United Nations (UN) inspection regime was working thereby eliminating the need for invasion. Alternatively, UNMOVIC's failure to find WMD was either evidence that none existed, at least not in any significant quantity, or evidence that the Iraqis were deceiving the international community by hiding their weapons and programmes. Regardless of the conclusions drawn by UNMOVIC and the evidence used to support them, the values driving the declared policy choices of the various protagonists would remain unchanged, as would, therefore, the policy choices themselves.[3] The issue of values then, and how they colour perceptions of uncertainty and risk, is of central importance in understanding the limits of both expert advice and rationalist expectations of evidence-based policy making. As James March and Johan Olsen have noted, the concept of knowledge informing and largely defining a rational, apolitical process of policy and decision making is made particularly dubious by the separation of knowledge and politics that it requires, a separation that is 'impossible to sustain, either conceptually or behaviourally':

> *Expert knowledge clearly rests on values that regulate the way knowledge is organized and validated... Like other people, experts seem to find facts and theoretical implications consistent with their policy preferences and forget facts and theoretical implications inconvenient for their purposes. For their part policy makers often seem to use advice from specialists as an excuse for doing what is unpopular with some groups. They often seem to be inattentive to the cautions and fine details of expertise... When experts disagree, policy makers often seem to view the disagreement as justification for accepting whatever advice is convenient. Agreement among specialists, on the other hand, is likely to be treated as a sign of conspiracy.*[4]

Exposing the falsity of this separation and the ways in which it inhibits rather than promotes agreement on 'legitimate' policy is an essential part of attempting to bring politics back into not only our understanding of policy decision making, but also the process by which one decision rather than another is legitimized. Broader and more rigorous public debate on complex, high stakes policy issues – as envisaged by liberal notions of a 'marketplace of ideas' – is the mechanism by which the 'political' is given life and power in liberal democratic societies.[5] Moreover, it is their essentially political character that defines them as free and open. But policy debates are unable to be framed in the context of the values and uncertainties that drive disagreement when competing knowledge claims take centre stage. The values underpinning particular positions on an issue are instead made obscure by an ostensibly science-driven discourse where different knowledge claims are used by various protagonists to support their policy preference and discredit the competing knowledge claims supporting other normative positions. Thus, the fundamental challenge, in terms of building broader and more effective policy debates, is for us to admit that our values and interests not only shape the way we look at science and expert advice but also drive disagreement over how problems should be identified, prioritized and responded to.

The sooner these values can be openly debated, the sooner competition between goals and priorities can be resolved, thereby allowing science to concentrate on the task of how best to achieve, as opposed to expecting it to somehow determine, what is politically acceptable. If we are to conduct policy debates of the kind used to argue the superior policy making ability of liberal democracies, which in the context of wicked policy problems are infrequent at best, it is the competing values behind the various expert advice on offer that must be openly debated so that the *actual* sources of disagreement can be identified and then negotiated on *both* the merits of the competing normative judgements that drive them and the expert advice/knowledge claims invoked to support them. In such a context, the limits of specialist advice and its susceptibility to differing uncertainty claims, regardless of the type of advice on offer, are much more likely to become clearer, allowing debate to move beyond the pointless claim and counterclaim over who has the 'real' science/knowledge, which occupies much of what has come to be accepted as public policy debate. Moreover, and contrary to rationalist claims, the problem is that policy debate is *under* 'politicized', since politicization means openly stating and contesting values rather than attempting to manipulate or pervert the quest for objective, evidence-based policy in order to achieve self-serving ends. Indeed, the 'post-normal' character of complex policy challenges like determining the level of threat posed by a WMD-armed Iraq or an appropriate response to the potential consequences of a changing climate makes politicization of the policy decision process both essential and inevitable.

Uncertainty defines 'wicked' policy problems, preventing policy debate from being decisively influenced by science or other privileged claims to knowledge, thereby eliminating any recourse to 'the truth' as the sole provider of legitimacy for the policy decisions taken. Nonetheless, the authority generated by a decision taken on the basis of objective knowledge and evidence compels policy makers to still claim the mantle of objective rationality by using uncertainty to erode the credibility of conflicting knowledge claims and invoking plausible nightmare scenarios to counter or trivialize the uncertainties that underlie their own positions. It is then the rationalist policy project's demands for objectivity and truth that create a legitimacy vacuum for policy makers confronted by irreducible uncertainties. The ensuing debate becomes 'scientized' as a result of this but cannot be resolved through any resort to expert authority or knowledge, preventing policy makers from deflecting responsibility for unpopular or contested decisions to the 'rationality' of science and the reality it purportedly unveils. However, the uncertainties that deny recourse to knowledge-based legitimacy also allow the raising of various plausible nightmare scenarios, which can be used to counter uncertainties over what will happen and why with catastrophic 'what if' possibilities that, under the logic of the precautionary principle, demand action regardless of the uncertainties. At this point, the close relationship between uncertainty, values and risk perceptions becomes clearer, in particular the important influence exerted by values on how uncertainty and risk are conceptualized in decision making contexts.

> *The way you cope with uncertainty goes directly to your own risk propensities and values – the extent to which you can tease that out is a political question. If I believe the reason that George [W.] Bush was unwilling to accept the wave of evidence on climate change is because the economic costs he referred to were essentially going to be paid by rich people in the oil industry, I want to tease that out, because he's talking about a risk propensity that's connected to a political interest. So in public policy terms, the question of how you deal with uncertainty deserves to be teased out.[6]*

As both the Iraq and climate change case studies demonstrate, uncertainty only becomes an issue in decision making when important values come into conflict. Uncertainty over key issues, then, leads to the scientization of policy debates so long as positivist ambitions to eliminate uncertainty through further research/ information gathering remain dominant. But once the irreducibility of such uncertainties becomes more widely accepted, uncertainty begins to play a very different role – one that makes the competing values and world views of the various protagonists more explicit, thereby allowing debate to be reframed in ways that force the values themselves, rather than only the knowledge claims used to support them, to be openly recognized and negotiated.

Uncertainty, precaution and the whaling deadlock

As discussed so far, the knowledge normal science produces, due to the various epistemological problems its production involves, makes uncertainty unavoidable in any research. Scientific advice, therefore, is always open to attack by either: (a) invocation of uncertainty to argue the evidence is insufficient to conclude harm will not occur (i.e. the precautionary principle in its current form); or (b) invocation of uncertainty on the grounds of a lack of scientific evidence to say harm will occur (i.e. the inverse of the precautionary principle in its current form). And as the Iraq and climate change case studies presented here indicate, the degree to which either of these interpretations is applied is a function of the political interests of the parties involved and the extent to which these interests conflict.[7]

What the International Whaling Commission's (IWC) experience with uncertainty issues and problems also suggests, however, is that the latitude for interpreting uncertainty in differing ways can diminish over time once uncertainty is accepted as an unavoidable factor in the policy process as occurred in the IWC during the 1980s and 1990s. The effect of seeking to manage, as opposed to reducing, uncertainty in the Commission during this time was to force the underlying values and interests driving disagreement to the forefront of the whaling debate as opposition to whaling on scientific grounds alone became less compelling. Until the late 1970s, cetacean science had been guided by positivist expectations that it was possible to base management on reliable estimates of how many whales of a particular stock or species existed, how quickly a given species and population reproduced and matured, and how many whales could, on the basis of these data, safely be taken by aboriginal and commercial whalers. Prior to the IWC Scientific Committee's completion of the Revised Management Procedure (RMP) in the early 1990s – an approach designed specifically to *manage* uncertainty in stock estimates and catch quotas – policy debate had focused almost entirely on the Scientific Committee's failure to resolve the myriad uncertainties surrounding earlier attempts at *knowing* safe population and catch levels. But when the need for such a range of accurate management data was made redundant by the RMP, which operates only on the basis of obtainable catch and population data that must be constantly updated and is assumed to be flawed, the nature of the debate changed as arguments against a resumption of commercial whaling focused more on moral and legal issues concerning international public opinion and the 'specialness' of whales than the disputes over science and the uncertainties it involved that had divided the IWC for nearly four decades.

The emergence of a precautionary principle (PP) approach in the IWC during the early 1970s, therefore, was positive in that it contributed to the Commission finally producing a serious attempt to better account for uncertainty issues, following the moratorium on commercial whaling's adoption in 1982, through what became known as the Comprehensive Assessment of whale stocks. This initiative later led to the creation of the highly risk-averse RMP – an algorithm designed to establish under conditions of uncertainty what, if any, catches could 'safely' be taken from a given stock – which was accepted by the IWC in 1994 after having been rejected by some members the previous year. Until the early 1990s, when determined attempts by some in the Commission to derail the RMP's future implementation began in earnest, it seemed likely that the pay-off from the Comprehensive Assessment would be the Commission finally establishing a broadly acceptable balance somewhere between its previous management extremes (i.e. unsustainable commercial hunting in the 1950s and 1960s versus no commercial hunting under the 1982 moratorium). The realization of this elusive balance so far has been prevented by the serious disagreement that surfaced along with the RMP in the early 1990s over whether the IWC's goal was in fact to manage uncertainty issues with *both* the interests of commercial whalers and the future survival of whale stocks in mind. The longevity of this stalemate on the IWC's fundamental purpose demonstrates the inability of science to resolve political disputes. It can, however, through its failure to resolve uncertainties, make the political nature and dimensions of such disputes clearer.

As an approach to managing uncertainty, the PP is, as discussed in Chapter 3, vague and therefore open to broad interpretation, but the IWC's ongoing impasse is not simply the result of the principle's vague character. The willingness shown by various governments in the IWC to selectively interpret and apply the principle in ways that complement and support predetermined political objectives – *vis-à-vis* their selective interpretations and treatment of scientific uncertainty – is what has most undermined compromise and negotiation in the Commission. The ambiguous and obscure nature of the PP certainly provides ample opportunities for stalling, equivocation and political posturing, but ultimately it is the policy makers themselves who choose whether to do so.

By 1993, when a majority of members rejected the Scientific Committee's unanimous advice to adopt the RMP, it became clear that a growing number of influential IWC governments were now opposing any return to commercial whaling – regardless of the scientific advice on offer – and were increasingly being perceived by pro-whaling governments and groups to be making demands for excessive levels of precaution. This division over goals and acceptable levels of risk has persisted, in spite of the Commission's adoption of the RMP, and is now delaying agreement on the Revised Management Scheme (RMS), which provides the inspection and verification rules under which the RMP must operate. The continuing dearth of compromise over the level of precaution the rules of the RMS should provide for (e.g. international observers on all or some whaling vessels; DNA testing of whale meat) has led to hunting continuing, both commercially and for research purposes, outside of the international management controls the IWC is supposed to provide – thereby making the IWC largely redundant as a wildlife management organization. Furthermore, the ongoing impasse may well result in the whaling nations eventually leaving the Commission to whale under regional organizations – a move that effectively would eliminate any further prospect for global regulation of any future commercial whaling.

Three key issues raised by the IWC experience in its attempt at *managing* uncertainty through a precautionary approach are:

1   the precautionary principle's openness to a wide range of interpretations that allow it to be selectively invoked by policy makers to emphasize uncertainty issues when scientific advice clashes with non-negotiable policy positions/goals; thereby leading to
2   its potential for highlighting, rather than reconciling, values disputes, especially when applied in highly conflicted environments like that of the IWC; and, therefore,
3   the need for broad agreement on fundamental values and objectives before the precautionary principle can successfully be applied as a management tool rather than as a quasi-scientific rationale for the promotion of political preferences.

What role then has the precautionary principle played in the IWC since its invocation more than three decades ago? Rather than having led to better and more cooperative management of the world's whale stocks, it instead became instrumental in exposing a *political* deadlock that continues to undermine any real chance of whales being globally managed. The PP played a crucial role in the creation of the moratorium in 1982 by providing the framework for the arguments the US-led opponents of whaling used against the IWC Scientific

Committee's view that a complete pause on all commercial whaling was not based on scientific evidence.[8] Its successful application during the 1970s by the IWC's majority of anti-whaling members eroded the credibility of the positivist methodologies the Scientific Committee had applied to uncertainty in whale management and later provided the catalyst for the RMP's development as a part of the overall Comprehensive Assessment of Whale Stocks, which was called for by the IWC following the moratorium's adoption.

But it was the RMP's eventual acceptance by the IWC in 1994 as an acceptable means of managing uncertainties in the available data that more clearly exposed the extent to which values had been driving disagreement and debate in the IWC. With the scientific basis of anti-whaling policies (i.e. the need for more certainty) now undermined by the Scientific Committee's unanimous support for the RMP, whaling's opponents were forced to fall back on the moral and ethical foundations of their opposition. Indeed, by the time of the RMP's completion and adoption by the IWC, some members had even gone so far as to say scientific uncertainty was not even relevant to the question of whether or not commercial whaling can recommence. In its opening statement to the IWC's 1994 meeting, the New Zealand government stated its intention to participate in negotiating the rules under which the RMP could be implemented (i.e. the RMS) even though its opposition to whaling would continue:

> We will work to maintain the moratorium on commercial whaling because it reflects the current reality of world opinion. We will participate fully in the dialogue about the Revised Management Scheme because it is essential to have the best possible rules for whaling, whether or not they are required in practice.[9]

Despite the growing anti-whaling mood within the Commission during the 1970s and 1980s, the issue of permanently banning commercial whaling still had not formally been raised in the IWC and the moratorium itself was voted on as only a *temporary* pause until the concerns regarding scientific uncertainty were resolved – thereby implying, at this stage at least, that the Commission felt it was possible to reduce scientific uncertainty to acceptable levels. Accompanying the moratorium's entry to the Schedule to the Convention was a clause stating that:

> ... This provision will be kept under review, based upon the best scientific advice, and by 1990 at the latest the Commission will undertake a comprehensive assessment of the effects of this decision [i.e. the imposition of zero catch limits] on whale stocks and consider modification of this provision and the establishment of other catch limits.[10]

Thus, the Scientific Committee had begun work on the comprehensive assessment programme on the assumption that the moratorium's main objective was the acquisition of more reliable cetacean research and management methods with the intention of considering a return to commercial whaling at some point.[11] However, the question of how much certainty was required or how little uncertainty could be tolerated before commercial hunts could recommence was never addressed by the IWC in any detail and its failure to do so allowed further division in the Commission regarding its purpose and objectives to develop.

For several years after the moratorium's inception, and even during the negotiations prior to the vote being taken in the Commission, the means by which the moratorium was to contribute towards more and better cetacean research remained unclear, with even the proposal for a Comprehensive Assessment of whale stocks being added as an apparent afterthought to the original moratorium proposal. Between the moratorium's adoption in 1982 and 1985, the Scientific Committee repeatedly told the Commission it did not understand what the Comprehensive Assessment was intended to mean and asked for an explanation and definition at each annual meeting. No answer from the Commission, however, was forthcoming. In 1985 the Scientific Committee 'decided that if progress was to be made it [the Scientific Committee] would have to define what it thought was a 'comprehensive assessment' and establish how it might be accomplished'.[12] In April 1986, almost five years after the moratorium's adoption, a special meeting of the Scientific Committee was held in Cambridge, England, to develop a working definition of the Comprehensive Assessment and its aims. The IWC report of that meeting defined the Comprehensive Assessment as:

> *... an in-depth evaluation of the status of the stocks in the light of management objectives and procedures. This could include examination of current stock size, recent population trends, carrying capacity and productivity. In order to achieve this the Committee agreed that it would need to:*
>
> *(a) review and revise assessment methods and stock identity; review data quality, availability requirements and stock identity;*
> *(b) plan and conduct the collection of new information to facilitate and improve assessments;*
> *(c) examine alternative management regimes.[13]*

The task of defining 'Comprehensive Assessment', a concept intended to reflect the reasoning behind the moratorium, was largely ignored by those supporting the moratorium who appeared content with simply proscribing commercial whaling as a solution to the Commission's management problems. A significant characteristic of the Commission's resolutions and schedule amendments relating to the moratorium was the vague nature of the wording of key concepts and provisions. In addition to the Scientific Committee's inability to understand what 'Comprehensive Assessment' meant, even the long-awaited definition included wording which left a great deal open to various interpretations, in particular, its description of the Comprehensive Assessment as an evaluation of whale stocks 'in the light of management objectives and procedures', which to this day remain far from clear.

By 1986, when the Scientific Committee provided its definition of what the moratorium was intended to provide in terms of a comprehensive assessment, the IWC's management objectives had become more confused than ever as the Commission by this stage was openly divided on the interpretation of the IWC's parent treaty, the International Convention for the Regulation of Whaling (ICRW). Some governments which had supported the moratorium were now openly calling for a permanent end to commercial whaling on the basis of a recently developed interpretation of 'sustainable utilization' that excluded killing, while those who had opposed it continued to insist that hunting should resume after the Comprehensive Assessment's completion. Thus, the environment in which the RMP was to be developed could offer no consensus on why it was needed or to what ends it would be used, if at all.[14]

The need to avoid extinction of any species has remained a commonly understood political objective shared by all IWC members (probably the only one in fact) and as a result the level of scientific uncertainty involved with the decision to label some species and stocks (e.g. blue, fin and sei) as protected has not been used to question that decision. And although protecting these species conflicted with the need to hunt for social and cultural reasons in some societies, the long-term possibility of over-hunting causing the collapse of the industry was enough to over-ride these concerns. The indirect protection of other stocks (in particular, the minke) through sanctuaries and the moratorium, however, raised disputes over scientific uncertainty precisely because there was no political agreement that these stocks required protection. Protecting stocks the Scientific Committee believed could sustain some hunting caused strong opposition from pro-whaling members because the industries in their countries wanted to turn a profit and the governments were keen to keep whalers in work. Similarly, the differing interpretations of 'sustainable utilization' within the IWC mean that the disagreements over the conditions to be enforced under the RMS remain unresolved due to the conflict its acceptance would create with the priorities of anti-whaling governments and non-governmental organizations (NGOs) by allowing a return to commercial whaling. As a consequence, the proposed rules the RMS would impose on any future commercial whaling have been challenged and scrutinized on the grounds that they either cannot provide enough certainty, or that they demand too much certainty, since *the level of certainty required by policy makers generally is inversely related to the level of political support available for the policy in question*.

In extreme cases, such as in the late 1950s and early 1960s, when rapidly declining pelagic catches convinced whaling governments that many stocks had been severely depleted, the Scientific Committee's advice to reduce catch limits was eventually accepted because of broad political acceptance of a recognized certainty – rather than uncertainties. But even in such cases, political agreement on the issue (i.e. species should not be driven to extinction) was still required before scientific advice was able to directly influence the Commission's policies. No political consensus on the desirability of the RMP as a means of actually managing commercial hunting existed at any time during its development and, despite its belated adoption by the Commission in 1994, anti-whaling governments continue to oppose its implementation.

The popularity and importance of whales within Western societies, as both a symbol for the fight against environmental destruction and also as a commodity to be enjoyed in unprecedented ways (i.e. whale watching, whale books, whale movies, whale songs), grew rapidly during the 1980s. So much so that by the early 1990s, when the RMP and some elements of the Comprehensive Assessment were nearing completion, the status of 'the whale' was such that any research aimed at sustainable hunting was by now anathema in the eyes of the many governments and environmental NGOs who were invoking international and domestic public opinion to support what by now had become an entirely protectionist position on whaling. When the RMP finally was presented to the IWC in 1993 with the unanimous support of the Scientific Committee – a rare enough occurrence in itself – anti-whaling governments voted against its adoption, ostensibly on uncertainty grounds but mainly because of fears that its adoption would lead to an ending of the moratorium. Immediately following the Commission's rejection of the RMP, the Scientific Committee's Chairman, Dr Philip Hammond, resigned as chairman in protest. In his letter of resignation to the IWC, Hammond wrote:

> What is the point of having a Scientific Committee if its unanimous recommendations on a matter of primary importance [the RMP] are treated with such contempt?... I have come to the conclusion that I can no longer justify to myself being the organizer of and the spokesman for a Committee whose work is held in such disregard by the body to which it is responsible.[15]

By the early 1990s, whaling opponents were increasingly diluting science-based arguments over uncertainty issues with ethical arguments about inhumane killing methods and the immorality of killing allegedly highly sentient creatures such as cetaceans – arguments which identified their proponents with a protectionist rather than conservationist approach to wildlife management. By definition, a protectionist – as opposed to a conservationist – position makes irrelevant any scientific evidence in support of sustainable hunting, which in effect means that even if uncertainty could be reduced to zero, which science cannot do, protectionists still would not accept any return to hunting. Driving this argument is the perception of whales as highly intelligent creatures that are different from other animals in addition to their status as a major symbol in the war against environmental degradation. Thus, the idea of 'the whale' became an effective tool in downgrading the relevance of scientific research intended to create a sustainable whaling regime (i.e. whales are special, therefore it is wrong to hunt them regardless of the level of uncertainty involved). Uncertainty, meanwhile, continues to be invoked by protectionist-orientated opponents as a means of highlighting the kinds of risks a return to commercial whaling may produce – most recently in the context of climate change. The duality of this approach allows protectionist opponents – most notably

Australia, New Zealand, UK and France, in addition to NGOs such as Greenpeace, the International Fund for Animal Welfare and the World Wide Fund for Nature – to keep one foot in the protectionist camp and the other in the conservationist camp in the course of unconditionally opposing whaling. The most likely explanation for this strategy is reluctance on the part of these governments and groups to divorce themselves entirely from the credibility that 'science-based' arguments can offer.

Both Douglas Butterworth and Arne Kalland, among others, have accused whaling opponents of duplicity in their use of scientific uncertainty.[16] Kalland, for example, points out that science-based ecological arguments are 'more palatable for various reasons than are ethical and moral ones to a number of people, corporations, and government agencies' and argues that:

> Many protectionists are more than reluctant to change their rhetoric from an ecological discourse to animal welfare or animal rights arguments. Thus the myth of the endangered whale is sustained by charging scientists producing new and larger stock estimates of being incompetent, biased and 'bought' by governments of whaling nations, by refusing to accept these new population estimates or refuting their relevance, or by introducing new arguments into the ecological discourse.[17]

Clearly the uncertainty arguments made against research supporting a limited return to whaling under the RMP inspire little confidence in scientists and their ability to gather and accurately interpret empirical data. It is important to note, however, that both sides have used the mantle of scientific credibility in order to justify their actions. In the course of applying the precautionary principle to the RMP – despite the RMP itself being a product of the PP's application to whaling – scientific argument based on alternative analyses of the same data has helped persuade some policy makers and the public that sufficient uncertainty does indeed exist to justify postponing its implementation, particularly when the onus of proof that over-hunting will not occur lies with those who support the RMP's use. Opponents of whaling also have used various research efforts to support their claims about the specialness of whales (i.e. their intelligence, human-like behaviour, etc), thereby lending scientific credence to moral arguments against whaling and, in particular, the perception that little or no uncertainty is acceptable and, therefore, the moratorium, should remain in place. In an attempt to counter the popularity of the 'whales are special' argument, pro-whaling governments (in particular, Japan) and NGOs have responded by promoting the cultural importance of whaling to their societies. This approach, however, has been largely unsuccessful and has left the pro-whaling lobby in a position where they have had to rely on the strength of their scientific arguments in order to force change, but such efforts are hamstrung by both the inability to remove uncertainty entirely and the ultimate irrelevance of science to the protectionist position on whether commercial whaling should recommence.

The reliance of the whaling governments on science as the basis of their arguments has been useful in justifying limited hunting after the moratorium took effect under the ICRW provision allowing governments to issue permits for scientific whaling. The practice of taking whales for scientific research has become one of the major controversies within the IWC and, with the exception of the debate over the RMP and its implementation, represents the clearest manifestation of how the Commission's polarized political environment has problematized the issue of what is or is not valid science. In the view of the Japanese government, which has been the most enthusiastic IWC member in issuing scientific permits to its nationals and conducting both lethal and non-lethal research, the research it conducts is scientifically valid and completely legal (the ICRW allows governments to issue permits for scientific whaling to nationals). But in the view of the anti-whaling governments and NGOs, Japan is simply using science to exploit a 'loophole' in the moratorium and continue whaling.

The two defining elements of the whaling debate have been political conflict and uncertainty's role as a double-edged sword in disputes over the reliability of scientific advice and data. The protectionist strategy of employing the precautionary principle to demand more proof that whale stocks are robust enough to justify the RMP's implementation necessarily implies the need for more research, thereby providing the Japanese with some justification for issuing scientific permits. The problem, however, is not simply that more information is needed but what kind of research is needed and what kinds of questions need to be answered. Scientific method alone cannot answer these questions, since value judgements concerning what is desirable are required to define the policy objectives scientists need in order to prioritize their research goals. It is, perhaps, more than coincidental that the ambiguity and controversy surrounding Japanese scientific whaling resembles the disputes that characterized the goals of the moratorium and the lack of direction provided by the Commission for the Comprehensive Assessment. In the absence of clearly defined policy objectives, scientists can hardly be expected to provide relevant advice, and the inability of the IWC membership to provide this direction may go some way toward explaining the increasing irrelevance of the Scientific Committee's work. As Butterworth has observed:

> The real debate in the IWC has been between some countries wishing to preserve industries, employment and a food source based on whales, and others wanting these animals classed as sacrosanct. The terms of the convention [the ICRW] have required that this debate be conducted in a scientific guise, so that these hidden agendas have had to be played out in the scientific committee.[18]

Conclusion

The role of science in the IWC and the interpretation of uncertainty has been left in a form of limbo since the early 1990s when ethical and moral issues were first introduced to seriously question the usefulness and appropriateness of the research undertaken during (and after) the Comprehensive Assessment. As debate over the future of the RMS continues, scientific advice appears to be both relevant and irrelevant to varying degrees, depending on the argument being made and the objective in question. Indeed, the extent to which scientific advice, rather than the various political objectives of the Commission's members, has influenced the IWC's policies is very much open to doubt; the role of science and the ends to which it is used has become equally problematic in climate change policy and its negotiation. If, for example, science is commonly expected to be able to accurately describe and predict the real world (as per the conventional view of science), then it is not difficult for governments and organizations, with an interest in doing so, to selectively criticize and reject scientific advice on uncertainty grounds when it conflicts with their values and priorities, as occurred with the treatment of uncertainty in the specialist advice on Iraq's WMD and the causes and potential effects of climate change. But if it is accepted from the outset, for the reasons discussed in Chapter 1, that uncertainty must be dealt with by making political decisions concerning how much risk is acceptable (because certainty is beyond the grasp of science), it becomes more difficult for participants to hide political and economic interests behind arguments made ostensibly on scientific grounds.

On the few occasions when relatively high levels of certainty over the depletion of stocks existed, such as the Antarctic collapse during the early 1960s,[19] the Japanese and Soviet delegations to the IWC were quick to point out the increasing hardships being suffered by their industries in order to bolster their positions against reductions, but only after it had become clear that uncertainty arguments alone no longer would suffice. This pattern of shifting justifications when uncertainty arguments become weaker in the face of contradictory evidence or circumstances was again repeated in the early 1990s, this time by anti-whaling governments and groups trying to reorganize the basis of their opposition in response to the decreased risk offered by a new and more risk averse management procedure for the hunting of baleen whales. In both instances, the erosion of uncertainty as a basis for opposition helped to reveal the underlying political judgements and priorities informing the policies being pursued. A similar unveiling of political motivations through shifting policy justification followed the coalition of the willing failure to uncover Iraq's alleged WMD or any evidence of active WMD programmes. The Iraq Survey Group's (ISG) failure to find WMD in Iraq forced the Bush, Blair and Howard governments to switch their primary justification for military action in Iraq from an existential threat to national and international security to alternative arguments citing the case for humanitarian intervention against Saddam's regime. John Howard, during the lead up to war, had denied himself this avenue of alternative policy legitimacy by stating that he could not support military action on the grounds of regime change alone.[20] Howard instead emphasized the threat of Iraq's WMD and the importance of the Security Treaty between Australia, New Zealand and the United States of America (ANZUS) as justification for supporting the US-led invasion.[21] The practice of shifting policy justification in the face of contradictory empirical evidence or specialist advice is also reflected in Chapter 6's discussion of how policy elites in the Bush administration and World Bank employed what became known as the 'augmented Washington Consensus' to deflect criticism of the original Washington Consensus's failings as a universal development model and to justify the augmented version's adoption as an economic blueprint for rehabilitating failed and failing states.

The widespread public opposition to whaling among many, but not all, Western states and the direct influence it has had on the foreign policy of those states is in many respects the product of exactly the kind of public interest and debate that a mature marketplace of ideas is expected to produce. It is also an example of both the strong interest foreign policy can generate domestically and the ability of domestic public sentiment to impose itself on foreign policy decision making. On closer inspection, however, in so far as the influence of domestic public opinion on government positions in the IWC can be attributed to public discourse and engagement on whaling in a functioning 'marketplace of ideas', the nature and scope of any public debate on whaling has been made very narrow by its openness to manipulation by various interest groups, most notably environmental NGOs and, to a lesser degree, government policy elites. Such is the current breadth and depth of anti-whaling sentiment that the marketplace of ideas – in so far as one has existed – has effectively become a 'monopoly on ideas' unable to tolerate any opposing or alternative viewpoints and arguments. Expectations for science to act as a neutral magistrate guiding IWC policy have been seriously undermined over the last four decades by both the numerous uncertainties surrounding the status and vulnerability of various whale stocks, and also the inability of science to comment on the many inherently political issues actually driving debate and disagreement – ranging from national interest considerations involving trade and security to broader issues involving what effective wildlife management should represent and the 'specialness' of whales.

Contrary to Pielke Jr's view in which science can or should create a space for 'honest brokers' to act as arbiters of competition between competing viewpoints and the values they represent,[22] scientific advice on whaling remains an advocate of differing values in the whaling debate but it is inevitable that science will play such a role. Indeed, the strategy of arguing against a preventive or alternative course of action because we do not know or cannot prove a particular set of outcomes will occur is common enough, as is the more recent strategy of arguing against other courses of action because we cannot prove undesirable outcomes will not occur. But both of these strategies become that much more difficult to implement when it is recognized from the outset that certainty is not available: a situation which forces the political interests that lie at the heart of the issue to the surface in order to argue why one course of action over another is more desirable. Put another way, uncertainty only need be a problem when people believe they can achieve their goals by demanding more certainty.

8
Alternative Responses to Uncertainty: Bringing Politics Back In

So how can values be made more explicit in policy debates? And how can the various actors, including the scientists and experts themselves, be dissuaded from attempting to hide their relative, and essentially normative, preferences behind competing claims of expert knowledge and rationality? At the very least, a more explicit understanding and acknowledgement of the necessary limits of science and the often dominant role played by values in post-normal issue areas is required, and this has already begun to take place, to some degree at least, in developed 'risk' societies as people become increasingly concerned with what science doesn't know and what its methods cannot predict. However, core disagreements on ultimate goals and the vastly different perceptions of progress, sustainability, risk and potential costs and benefits that fuel them often remain as obscure as ever in terms of public discourse and perception. Thus, it is upon these very issues that a form of broad and open 'meta-debate' is required if more useful, values-specific debates on policy, as per the marketplace of ideas concept, are to take place. Open political debate is, as Bernard Crick has argued, not only essential to notions of legitimacy in liberal democracies but also the defining difference between 'political and authoritarian rule':

> The political method of rule is to listen to these other groups so as to conciliate them as far as possible, and to give them a legal position, a sense of security, some clear and reasonably safe means of articulation, by which these other groups can and will speak freely. Ideally politics draws all of these groups into each other so that they each and together can make a positive contribution towards the general business of government, the maintaining of order. The different ways in which this can be done are obviously many, even in any one particular circumstance of competing social interests…

> *But, however imperfectly this process of deliberate conciliation works, it is nevertheless radically different from tyranny, oligarchy, kingship, dictatorship, despotism, and – what is probably the only distinctly modern type of rule – totalitarianism.*[1]

The two essential ingredients in a post-positivist approach to managing uncertainty then are firstly a broad recognition among policy makers, the media and the public that normal science is unable to solve many unknowns, or sometimes to even identify unknowns, and that while positivist expectations that the 'truth is out there' may at some point become well founded, we currently remain incapable of recognizing 'the truth' as such in any definitive way even if we were to come across it. Secondly, a similarly broad recognition that knowledge claims made under conditions of uncertainty are, therefore, being made for reasons informed at least as much (and often more) by normative values and preferences as they are by reliable evidence, testable assumptions and theories, or repeatable experimentation. The establishment of these two conditions is clearly a huge challenge that may never be achieved but, as noted earlier, the increasingly questioning attitude of many in society of science and what it represents indicates that some progress toward this end has already been made. The point I am making here, however, is more about the conditions that need to exist *if* we are to move beyond positivist expectations of policy making and the kinds of problems that emerge from continuing to entertain such 'rationalist' expectations. As I argued in Chapter 1, the 'rationalist model' of policy making and the kinds of expectations from policy making it encourages, particularly in terms of legitimacy and effectiveness, become 'irrational' under conditions of irreducible uncertainty since there is nothing *rational* about continuing to demand certainty when there is none to be had. Moreover, maintaining the expectation of more certainty in the face of uncertainties made irreducible either by time constraints (normally the case in policy) and/or the complexities of an open system leads only to the opportunity for policy advocates to 'construct' empirical cases for one policy or another as a smokescreen for unspoken political motivations behind the policy – as occurred with the US case for invading Iraq and is occurring among the various 'science-based' arguments for and against an immediate cut in greenhouse gas (GHG) emissions.

Through the creation of these two essential conditions, which allow for the framing of complex, wicked policy problems in post-positivist terms, the relevant uncertainties will become more explicit, making the masking of the values and interests underlying differing policy positions behind claims of objective or scientific knowledge much more difficult. As a result, questions of legitimacy will necessarily become more political as debates contesting differing priorities and perceptions of risk take centre stage and begin to change a political context in which competing knowledge claims can be more openly judged in terms of both their veracity and their relevance to the values that define the debate. Should, for example, regime change in states like Iraq be a policy priority and, if so, why, under what conditions and to what ends?

Is regime change possible in a way that will not produce greater uncertainty and risk? Alternatively, is the welfare of current generations more important to us than that of future generations? What level of certainty do we require that future threats are real or that we know what will produce them before it is legitimate to impose penalties and costs on contemporary societies for the (possible but unknown) benefit of future societies?

Preventing the *scientization* of wicked policy issues, like Iraq's alleged threat potential or the future impacts of climate change, by highlighting uncertainty and the values that determine its treatment, therefore brings competing values – the essence of 'politics', to the forefront of debate, making it possible for hedging strategies to be raised and considered both as a means of reconciling values disputes and managing, rather than only attempting to reduce, uncertainty. However, attempting to promote a hedging approach as an alternative without first uncovering the various value positions will fail to compel agreement on its adoption, as the Security Council debate on how to manage Iraq's alleged weapons of mass destruction (WMD) demonstrated, because positivist-type policy 'solutions' (we have 'scientifically' identified and studied the problem and its cause(s) and we now know how to fix it) remain impervious to being 'delegitimated' in the absence of any way of convincingly falsifying their claims of objectivity, which is normally the case in post-normal-type policy issues. Moreover, and as I argued in Chapter 3, risk perceptions are themselves an expression of the values and importance we attach to 'not knowing' (i.e. uncertainty). Thus, the creation of a politically acceptable and, therefore, implementable hedging strategy requires values firstly to be made explicit through open debate, allowing the relevant risks to then be identified and prioritized within the policy process.

Case Study Redux: The invasion of Iraq

Richard Clarke and others have said the arguments made within the Bush administration for invading Iraq were made within days of the 9/11 attacks.[2] The point at which this form of military action actually became an *unstated* policy decision appears to have occurred at some point in the months between President Bush's 'axis of evil speech' identifying Iraq, Iran and North Korea as threats to US national security in January 2002[3] and a London meeting later that July between senior UK policy and intelligence figures where, according to what became known as the Downing Street Memo, both the Bush administration's decision to invade Iraq and its strategy of fixing the intelligence around this policy were communicated to the Blair government by MI6 Head Sir Richard Dearlove following his recent meetings with US policy makers in Washington, DC.[4] Regardless of precisely when the decision to invade Iraq was made, the important point is that it occurred well before the debate regarding the need for a military occupation had even begun. What this means, of course, is that policy was indeed running strong in the US executive's treatment of the intelligence on WMD it received from this point on at least, and this soon became the case in the Blair and Howard cabinets as well. As a consequence, uncertainty over the existence of Iraqi WMD programmes was always going to be downplayed by the executives of each government, since a decision based on a mixture of prior assumptions, ideology and circumstantial evidence already had been made. The BBC documentary *Road to War – The Inside Story* described the policy environment within the Bush administration in the aftermath of the 9/11 attacks on the US as one where: 'Policy and emotion were fused in the aftermath of the [9/11] attacks. The President brought the feelings he found in New York with him to the Cabinet table, and his advisors forged them into a new political philosophy.'[5]

Regime change in Iraq had become a bipartisan policy objective in the US, but the use of military intervention, rather than sanctions and the many airstrikes that had been carried out on Iraq, as the policy instrument for precipitating Saddam's removal did not become a publicly-stated policy option in the US, despite its earlier support among neo-conservatives,[6] until after the 2001 al Qaeda attacks. As Paul Pillar has noted:

> *The tremendous change [9/11] engendered in the mood of the American public finally made it politically possible for the neo-con stars to come together along with a president who was yearning to be a war president... Without 9/11 [invading Iraq] wouldn't have been politically possible but the aspiration was still there and certainly the [Paul] Wolfowitzes and the [Richard] Perles were champing at the bit to make it happen and they'd been champing for some time but the political reality was otherwise.*[7]

The challenge that supporters of an invasion faced, however, was the need to construct Saddam's regime as a developing existential threat in the present in order to make future threat scenarios more compelling, since an occupation of Iraq could not be legitimized only by pointing to Saddam's past behaviour as evidence of his future threat potential, regardless of how well-founded such fears were believed to be. Overcoming this challenge, then, depended on the Bush administration's ability to produce a body of contemporary evidence of Iraq's ongoing development of proscribed weapons that would support the kind of threat scenarios needed to justify precautionary action against Iraq.

The Bush, Blair and Howard governments attempted to 'objectify' the argument for war by selectively introducing facts that could be interpreted as supporting the threat thesis against Iraq and then bolstering the strength of that interpretation by emphasizing the scale of the threat itself. Indeed, there was little doubt among even opponents of the invasion that Iraq had retained at least some of its chemical and possibly biological weapons capacity, due to Saddam's past duplicity and resistance to weapons inspections. The key issue debated in the Security Council and elsewhere was whether Saddam's possession of 'some' so-called WMD provided a sufficient 'factual' basis for invading Iraq. The Bush administration and its allies in London and Canberra exploited uncertainty over the kind and level of threat posed by Iraq by extrapolating from the available, but still ambiguous, evidence various nightmare scenarios involving mushroom clouds and WMD-armed transnational terrorist groups – all of which were made so much more credible by the 9/11 attacks in New York and Washington. And, in lieu of any indisputable evidence that Iraq had already abandoned its chemical, biological and nuclear programmes as Saddam was claiming, there was little prospect of undermining the Bush administration's argument for precautionary action. In addition to reversing the burden of proof and allowing much greater scope for speculation over what may exist or happen, introducing a precautionary approach, as noted in Chapter 3, also allows, due to the uncertainties involved, much greater scope for how the available evidence may be interpreted. Thus, proponents of military action needed only to produce often untestable evidence that *suggested* the possibility of Iraq maintaining proscribed weapons whereas the Iraqi government needed to *prove* that it did not have them, which, as Hans Blix, former Head of the United Nations Monitoring, Verification and Inspection Commission (UNMOVIC), observed, introduced the impossibility of proving a negative:

> *You cannot prove a negative, that's what we [UNMOVIC] said, but we sometimes get too much credit ... 'you were the ones who said there weren't any weapons ... and they should have listened to you'. But we didn't say so. There was a thick document, the Cluster document, we gave to the Security Council the day after the invasion and we said these things are unaccounted for, but we did not draw the conclusion that they were there. So we had intellectually a much more viable position than those who claim there is something or those who claim there weren't any [WMD]. There was a residue of uncertainty.*[8]

The argument for military action against Iraq was based on selective interpretations of uncertainty that promoted the credibility of some evidence over other evidence depending on its compatibility with the case for war. But what gave credibility to how the many uncertainties surrounding the evidence were being either downplayed or emphasized among policy makers, various analysts and much of the media reporting was the precautionary logic the threat posed by a WMD-armed Iraq under Saddam's control could invoke. Underlying the Bush administration's justification of its Iraq policy was an uncomplicated view of past and current intelligence in which the facts had in effect spoken for themselves on the question of Iraq and the threat it posed to Western interests, which left little room for alternative inferences to be drawn on Saddam's future intentions. Furthermore, the various known risks posed by toppling Saddam's regime, many of which now have been realized, were – like the initial uncertainties that created them – given low priority by the Bush administration and its allies also because of the confidence they placed in their own assessments of not only the evidence for and against Iraq's continued possession and development of WMD, but also the costs involved in removing him from power. Put simply, the cost–benefit analysis was presented by policy makers as an evidence-based assessment that demonstrated military action was a low-risk option that would yield many contemporary benefits at little cost.

Former US Defense Intelligence Agency (DIA) analyst Jeff White believes that attempting to legitimize the invasion by establishing Saddam as a threat on the basis of Iraq's alleged WMD capability and terrorist links was a mistake. The first argument, according to White, used by President Bush for military action instead should have been that Saddam's regime was evil and would become more difficult to contain in the future, '... if that didn't work politically, we should have waited for the sanctions and inspections regime to play out'.[9] Indeed, allowing the UNMOVIC inspections to have continued would likely have further weakened support for an invasion, since there were no WMD to be found. But allowing the inspections to 'play out' also would have allowed the opportunity for greater international support for regime change to be gathered if Saddam's government had failed to cooperate with the inspections, as any further obstructive behaviour by the Iraqis no doubt would have strengthened the legal case for an invasion. In retrospect, it is now obvious to all, except perhaps those most responsible, that the US policy shift on Iraq from containment to invasion was neither warranted in terms of the justification put forward nor in the best interests of the US and its allies. Apart from the obvious loss of life and political instability in Iraq, the decision to invade also diverted attention and much needed military resources from Afghanistan and significantly eroded the legitimacy and credibility of US policy. Even more worrying is the prospect that both Iraq and Afghanistan look likely to remain heavily dependent on Western military and financial support for many years to come if they are to avoid falling either into protracted civil war or the control of Islamic extremists.

A hedging strategy based on further inspections by UNMOVIC and the assumption that an absence of evidence of any continuing Iraqi WMD programmes or stockpiles might indicate an absence of WMD rather than an Iraqi concealment strategy, as proposed by opponents of the war in the UN Security Council and elsewhere, would have allowed for the same conclusion reached by the Iraq Survey Group (ISG) to have been reached without the ongoing costs incurred by invasion and occupation. It was an argument forcefully made during the Security Council debate on Iraq by the French Foreign Minister Dominic de Villepin:

> We were in a process where the [UNMOVIC] inspectors were telling us that things were better, they were doing progress [sic]. We have a chance to disarm Iraq peacefully. Why take the risk of a war in this region? Why take the risk to have ... unity of Iraq at stake? Why take the risk to have the Arab world put on fire? Why should we do that if we can work through a peaceful disarmament?[10]

The only likely obstacle to UNMOVIC achieving the same outcome as the ISG would have been further recalcitrance on the part of the Iraqis, which would have at least given the coalition case for war greater legitimacy and, therefore, international support. But given the inability of the debate to move beyond its positivist framing by the Bush administration's use of 'solid' intelligence (i.e. we know Iraq has WMD and terrorist links), which could not easily be dismissed due to its secret status, the case for hedging against uncertainty effectively was made irrelevant by untestable claims that no uncertainty existed. Ironically, the only available empirical test for these claims was the UNMOVIC inspections but their findings were neutralized by the Bush administration interpretation that UNMOVIC's failure to locate WMD was only evidence of Saddam's deceit rather than evidence that Iraq's claims of already having destroyed its WMD were valid. This essentially precautionary interpretation of UNMOVIC's conclusions was difficult for even the French and German governments to refute since they too, like most observers at the time, believed that Iraq had maintained at least some of its former WMD programmes and capability. The impossible task faced by UNMOVIC (and Saddam) of empirically demonstrating negative propositions as true (Iraq has no WMD/is not hiding WMD; Iraq has no al Qaeda ties; Iraq is not an existential threat), or falsifying the speculative assumptions underpinning the Iraq threat thesis, therefore, opened sufficient space for an *unfalsifiable* collection of empirical bits and pieces to be gathered together under the logic of ideologically motivated and informed suppositions that could be supported by that evidence, both past and present. And it was from within this space that Colin Powell's own belief in the truth of the material he presented to the UN apparently emerged, giving him the confidence to argue the US case against Iraq with 'certainty': 'My colleagues, every statement I make today is backed up by sources, solid sources... These are not assertions. What we are giving you are facts and conclusions based on solid intelligence.'[11]

What then could be done to make the influence of values and ideological predispositions of policy elites on the treatment of uncertainties in intelligence assessments either more explicit in policy debate or, at the very least, a recognized factor in how policy decisions are arrived at? As the treatment by the US, UK and Australian executives of uncertainty over the question of Iraq's alleged WMD programmes has demonstrated, the rationalist policy model and the standards it produces for 'legitimate' policy decisions encourage more than only unrealistic expectations of specialist advice and the role it plays in policy making, especially under conditions of high uncertainty. The rationalist depiction of the policy process also, by encouraging such expectations, often allows executive decision makers to deflect scrutiny of their choice of evidence, and therefore also their treatment of the uncertainties involved, simply by arguing that the decision taken was rational and therefore legitimate given the advice or information they received; questions about why they 'received' some advice rather than other advice, how they judged some advice or evidence to be more or less reliable, or why they interpreted uncertainty as grounds for precaution in one case but not in another are seldom raised and almost never answered. We are instead still encouraged to accept that good policy is, as the rational policy model insists, primarily about rational decision making based on accurate information and assessment; if policy doesn't produce the expected outcomes, the problem, therefore lies with either the quantity or quality, and sometimes both, of the information provided rather than how the decision makers selected, interpreted and used the information they received.

As Chapter 4 shows, this is precisely what occurred when President Bush and Prime Ministers Blair and Howard were confronted with the ISG's failure to find any evidence of chemical, biological or nuclear weapons development in Iraq. Almost all of the investigation into why the central reason for invading Iraq was completely wrong, that is Saddam's ongoing possession and development of proscribed weapons, focused only on why the intelligence *used* by policy makers was inaccurate and how it could be made more accurate in the future. Only the Australian Joint Parliamentary Committee (AJPC) and the long-delayed Phase II investigation under the Senate Select Committee on Intelligence in the US (released in June 2008) addressed the many questions surrounding the evidence chosen by their respective executives and the manner in which it was presented as supporting the case for war. The AJPC, however, was limited by both its inability to access all of the relevant secret intelligence available to the Howard cabinet during 2002 and early 2003, and also its essentially preliminary status to the Flood Report set up by John Howard in response to the AJPC's recommendation for further investigation. The terms set for the Australian investigation under former Office of National Assessments (ONA) Chief Phillip Flood, like the UK's Butler Report, did not address the issue of how the executive chose and presented the intelligence underpinning its decision to support the US. Flood's brief was, as a consequence, limited to examining the failed rationale for war used by Howard and his ministers as an *intelligence* rather than *policy* failure.

The Phase II report in the US, meanwhile, did not, as the Select Committee's director of research and former State Department intelligence analyst Greg Thielmann has since argued, take into account the full range of evidence and sources available to the Bush administration prior to the March 2003 invasion, which contradicted much of the evidence presented in support of the war cited or relied on by the administration between October and December of 2002 and included key issues such as the aluminium tubes, the Niger claim and the absence of evidence of WMD development activity at any of the sites inspected by UNMOVIC. Moreover, the Phase II report did not examine the administration's public statements in the context of the evidence and testimony demonstrating that the decision to invade Iraq had been made prior to much of the intelligence used in making the case for war becoming available. In Thielmann's view, 'An administration hoping to avoid war rather than trying to justify it would have revisited many of the intelligence judgements reached in October 2002 [when the now discredited US National Intelligence Estimate was completed] based on the access gained following the inspectors' return in late November 2002'.[12]

But the kind of open debate over uncertainties and potential risks that could have more clearly exposed the normative agenda behind the Bush administration's policy and made hedging a much more compelling option is often impossible in the realm of national security policy making. Unlike other wicked policy problems, such as climate change, where the credibility of evidence and arguments is exposed to independent scrutiny, national security policy exists in a very different domain. The information used in national security and sensitive areas of foreign policy, and the sources and means used to obtain it, often cannot be (or are not) made available for wider examination for what are often undisclosed reasons of national security, making any external scrutiny of government decision making in these areas, especially in terms of the uncertainties and values involved, very unlikely. The public is effectively forced to take policy makers at their word on issues informed by secret intelligence and the conclusions they draw from it, as occurred during Colin Powell's presentation of the US case for regime change in Iraq when he prefaced his presentation by saying: 'I cannot tell you everything that we know. But what I can share with you, when combined with what all of us have learned over the years, is deeply troubling.'[13]

Conflict between the need to keep intelligence sources and information secret and out of the public domain and the need for independent assessment of the policy arguments made by policy makers often is unavoidable, making open debate on such issues impractical; the national security policy arena, therefore, is of a fundamentally different nature to the kind of debates occurring in other policy domains. As a consequence, interpretation of the uncertainties and potential risks that intelligence presents normally is limited only to those of the policy elites, causing policy within this environment to be debated and framed within a very narrow band of values and assumptions. But in spite of these restrictions, the policy process by which decisions are arrived at still claims its legitimacy by reference to the objective facts the relevant intelligence is argued to have provided as per the rationalist policy model, making it very difficult to contest since access to the knowledge underpinning such claims is often delayed well beyond the point at which policy decisions are made and implemented. Had Curveball's background, behaviour and status (both as a defector and as the only human intelligence source the US had outside of the Iraqi National Congress) been exposed to external scrutiny much earlier, for example, the US argument for why Saddam presented an objective threat would have been severely undermined. Again in retrospect, it also has become obvious that, because the decision was made well before the evidence presented as the basis for the decision was even assembled, the rational actor model was irrelevant to the policy process within the Bush administration and Howard and Blair governments. Furthermore, the kinds of information, evidence and analysis that did inform the decision to go to war were both speculative and circumstantial, and assembled mainly to legitimize the pursuit of a policy judgement (Iraq is an immediate threat) rather than to attempt an assessment of *whether* that judgement was sufficiently supported by the available evidence for it to qualify as 'legitimate'.

Given the constraints of secrecy in national security related policy, measures aimed at ensuring the kind of rational approach to managing uncertainty I am arguing for – that is, recognizing irreducible uncertainties as *irreducible* and making the values informing their treatment an explicit part of the policy debate – will need to be internally implemented. Doing so, however, will require some form of institutional incentive to ensure that these measures are not circumvented or ignored by policy elites. In the aftermath of the Iraq debacle, there are many lessons to be learnt for intelligence analysts and policy makers alike, but perhaps none more so than the folly of relying so heavily on tactical intelligence at the expense of strategic assessment. As I argued in Chapter 4, the disdain shown for strategic assessment within the Bush, Blair and Howard executives, in particular, on the question of Iraq's threat capability, was a major contributor to allowing 'suppositions to be piled on suppositions' by promoting an almost 'anything is possible' range of possibilities for how the tactical intelligence was interpreted. The myriad uncertainties surrounding tactical intelligence, due to its current and often untestable nature, mean that various interpretations are always going to be possible and this should be encouraged, but not in isolation from the bigger picture provided by strategic analysis and certainly not in a way that allows such untestable (at the time) interpretations to exist independently of conflicting evidence or assessments without a clearly stated rationale for doing so.

The only sanction currently faced by the US, UK or Australian executives for the policy justifications they adopt that is beyond executive control or influence is the prospect of electoral defeat when policy fails to achieve its stated goals or produces other, less desirable, outcomes. The problem here though is that electoral penalties tend to be enforced, as Wayne Parsons points out,[14] less in response to issues of misrepresentation or error in the *means* by which policy *is* produced than by dissatisfaction with the *ends* that policy produces. It is, for example, very likely that the Republicans would not have been so severely punished in the 2006 Senate elections and that Tony Blair would not have come under pressure from his own party to resign as Prime Minister and Labour Party Leader for fear of losing the next election if at least some of the proscribed weapons that President Bush and Prime Minister Blair claimed Iraq had been hiding were found prior to 2006. Measuring policy legitimacy only by its outcomes while ignoring the reasoning that devised it, however, only further encourages the kind of speculative thinking that prompted the Bush administration and its allies to substitute preconceptions and ideological conviction for evidence and measured prudential judgement of uncertainty and the potential costs of being wrong. Moreover, had the Bush administration been proven right, the policy process no doubt would have become an example of rational policy making at work and been left largely, if not entirely, unquestioned.

Various recommendations already have been made by investigations, such as the Silberman-Robb Commission in the US, the UK's Butler Inquiry and the Flood Report in Australia, on how the intelligence side of the equation can be improved. These investigations have reinforced an awareness within the intelligence community that close scrutiny of its performance will follow any major inconsistencies or failures, thereby creating a strong incentive for intelligence analysts and managers to exercise caution and responsibility when providing assessments to policy makers. But as the investigations into the intelligence available prior to the Iraq invasion have demonstrated, the accountability imposed by retrospective inquiry is almost entirely restricted to the activities of the intelligence community; the conduct and accountability of the policy makers in their use of that intelligence remain unexamined. As noted earlier, only the AJPC and the Senate Select Committee's Phase II investigation made any attempt to examine how the executive interpreted conflicting assessments and the various caveats they contained, and the extent to which policy statements accurately represented the assessments that were available.

The obvious alternative to invasion was, as noted above, to hedge against the uncertainties by allowing the recently recommenced United Nations (UN) inspections to continue while maintaining the threat of military action if Iraq did not cooperate. President Bush and his allies dismissed this approach even before debate had begun, creating a situation where the intelligence is now broadly agreed to have been fixed around the policy. There has been no formal accountability imposed on the policy elites who were involved with building the case for war, although it is clear that their own reputations have suffered. But if policy elites were, like the intelligence community, aware that in the aftermath of major policy decisions, such as taking their country to war, their judgements and policy rationales would be revisited in great detail by investigations independent of executive influence, would they be less likely to try and 'fix' the intelligence around predetermined policy goals? If policy elites knew that these investigations would give equal weight to *both* the performance of the intelligence community and quality of assessment it provided *and* the policy judgements and decisions of the policy elite in relation to how those assessments were incorporated into the policy process, would they be more careful to accurately reflect the uncertainties within the expert advice they received in the policy justifications they publicly presented?

Given the difficulty of imposing accountability onto the policy process when national security concerns are invoked by the executive, legitimately or not, the most effective way to ensure a more 'rational' approach to *managing* uncertainty – through a broader and more balanced recognition of not only the various risks involved but also the values informing them – is, I argue, to ensure that policy elites know they will be made accountable for their policy decisions and arguments after the fact by open and transparent investigation of the advice they received and the decisions they made in relation to that advice. The task of appointing appropriate, non-partisan people to lead these investigations, in addition to deciding how the appointments are made and by whom (other than the executive), will be a difficult challenge and it is beyond the brief of this book to go beyond the *what* and venture into the *how*. Others, however, have made similar observations concerning the need for broader accountability in and oversight of the intelligence-policy relationship and have suggested various ways in which this might be achieved.[15] The most important precursor for reforming the intelligence-policy interface in ways that could prevent policy failures like the decision to invade Iraq is, as I have argued, a public recognition of the ways uncertainty in specialist advice more broadly, and in intelligence more specifically, can be utilized and interpreted for a variety of ends in the policy process. Without such recognition, public perceptions and expectations of policy legitimacy will remain locked within the rational policy model's positivist mindset, thereby leaving politics locked out of our understanding of what it means for a policy to be 'rational'.

Case Study Redux: Reframing climate change negotiations

What, then, can a retrospective analysis of uncertainty and its role in building the case for military action against Iraq tell us about the ongoing contemporary debate over climate change and its status as a policy issue? One lesson from the Iraq experience is the ease with which precautionary logic can lead to threat exaggeration and the enlistment of the 'power of nightmares' in policy debate. Another observation, highlighted by this book's interpretation of uncertainty's treatment by the Bush administration and its allies, is that the only truly 'rational' approach to profound uncertainty and serious risk is to hedge against getting things wrong, a likely outcome when uncertainties are high, rather than basing decisions on the expectation of getting things right. Hedging strategies in the context of public policy, however, require a shared understanding of what is important and what is to be prioritized (i.e. the risks to be avoided or accepted) if they are to receive political support and agreement. Such understandings are, as I have argued, the product of openly debating and negotiating the values and interests that underpin conflicting policy positions and the kinds of outcomes they are expected to bring. They are, in other words, the product of a negotiated political process that *explicitly* deals with competing values rather than a so-called 'evidence-based' process that instead attempts to exclude 'politics' with claims of objective knowledge and facts.

In the context of my analysis of how values inform perceptions of uncertainty and risk, the major obstacle to climate change policy agreement remains the failure among governments and societies to explicitly address and negotiate the competing sources of concern driving disagreement. Indeed, a variety of fundamental values and interests are believed to be at risk as a result of either potential climate change impacts or the potential economic and social costs of attempting to reduce these impacts. Moreover, conflict arises over not only which issues should take priority in dealing with climate change, but also the kind of issues that define how climate change is, or should be, understood or 'framed'. And the more complex the issue, the greater the proliferation of competing perceptions or framings.[16] Steven Ney sees 'messy' policy problems such as climate change constituting what is really an 'argumentative' policy process, one in which almost everything is contested, or contestable, as a result of the many differing perceptual frames that can emerge in post-normal policy situations when uncertainty is high and values are in dispute:

> *What kind of policy issue is climate change? Is it an issue of poverty and inequality, as many of the developing countries claim? Is it an issue of technology? Is it an issue of control and regulation? Is it an issue of profligate consumption? Or is it all of these things? If so, how do they interact? This is why conflict is intractable: policy actors cannot actually agree what is at issue,*

let alone negotiate a compromise between different preferences. In an argumentative policy process, policy actors need to learn as they try to make sense of messy policy issues. So what we want is likely to change as we learn. Yet, what we learn, in turn, will depend on what we want.[17]

Framing climate change primarily as a human-induced phenomenon that can, therefore, also be moderated or controlled by human endeavour, as the United Nations Framework Convention on Climate Change (UNFCCC) has, betrays a lingering positivist belief in human kind's ability to master the natural environment. According to this view, science has told us what is wrong and how to fix it; the only obstacle to action on GHG mitigation is then the political will of governments to do what climate science tells us is rational, that is reducing GHG emissions. But in addition to overstating our understanding of climate change and the extent and nature of our contribution to it, presenting climate change in such stark, rationalist terms invites disputes over who should sacrifice what and why, and to what end, with little scope for policy ideas that may be able to focus on benefits rather than only costs. The logic of climate change debate and negotiation to date has been that all societies – although the issue of historical responsibility remains a major point of disagreement between developed and developing states – must accept the social and economic costs of mitigation because, according to the mainstream climate science consensus as presented by the Intergovernmental Panel on Climate Change (IPCC), there is no choice other than suffering larger social and economic consequences in the future. This narrow framing of climate change and the policy response required was clearly reflected in a statement by the G77/China group of nations in September 2009 during the lead up to the Copenhagen negotiations when Sudan's delegate, speaking on behalf of the group 'stressed that the overall emission reductions pledged by Annex I countries [i.e. industrialized countries] were still below levels demanded by historical responsibility and science'. The delegate went on to add that 'agreement in Copenhagen will not be possible without Annex I leadership'.[18]

But this is a false logic because climate change science cannot resolve uncertainty concerning the extent of our contribution to climate change nor its causal linkages to current and future climate behaviour, due to the immense complexities of global and regional climate behaviour – at least not to an extent where all, or even most, governments would be compelled to act on the conclusions of climate science alone. It is hardly surprising then that governments and groups facing the greatest potential costs have pointed to such uncertainties as reason to resist taking action on mitigation, or at the very least delay such action, since there is little immediate benefit to doing so in comparison with the immediate costs, and also the potential for little or none of the expected long-term benefit being realized should the impact of human emissions on climate behaviour be less than the current climate science consensus claims. What would, however, make the case for policy action on climate change logical – given the uncertainties involved over what will happen and why – is adopting policies that:

1 seek to manage climate change impacts (both current and expected) regardless of their possible causes; and
2 will pay dividends now and in the future regardless of how accurate or inaccurate the claims of the current climate science consensus later turns out to be.

The Bali negotiations on the framework to replace the Kyoto Protocol when it expires in 2012 were roundly applauded as a success, but in reality no major commitments were made. The Roadmap's biggest achievement was an agreement among its participants to *try* and negotiate a replacement for Kyoto over the next couple of years along with agreement on some basic guidelines and principles for doing so. But the prospects for a comprehensive, binding, and above all 'effective' agreement will be severely weakened if governments continue down the same road as the Kyoto Protocol by continuing to focus primarily on cutting emissions instead of finding ways to eliminate what produces them. Furthermore, governments in developed states need to take the lead in both the formulation and implementation of climate change policy at home and move beyond their almost slavish faith in the ability of market mechanisms and business and technology to provide emission reductions and make fossil fuels cleaner. There exist many policy initiatives that not only would contribute directly to managing the potential for future climate change impacts but also could be justified independently of climate change science, thereby opening up much greater space for political negotiation and policy agreement. The climate change debate's unyielding focus on 'man-made' climate change, however, so far has excluded such alternatives, or reduced them to a low order of priority.

The policy dilemma governments face, particularly in developing countries, in charting a course beyond the Kyoto Protocol's 2012 expiration is essentially a choice between:

1 accepting economic and political pain today by making substantial emission reductions (high level of certainty) in the hope that doing so will significantly reduce the possible (but unknown) costs of global warming in the future (comparatively low level of certainty);
2 adopting a mostly business-as-usual approach in the hope that the scientists predicting worse case scenarios have got it wrong (as occurred, for example, with the Howard government's Asia Pacific Partnership initiative); or
3 finding an alternative approach that hedges our bets against the many uncertainties we face over various possible future outcomes.

The stakes are indeed high, as are the associated uncertainties. But because the stakes are so high, it is imperative that we do not make the error of confusing 'consensus' with 'certainty' or 'scepticism' with politically motivated 'contrarianism' in the course of debating appropriate policy responses to climate change. A clue to how we might avoid such mistakes is provided by Bertrand Russell's support for a 'middle position' on scepticism. In *Sceptical Essays* (1935), Russell wrote that:

Even when the experts all agree, they may well be mistaken. Einstein's view as to the magnitude of the deflection of light by gravitation would have been rejected by all experts 20 years ago, yet it proved to be right. Nevertheless the opinion of experts, when it is unanimous, must be accepted by non-experts as more likely to be right than the opposite opinion.[19] [my emphasis]

The problem here, of course, is that expert opinion is very seldom unanimous when 'uncertainties are high and values are in dispute' as the various ongoing global warming debates demonstrate. In fact, the more important the issue and the greater the political and economic costs involved, the less likely unanimity becomes. The best that can be hoped for with specialist advice then, whether it be scientific or otherwise, is a simple majority consensus, which is a good deal less comforting than unanimous opinion when important decisions need to be made. In this situation, Russell advised 'that when they [the experts] are not agreed, no opinion can be regarded as certain by a non-expert'.

As Gwyn Prins et al have observed, there are only four macro-level policy 'levers' available for reducing the level of carbon emissions: population, wealth, energy intensity and carbon intensity. Of these four potential areas where reductions would reduce emission levels, population and wealth reductions are so politically sensitive as to make the prospect for any meaningful cut in emissions all but impossible, leaving only energy and carbon intensity as potential policy instruments. The key then to emission reductions is to be found in these two domains, but not with emission reductions as the main objective; doing so to date has resulted only in political stalemate and an overall increase in global emissions over the last decade,[20] as the following graph on global emissions increases demonstrates (Figure 8.1):

Policy instead needs to be focused on eliminating possible cause rather than seeking only to limit its unwanted effect:

The lesson of the recent past is clear to us. In the first instance, policy should focus directly on decarbonization rather than on emissions; on causes instead of consequences. Developed countries' emissions targets, which are now under negotiation in the UNFCCC, should be backed by solid calculation of possible efficiency gains and decarbonisation [sic]. Among the major economies only ... Japan ... has set a concrete target ... to be met by real-world efficiency gains and decarbonization through deployment of efficient and low-carbon technologies. The Japanese target does not depend on the froth of purchased offsets.[21]

Reframing climate change mitigation to focus on phasing out fossil fuel use rather than reducing carbon emissions, for example, would make uncertainty over human influence on the climate largely redundant in policy terms since eliminating industrial carbon output would, in addition to *certainly* reducing carbon levels, also help address a number of other uncontroversial,

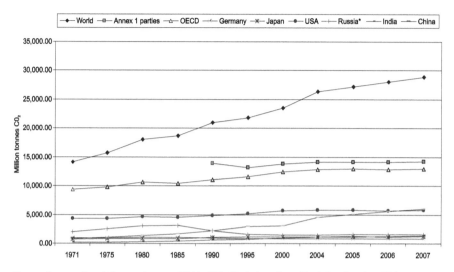

Source: International Energy Agency (IEA), CO_2 *Emissions from Fuel Combustion* (IEA Statistics, 2009), pp44–45

Figure 8.1 *Change in global CO_2 emissions, 1971–2007*

broadly recognized policy challenges ranging from energy security concerns about future energy supply and competition to the health and environmental impacts of air pollution. Adaptation measures such as more energy efficient buildings and infrastructure implemented alongside more careful planning of where and how they are built offer numerous benefits that would apply regardless of whether carbon emissions will cause sea levels to rise or more destructive weather events.[22] And because the benefits of such measures are not dependent on the accuracy of climate science and its predictions, adopting such a change in focus also would greatly reduce the impact of climate science uncertainties on policy action in addition to providing us with some insurance against being wrong in our current assessment of how and the extent to which human activity alters climate behaviour. Climate change research in the meantime should continue – not as a justification for delaying policy action until the 'facts are in' or in the belief that the certainty policy makers demand can be achieved – but rather in the hope that it will at least explain how some of the many uncertainties we necessarily face in policy making may be better managed in the future. Another, more obvious, argument for prioritizing the development of renewable energy sources rather than focusing our efforts on reducing fossil fuel emissions and making them cleaner is that a shift away from fossil fuels is inevitable over the next century since they are finite resources that cannot be renewed.

In addition to focusing more on adaptation measures, climate change policy should aim to replace fossil fuels with a more diverse and cleaner array of renewable energy sources as quickly as possible, as opposed to trying to figure out ways to limit fossil fuel use and make it cleaner, a major objective of current mitigation thinking. Doing so not only would greatly reduce human GHG emissions but would also, with a relatively high degree of certainty, provide a host of important benefits that – unlike investment in clean(er) coal and carbon sequestration technology – would still be available even if our current assessments of global warming's causes and the severity of its impacts turn out to be wrong. Adopting such a 'no regrets' approach to risk and uncertainty is entirely compatible with the decisions taken for the Bali Roadmap and would require all of the same provisions concerning technology transfer, funding and monitoring. Moreover, making the phase out and replacement of fossil fuels the main goal of mitigation would produce additional benefits by making the monitoring of compliance and transfers far less complex.

The essential difference is that these measures instead would be focused on accelerating the phasing out of fossil fuel use. As an added benefit, monitoring the effectiveness of policy and its implementation would become less complicated and therefore more reliable since the task of measuring and observing fossil fuel use, pricing and taxation is a far less difficult proposition than measuring emissions, creating and implementing emissions trading markets, and calculating the relative worth of carbon offset programmes. Rather than attempting to offset carbon emissions through corruption prone schemes such as the Clean Development Mechanism[23] or difficult to monitor and administer emission trading schemes, a revenue neutral tax on carbon producing fuels could not only be more cheaply and effectively implemented (i.e. directly by government), but would also offset the higher cost of fossil fuels to consumers. Taxing fossil fuel use in this way would make renewables cheaper, relative to the cost of fossil fuel, while also compensating for higher energy costs by using the tax revenues to subsidize other essential products and services such as food, water, education and health. Part of the revenue, depending on the needs and circumstances of particular societies, also could be used as additional funding for renewable energy development. IEA figures show that government investment in renewables is again on the rise since 2004 after a long period of stagnation over the previous 25 years. Investment spiked following the 1974 oil shocks but then fell sharply in the 1980s and failed to recover. But even the current rise in investment is still far short of 1970s levels, and current governments will need to spend a good deal more on renewable energy if our current reliance on fossil fuels is to be broken (see Table 8.1, Figures 8.2 and 8.3). As a percentage of gross domestic product (GDP), even the biggest total investors, Japan and the US, annually have spent far less than 1 per cent on the research and development of renewable energy, which indicates that there is scope for major spending increases on alternative energy without significantly detracting from other areas of spending, particularly if additional investment from the private sector is also encouraged.

Such a strategy for drastically reducing oil and coal reliance over the next 20 years, for example, would require replacing them where possible with readily available, short-term alternatives such as natural gas and nuclear energy but would also provide immediate opportunities for other, longer term

Table 8.1 *Comparison of R&D expenditure as percentage of GDP, 2007 (current 2008 USD)*

	Renewable energy	Energy sector	Gross R&D expenditure
IEA total	0.004	0.03	1.9
Canada	0.005	0.04	1.9
France	0.004	0.05	2.1
Germany	0.004	0.02	2.5
Italy	0.004	0.03	1.1*
Japan	0.005	0.09	3.4
Korea	0.007	0.05	3.5
Spain	0.003	0.01	1.3
UK	0.005	0.01	1.8
USA	0.003	0.03	2.7

Note: * 2006 data. No recent comparable data available for Australia.
Sources: Calculated from IEA, 'R&D Statistics', 2009, www.iea.org/Textbase/stats/rd.asp; Organisation for Economic Co-operation and Development (OECD), *National Accounts of OECD Countries Volume I: Main Aggregates 1996–2007* (Paris: OECD, 2009), p325; OECD, *Main Science and Technology Indicators*, 2009/1 (Paris: OECD, 2009), p25

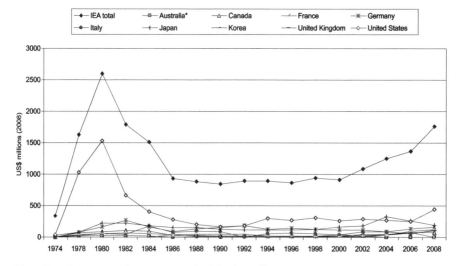

Note: Data for nearest subsequent year cited for Australia.
Source: IEA, 'R&D Statistics', 2009, www.iea.org/Textbase/stats/rd.asp/

Figure 8.2 *R&D investment renewable energy (selected IEA members)*

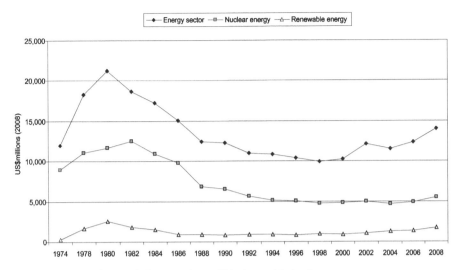

Note: OECD members with the exceptions of Mexico and Iceland.
Source: IEA, 'R&D Statistics', 2009, www.iea.org/Textbase/stats/rd.asp

Figure 8.3 *R&D investment in energy, sectoral comparison (total IEA members)*

alternatives already in use such as hydroelectric, wind, geothermal and solar while boosting their development. Nuclear power will, in any case, remain as an important source of electricity generation in countries such as France, China and Japan, but its adoption by other states will continue to be problematic, spurring debate over its potential risks and the huge investment involved with building, running and dismantling reactors, given their relatively short operating life, and also the relative ease with which civil nuclear programmes can be adapted to producing nuclear weapons. Indeed, the possibility that GHG emissions are the major cause of global warming – as 'likely' as this may or may not be – should stand as only one of several other equally compelling reasons for pursuing an accelerated shift away from fossil fuel reliance. Aside from the obvious environmental and health impacts of fossil fuel use, oil in particular poses major challenges for developing and developed economies alike. In addition to the economic burden imposed by escalating oil prices, some examples of the risks and problems posed by its future scarcity include higher levels of exposure among developing economies to energy price rises (as the fall of the Suharto government demonstrated following the 1997 Asian financial crisis);[24] increasing energy competition between states; financial and political support for dictatorial/authoritarian, and often hugely dysfunctional, regimes in resource rich states as has occurred with China's 'aid for energy deals' in Burma, Sudan and elsewhere; and further nuclear proliferation and weakening of the Non-Proliferation Treaty under the current deadlock between established and aspiring nuclear weapon states.[25]

Focusing only on emissions reductions has been demonstrably unproductive as the ongoing increase in global GHG emissions shows. Moreover, this approach also has delayed the emergence of a clear policy response – either domestically or internationally – by limiting policy negotiations to a set of responses no government seems willing to pursue; climate change negotiations in their current form are essentially about governments attempting to talk each other into commitments that they themselves are reluctant to adopt, as illustrated by the Copenhagen meetings failure to produce any form of binding commitment among states. According to Daniel Bodansky:

> *Although many negotiators left Copenhagen with a sense that the UNFCCC process is broken, there is no viable alternative at the moment, so the AWGs [Ad Hoc Working Groups] will continue to meet and the negotiations will continue to revolve around the COPs [Conference of the Parties]. But if world leaders were unable to make further progress through direct negotiations, under an intense international spotlight, there is little reason to expect mid-level negotiators to be able to achieve a stronger outcome anytime soon. As a result, the Copenhagen Accord may well represent the high-water mark of the climate regime for some time to come.*[26]

The gap between what governments say about the importance of climate change policy and what they actually do is reflected in the relatively small increase in funding for renewables research in response to climate change since 2000 compared with the much larger increase in funding that followed the oil shocks of the early 1970s. This gap clearly needs to close if any kind of coordinated international response to climate change is to occur. Assuming that government statements on the potential dangers of climate change are more than mere rhetoric, policy making in the developed world in particular needs to stop passing the job of implementing policy onto the private sector and market mechanisms like emission trading schemes, and instead begin taking responsibility for both the creation and implementation of policy measures. Supporters of the mainstream global warming view often argue that future generations will never forgive us if we fail to act against the future consequences. That is no doubt true, but this argument assumes that we know what the consequences are (which we don't) and also neglects the possibility that drastic action today – on the basis of little more than *untestable* assumptions about the future – may also have consequences that our great grandchildren will find equally difficult to forgive, such as development failures and worsening poverty, the neglect of other pressing environmental and social issues, and a heightened risk of military conflict.

9
Uncertainty as *Deus ex Machina*: Some Concluding Remarks

Uncertainty's interpretation by policy makers plays a key role in attempts at claiming one policy framing to be more objective and rational, and therefore more legitimate, than another. Indeed, uncertainty's double-edged character allows for it to be either highlighted or downplayed depending on the fit between the advice on offer and the policy preferences being pursued. And because uncertainty strips us of the ability to proclaim the 'best' course of action on the basis of evidence-derived knowledge alone in such situations – while simultaneously granting licence to speculate on various policy alternatives informed by more or less equally plausible notions of what may or may not happen – uncertainty itself becomes, therefore, something of a *deus ex machina* for those seeking to frame policy issues in particular ways and legitimize one course of action and set of priorities over others.

As I have argued in the preceding chapters, the differing framings of policy issues like climate change and Iraq's purported possession of weapons of mass destruction (WMD) – issues characterized by high complexity and uncertainty – are mostly the product of competing values and ideological preferences among policy elites and other policy protagonists. The many and significant uncertainties that characterized the specialist advice cited by the Australian, UK and US governments to legitimize the Iraq invasion were downplayed by all three governments. Unlike the policy position adopted in the case of climate change, where the lack of clear, uncontested evidence supporting its potential impacts was cited as good reason for not reducing emissions, both President Bush and Australian Prime Minister John Howard's support for military action against Iraq, like that of British Prime Minister Tony Blair, was based on expert advice that contained little in the way of clear empirical evidence, and in spite of strong opposition in the Security Council and elsewhere to such action being taken. Even the Blair government's position on climate change during this period, while less dismissive of global warming as a policy issue than Bush or Howard's, avoided any commitment to immediate emissions reductions.

In all three governments, the many significant uncertainties surrounding Iraq's alleged WMD and intentions clearly were interpreted in far more alarmist terms and presented very differently when compared with the policies and arguments made by each government on the question of global warming's arguably even greater, and potentially cataclysmic, consequences. Saddam's alleged chemical, biological and nuclear capability was framed as an immediate, existential threat by each government without reservation whereas the need for immediate greenhouse gas (GHG) reductions was instead perceived as an issue still too clouded in uncertainty to deserve becoming 'securitized' and, therefore, prioritized over other policy concerns, despite mounting public pressure and expert advice to the contrary. The United Nations Framework Convention on Climate Change's (UNFCCC) framing of climate change as anthropogenic global warming – a man-made phenomenon requiring an urgent and direct policy response – was in effect ignored by these and other governments who instead sought to reframe climate change in accordance with an already established policy paradigm, one that prioritized economic development and growth as a non-negotiable aspect of national security.

In contrast to the controlled environments and testing that characterize the practice of normal science, the sheer scale and complexity of 'wicked', post-normal problems mean that falsification (or verification) of predicted impacts or outcomes is limited to waiting to see whether or not they actually materialize within a given period of time. But even the occurrence of a predicted outcome may not resolve uncertainties regarding the methods and arguments used to predict it while alternative causal explanations remain possible. The untestable nature of climate change prediction, intelligence analysis, development models or wildlife management schemes prior to decision making means then that so called 'evidence-based' policy making approaches to these issues is always going to be based on factors other than objective facts or evidence. Policy making is necessarily forward looking, but in post-normal issue areas, where uncertainty is made irreducible by either complexity or time constraints, decisions are unable to be based on knowledge or findings that have survived repeated attempts at falsification under consistent and controlled conditions of testing. But despite the clear limits imposed on normal scientific methods by the many uncertainties such open and complex systems produce, objective knowledge remains the basis for legitimate policy making, thereby perpetuating the ongoing practice among governments, interest groups and the mainstream media of using science (and the competing expert advice it normally produces) in post-normal policy situations to legitimize one or another position. Doing so, as the Iraq and climate change case studies I have presented illustrate, inevitably obscures the various values and interests that are at the heart of policy disagreement behind an 'excess of objectivity', narrowing not only the framing of policy issues and debate in terms of what is important and relevant, but also the range of possible responses expert advice and science might produce.

The limits to what expert advice can contribute become greater if we add additional uncertainty over the potential opportunity costs of responding in a particular way to avoid a particular risk, which raises the classic precautionary principle

(PP) dilemma – acting to avoid potential risks *does not* eliminate risk, it merely alters the kinds of threat that may arise.[1] Moreover, adopting a precautionary approach also raises the question of whether such costs, assuming they are even known, are worth the expected, but not guaranteed, benefits of achieving one's original objective, assuming that it was clearly understood in the first place (e.g. what is an acceptable level of global warming and what costs are acceptable in attempting to achieve it? What are the criteria for making such judgements?). As a consequence, policy responses to complex issues like global warming and whaling, among many others, have been delayed by a denial in mainstream debate of the ways in which our values and interests shape the way we understand science and the advice it produces. The challenge then is to find political solutions to the values-driven controversies that fuel policy debates, since science cannot be expected to solve political problems.[2]

Another outcome of this scramble for the holy grail of scientific objectivity and rationality among the various actors is that a host of alternative policy options are overlooked, particularly those aimed at managing uncertainty. Rather than attempting either to downplay or exaggerate the significance of uncertainties and knowledge gaps – as is normally the case when competing interests seek to make their respective policy positions more science-based (read rational and objective) than alternative positions – hedging or 'no regrets' risk strategies instead recognize and accept the problems posed by the uncertainty dialectic discussed earlier and seek to manage system complexities and uncertainty through the use of feedback mechanisms and the recognition of a broad range of possible outcomes, both known and unknown. Sometimes referred to as 'adaptive management' or as a variation on muddling through, this approach to managing rather than (futilely) attempting to eliminate uncertainties operates within a flexible policy framework that is able to adjust its priorities and responses as new information becomes available or as circumstances change in unforeseen ways.

If, for example, the Bush administration had not been so strongly committed to military action against Iraq and the overthrow of Saddam Hussein, or had been less successful in its use of suppositions and uncertainty in building a false empirical case against Iraq, the debate on whether Iraq actually possessed or was producing WMD could have been conducted very differently, allowing the uncertainty to have been managed through further inspections rather than attempting to eliminate it through military action. The decision to do one rather than the other is a political decision, and needs to be presented and debated as such. The Bush administration instead attempted to 'construct' certainty over both the existence of Iraqi WMD and the threat Saddam posed as justification for the use of military force, and this was precisely the objective of US Secretary of State Colin Powell's presentation of the now discredited US case against Iraq at the UN shortly before hostilities began. As Robert Gallucci observed:

> *[The Bush Administration] had objectives for the Middle East ...*
> *which could not be realised so long as Saddam was in Iraq,*
> *and they needed him out. And you can't extract, you can't do*

a 'Saddamectomy' without having a threat. You can't do it as a foreign policy objective.[3]

Similarly, if the UNFCCC was not so narrowly focused on human-induced climate change in defining climate change as a policy problem, the policy options could be significantly broadened allowing more opportunity for common interests and values to be recognized and negotiated.

As this book goes to press, the Chilcot inquiry in the UK is attempting to figure out the lessons to be learned from the Blair government's now widely criticized support for US military action against Iraq. Like earlier investigations in the UK, the US and Australia, the inquiry's tone betrays a thinly veiled indignity that the values and ideological leanings of the Blair executive were somehow allowed to compromise the rationality, and therefore also the legitimacy, of British foreign policy. And one cannot help but think one of the main lessons being sought in Sir John Chilcot's investigation is how to keep 'politics' from again sullying the UK's normally 'objective' and evidence driven policy process. The Copenhagen meeting, meanwhile, created an unprecedented level of environmental fanfare but to no real effect. The climate change policies and positions of most governments, in particular the major GHG emitters, remain largely unchanged and non-committal. Whereas the policy process on Iraq delivered the wrong outcome, the UNFCCC policy framework has, in effect, failed to deliver any outcome.

Contrary to rationalist expectations, conditions of high complexity and uncertainty prevent policy debate from being negotiated and resolved on the basis of knowledge claims or the best available advice alone. Recourse to the rationalist model's vision of policy being objectively determined by the evidence is, as a consequence, blocked, leaving the legitimacy of policy decision making open to contest for those with an interest in questioning it. Nonetheless, the enduring appeal of rational policy making still compels policy actors both in and outside of government to claim the mantle of knowledge-based legitimacy by using uncertainty issues to undermine competing explanations of what is 'really happening' and invoking possible nightmare-like scenarios (WMD-armed terrorists and rogue states, economic decline/stagnation, cataclysmic climate change) as protection against uncertainty being used to undermine their own preferred policy choice. Uncertainty, then, essentially is what you make of it, since its import and relevance to any given issue is determined less by the strength of the available evidence than by whether or not the values of the various policy protagonists clash or are complementary. As I argue in Chapter 7, the level of certainty required by policy makers generally is inversely related to the level of political support available for the policy in question. Thus, when values conflict and the uncertainty is high, the rationalist model inevitable leads to a legitimacy vacuum within which *political* debate over competing values becomes disguised as scientifically-guided knowledge claims fighting it out to determine what the facts really are so that policy decisions can then 'rationally' be made. Chapter 7's discussion of the International Whaling Commission (IWC) further demonstrates why policy debate is often driven less by compelling knowledge claims adjudicated by the objective application of the scientific method, as per Enlightenment expectations, than it is by competing preferences derived from differing world views and ideological orientations.

Moreover, persisting with rationalist perceptions and expectations of policy making and the *deus ex machina* role they inadvertently give to uncertainty's interpretation also allows decision makers at the elite level to selectively dodge responsibility and accountability for the policies they adopt and the outcomes these policies produce. If a policy is broadly seen as a success, responsibility for its formulation and implementation is unequivocally accepted, indeed enthusiastically embraced, by the policy elite. Agency is writ large in policy explanations of such triumphs, attributing credit to the vision and prescience of the decision makers themselves. But when things go wrong, responsibility rather predictably becomes far more diffused and is usually distanced from those in the executive who nevertheless make the final call on what is or isn't policy. Attempts at introducing 'agency' operating at the elite policy level to the post-mortems of unwanted policy outcomes and erroneous policy rationales are vigorously resisted, as occurred with the intelligence inquiries into Saddam's phantom WMD programmes and capabilities, and the sources of policy failure attributed to organizational and structural causes.

Indeed, the need for politics to be made subordinate to knowledge in the policy process encourages a strong structuralist bias in our understanding of policy making. In the rationalist schema, legitimate, knowledge-based policy relies on disinterested experts and bureaucrats providing timely and accurate advice to policy elites from within organizational structures and hierarchies designed to promote objectivity and political neutrality. If the wrong policies are being implemented, then the fault most likely is with how these structures are operating since 'rational' policy makers can only make the 'right' decision if they are given the 'right information'. Objective rationality on the part of decision makers and experts is assumed, while questions about how their supposed or objective or even bounded rationality deals with uncertainty are largely ignored in the expectation that uncertainty can be eliminated or reduced – at least to the extent that the 'right' policy choice will become clear.

Rational choice-type models assume particular patterns of behaviour and take these patterns as their analytical starting point. Notions of agency, and the politics that inform and guide acts of individual or group agency, instead seek to explain – or at least recognize and accept – the political dimensions of policy behaviour and how values shape even our ideas of rationality. Thus, attempting to remove politics from our understanding of policy also leads to the removal of agency from policy explanations, and, as a consequence, an 'excess of objectivity' that in turn helps erode the accountability and responsibility of individual decision makers. Put another way, excluding 'politics' from policy analysis and explanation helps *rationalize* the prioritization of structural influences over the agency of policy elites in explaining the adoption of one policy over another. As a result, the individual political preferences that also influence acts of choice are seldom considered. But the world views and ideologies of executive elites and the political views they produce should be seen as an important element in any policy story. They are, as I have argued, central to gaining a more comprehensive and accurate understanding of policy decisions and the policy paradigms within which those decisions are made, or, conversely, the paradigm shifts they help to produce, since policy paradigms can only survive if they are compatible with the world views of the executive elite. A major shift in executive thinking will, therefore, lead to the kind of paradigmatic shifts in policy discussed by Peter Hall and demonstrated by various governments over the last three decades in critical policy areas such as the economy, foreign policy and international security.

As both the major case studies demonstrate, uncertainty only becomes an issue in decision making when particular values – made significant by their breadth and sources of support – are in competition and cause political conflict. At this juncture, the nature of the relationship between uncertainty, values and risk is at its clearest. Moreover, it is political disagreement over uncertainty issues that provides the grounds and motivation for invoking risk as justification for a particular policy, since uncertainty is a prerequisite of risk and perceptions of both are ultimately the product of the respective values and preferences of the relevant actors. Perceptions of risk are, as I argued in Chapter 3, essentially an expression of the values we attach to 'not knowing' (i.e. being uncertain), as seen through the lenses of our respective world views and ideological beliefs. Values inform us about what is important, what is at risk, and what needs to be better known or understood. But in the rationalist policy world, knowledge exists primarily to validate or invalidate these competing values; it acts as a value-neutral magistrate in a marketplace of competing world views and preferences, dispensing or withholding legitimacy in a rational and objective manner.

The rationalist policy model, then, expects knowledge, as determined by scientific inquiry, to sit in judgement on politics, regardless of the extent and nature of the uncertainties involved. On the big policy issues existing outside the very limited jurisdiction of normal science, however, it is politics that more often than not sits in judgement of science. If we are to adopt a truly 'rational' approach to policy and decision making, we need to abandon the positivist expectations of knowledge and the role it *should* play in legitimate policy making that have made our perceptions and understanding of it 'irrational'. Rational responses to wicked policy problems, and the many uncertainties they contain, are about openly recognizing and engaging in politics and accepting the many limits to what we can know. Indeed, a truly 'rational' approach to understanding policy making and what makes it 'legitimate', in the context of liberal democracies at least, demands recognition that legitimate policy decisions are made possible under conditions of uncertainty *because of* politics, not in spite of it. We must, therefore, embrace, rather than reject, politics if we are to liberate ourselves from the allure of 'irrational great expectations'.

Notes

Chapter 1

1 Described by Bertrand Russell as 'a particular blend of general and particular interests in the pursuit of science; the particular is studied in the hope that it may throw light upon the general'; Bertrand Russell, *Sceptical Essays* (New York: Barnes and Noble, 1961), pp28–29.

2 Stephen Bocking, *Nature's Experts: Science, Politics, and the Environment* (New Brunswick, NJ: Rutgers University Press, 2004), p21.

3 Yaron Ezrahi, *The Descent of Icarus* (Cambridge, MA: Harvard University Press, 1990), pp14, 17.

4 Ezrahi's main argument is very similar to my argument concerning the influence of utility perceptions on the treatment of expert knowledge or advice. Ezrahi writes that: 'In time I became increasingly convinced that the story of the relations of science and politics in the modern democratic state is not an account of the progressive rationalization of politics. It is, rather, a process through which liberal-democratic ideology and politics selectively appropriate and adapt science and technology for constructing political authority and legitimating the exercise of political power.' Ezrahi, *Descent of Icarus*, pvii.

5 Wayne Parsons, *Public Policy: An Introduction to the Theory and Practice of Policy Analysis* (Aldershot, UK: Edward Elgar Publishing, 1995), p14.

6 Quoted in Derek H. Chollet and James M. Goldgeier, 'The scholarship of decision-making: Do we know how we decide?', in *Foreign Policy Decision-Making (Revisited)*, Richard C. Snyder, H. W. Bruck and Burton Sapin (eds) (New York: Palgrave Macmillan, 2002), p170.

7 In the case of George W. Bush, Carl M. Cannon argues, the question of lying to the public is complicated by the issue of whether Bush actually believed his statements on Iraq and on other issues and was either unable or unwilling to accept contradictory evidence – that he had, as Bob Woodward put it, a 'habit of denial'. Carl M. Cannon, 'Untruth and consequences', *The Atlantic*, 299 (January–February 2007): pp56–67; see also Bob Woodward, *State of Denial: Bush at War Part III* (New York: Simon & Schuster, 2006), p488.

8 For an excellent treatment and overview of the policy literature and the different theoretical approaches, see Parsons, *Public Policy*.

9 For examples of alternative approaches, see Parsons, *Public Policy*; Cris Shore and Susan Wright, *Anthropology of Policy: Critical Perspectives on Governance and Power* (London and New York: Routledge, 1997); Frank Fischer and John Forester (eds), *The Argumentative Turn in Policy Analysis and Planning* (Durham, NC: Duke University Press, 1993), in particular John Dryzek, 'Policy analysis and

planning: From science to argument', pp213–232; Robert Hoppe, 'Policy analysis, science and politics: From "Speaking truth to power" to "Making sense together"', *Science and Public Policy*, 26 (1999), pp201–210.

10 Graham Allison and Phillip Zelikow, *Essence of Decision: Explaining the Cuban Missile Crisis*, 2nd edn (New York: Longman, 1999), p8.

11 These include rational choice and rational actor models, bounded rationality, political or bureaucratic competition, social learning, structural, social relations and pluralist perspectives.

12 One of the best known critiques of the rationalist model is Charles Lindblom's 'science of muddling though'. See Charles E. Lindblom, 'The science of muddling through', *Public Administration Review*, 19 (1959), pp79–88; and 'Still muddling, not yet through', *Public Administration Review*, 39 (1979), pp517–526. More contemporary examples include Sheila Jasanoff, *The Fifth Branch: Science Advisers As Policymakers* (Cambridge, MA: Harvard University Press, 1990); Deborah Stone, *Policy Paradox* (New York: W. W. Norton & Company, 2002); Roger Pielke Jr, *The Honest Broker: Making Sense of Science in Policy and Politics* (New York: Cambridge University Press, 2007); and Max Nieman and Stephen J. Stambough, 'Rational choice theory and the evaluation of public policy', *Policy Studies Journal*, 26 (1998), pp449–465.

13 Max Nieman and Stephen J. Stambough, 'Rational choice theory and the evaluation of public policy', *Policy Studies Journal*, 26 (1998), p450.

14 Max Nieman and Stephen J. Stambough, 'Rational choice theory and the evaluation of public policy', *Policy Studies Journal*, 26 (1998), p450.

15 Bernard Crick, *In Defence of Politics*, 5th edn (London: Continuum, 2000), Ch. 1.

16 See Michael Heazle, *Scientific Uncertainty and the Politics of Whaling* (Seattle: University of Washington Press, 2006), pp10–34 for a more detailed explanation of this argument.

17 My approach could be labelled constructivist in so far as it challenges positivist accounts of knowledge, accepting instead the proposition that knowledge claims are highly problematic, by arguing that individual utility perceptions are what actually inform the practice of knowledge demarcation in the absence of any direct and demonstrable human knowledge of the *real*; uncertainty is therefore unavoidable and open to a variety of competing interpretations. Constructivism, however, is, as Martha Finnemore and Kathryn Sikkink have already noted, a very broad church and its basic assumptions about the importance of ideas and social influences in understanding human behaviour and interaction have been widely used, often by scholars who would not (or did not) necessarily refer to themselves as 'contructivists'. Martha Finnemore and Kathryn Sikkink, 'Taking stock: The constructivist research program in international relations and comparative politics', *Annual Review of Political Science*, 4 (2001), pp391–416.

18 Thomas Kuhn, *The Structure of Scientific Revolutions*, 3rd edn (Chicago: University of Chicago Press, 1996), pp23–34.

19 Interestingly, opposition to commercial whaling holds no economic risk for the governments opposing a return to commercial hunting and in fact provides a political opportunity for establishing their 'commitment' to environmental protection at little cost. The important questions here of course are what can explain the selective way in which the precautionary principle (PP) often is applied and what does this tell us about how policy makers, experts and the general public deal with specialist advice and interpret uncertainty? In the case of the broad, but far from unanimous, Western opposition to whaling, disagreements between the pro- and anti-whaling

nations have reached a point where they are entirely driven by vastly different values and interests. As a result, science has become not only ineffectual as a voice of rational authority, but is also now a contributor to the political stalemate that continues to paralyse the IWC. See, for example, Heazle, *Scientific Uncertainty*, Chs 5 and 6; and Arne Kalland, 'Whose whale is that? Diverting the commodity path', in *Elephants and Whales: Resources for Whom?*, Milton M. R. Freeman and Urs P. Kreuter (eds) (Amsterdam: Gordon and Breach, 1994), pp159–186.

20 According to Suskind, Vice-President Cheney's 1 per cent doctrine meant that: 'If there was even a one percent chance of terrorists getting a weapon of mass destruction – and there has been a small probability of such an occurrence for some time – the United States must now act as if it were a certainty.' Ron Suskind, *The One Percent Doctrine* (New York: Simon & Schuster, 2006), p62.

21 Michael Heazle, *Scientific Uncertainty and the Politics of Whaling* (University of Washington Press, 2006), p13.

22 E. H. Carr, *What is History?* (Oxford: Oxford University Press, 1961), p131.

23 Lynn Frewer and Brian Salter, 'Public attitudes, scientific advice and the politics of regulatory policy: The case of BSE', *Science and Public Policy*, 29 (April 2002), p138.

24 John Howard's later in principle support for lowering carbon emissions *implied* acceptance of the dominant global warming view, but only in so far that policy responses did not disadvantage Australia's economy and exports. Moreover, since Australia negotiated an 8 per cent *increase* on its 1990 emission levels before then pulling out of the Kyoto Protocol, the Howard government's claim that it had nonetheless met its commitments under the agreement needs, therefore, to be seen in context.

25 For post-positivist related perspectives on science and technology and the role of expert advice in policy making, see also, for example, in addition to the works cited elsewhere in this chapter, Silvio Funtowicz and Jerome R. Ravetz, 'Science for the post-normal age', *Futures*, 25 (September 1993), pp739–755; 'The good, the true, and the post-modern', *Futures*, 25 (10) (December 1992), pp963–976; Jerome R. Ravetz, 'What is post-normal science?', *Futures*, 31 (1999), pp647–653; Lorraine Daston, 'Scientific error and the ethos of belief', *Social Research*, 72 (Spring 2005), pp1–28; Maarten Hajer 'Policy without polity? Policy analysis and the institutional void', *Policy Sciences*, 36 (2003), pp175–195; Maya J. Goldenberg, 'On evidence and evidence-based medicine: Lessons from the philosophy of science', *Social Science and Medicine*, 62 (2006), pp2621–2632.

26 Silvio Funtowicz and Jerome R. Ravetz, 'Science for the post-normal age', *Futures*, 25 (1993), p744.

27 Roger Pielke Jr, *The Honest Broker: Making Sense of Science in Policy and Politics* (New York: Cambridge University Press, 2007).

28 Daniel Sarewitz, 'How science makes environmental controversies worse', *Environmental Science and Policy*, 7 (2004), pp385–403; 'Science and environmental policy: An excess of objectivity', Center for Science, Policy and Outcomes – Columbia University, 1999, www.cspo.org/products/articles/excess.objectivity.html.

29 Jurgen Habermas, *Toward a Rational Society* (London: Heinemann Educational Books, 1971), p75. First published in German in 1968.

30 'Wicked' policy problems are broadly understood as policy issues of great complexity involving systems within systems, which not only defy any uniform definition but also are highly resistant to analysis and resolution due to the numerous system uncertainties (epistemic and variability) and multi-causal factors involved.

31 Daniel Sarewitz, 'Science and environmental policy: An excess of objectivity', Centre for Science, Policy and Outcomes (1999).

Chapter 2 notes

1   For an excellent example of why decision makers do not, and indeed usually *do not want to*, know all of the available facts and information, see Patrick Weller, *Don't Tell the Prime Minister* (Melbourne: Scribe Publications, 2002).

2   The Howard government and Bush administration used an identical approach to the global warming debate; their governments' policy response was that we need to know more before committing to major CO_2 emission reductions. The assumption here of course is that we can continue to reduce the uncertainties surrounding global warming and its future impacts through further research, a policy position which fits neatly with the research funding interests of climate change scientists. See Roger Pielke Jr and Daniel Sarewitz, 'Wanted: Scientific leadership on climate', *Issues in Science and Technology*, 19 (Winter 2002), pp27–30.

3   Harold Lasswell, 'The emerging conception of the policy sciences', *Policy Sciences*, 1 (1970), pp3–14. Lasswell's point in making this distinction between knowledge *for* and knowledge *of* was to further define and establish the role of the political scientist in public policy as an objective 'integrator of knowledge' unsullied by ideology or the attraction of power and, therefore, able to facilitate and help guide an increasingly rational policy process.

4   John Dryzek, 'A post-positivist policy analytic travelogue', *The Good Society*, 11 (2002), pp32–36.

5   Dryzek, 'A post-positivist policy analytic travelogue', pp33–34.

6   Dryzek, 'A post-positivist policy analytic travelogue', pp34–35.

7   Dryzek, 'A post-positivist policy analytic travelogue', p35.

8   Douglas Torgerson, 'Contextual orientation in policy analysis: The contribution of Harold D. Lasswell', *Policy Sciences*, 18 (1985), p242.

9   Torgerson, 'Contextual orientation in policy analysis', p243.

10 Daniel Sarewitz, 'How science makes environmental controversies worse', *Environmental Science and Policy*, 7 (2004), p400.

11 Charles E. Lindblom, 'The science of muddling through', *Public Administration Review*, 19 (1959), pp79–88.

12 Lindblom, 'Still muddling, not yet through', *Public Administration Review*, 39 (1979), p517.

13 Lindblom, 'Still muddling, not yet through', pp517–526.

14 Herbert Simon saw decision making as a rational process but one in which rationality was 'bounded' by various factors such as the fragmented nature of knowledge; uncertainty; and limits to human learning, memory and attention to specific issues or details. Simon, however, believed that rationality could continue to be improved through our ability to better manage these limits. Charles Lindblom, in contrast, was very pessimistic about the prospects for improving 'rationality' in any significant way, and instead stressed the importance of focusing on more efficient ways of reaching political agreement and consensus as the best way of both better understanding and improving decision making. See Parsons, *Public Policy*, pp273–293.

15 Lindblom, 'Still muddling, not yet through', p524.

16 Sarewitz, 'How science makes environmental controversies worse'.

17 Bernard Crick, *In Defence of Politics* (London: Continuum, 2000), p18.

18 See for example, Oran R. Young and Gail Osherenko (eds), *Polar Politics: Creating International Environmental Regimes* (Ithaca, NY: Cornell University Press, 1993); and Peter M. Haas (ed.), *Knowledge, Power, and International Policy Coordination* (Columbia, SC: University of South Carolina Press, 1997).

19 See, for example, John Mearsheimer, 'A realist reply', *International Security*, 20 (1995), pp82–93 for Mearsheimer's response to liberal institutionalist critiques of his earlier article in *International Security*, 'The false promise of international institutions'.

20 Peter Hall, 'Policy paradigms, social learning, and the state: The case of economic policymaking in Britain', *Comparative Politics*, 25 (April 1993), p292.

21 See, for example, Robert Jervis, *Perception and Misperception in International Politics* (Princeton, NJ: Princeton University Press, 1976); Robert B. McCalla, *Uncertain Perceptions: U.S. Cold War Crisis Decision Making* (Ann Arbor, MI: University of Michigan Press, 1992); Richard C. Snyder, H. W. Bruck and Burton Sapin (eds), *Foreign Policy Decision-Making (Revisited)* (New York: Palgrave Macmillan, 2002); and George A. Kelly, *A Theory of Personality: The Psychology of Personal Constructs* (New York: W. W. Norton and Company, 1963), for discussions and analyses of perception and misperception, dispositional versus situational perceptions, human agency and individual templates/world views.

22 Hall, 'Policy paradigms, social learning, and the state'.

23 Michael Freeden, *Ideologies and Political Theory: A Conceptual Approach* (Oxford: Oxford University Press, 1996), p76.

24 Judith Goldstein and Robert O. Keohane, 'Ideas and foreign policy: An analytical framework', in *Ideas and Foreign Policy: Beliefs, Institutions, and Political Change*, Judith Goldstein and Robert O. Keohane (eds) (Ithaca, NY: Cornell University Press, 1993), p8.

25 US House of Representatives Committee on Oversight and Government Reform, *The Financial Crisis and the Role of Federal Regulators*, Preliminary Hearing Transcript, 111th Congress, 23 October 2008, pp36–37.

26 'Alan Greenspan vs. Naomi Klein on the Iraq War, Bush's tax cuts, economic populism, crony capitalism and more', *Democracy Now*, 24 September 2007, www.democracynow.org/2007/9/24/alan_greenspan_vs_naomi_klein_on.

27 Hall, 'Policy paradigms, social learning, and the state'.

28 Robert B. McCalla, *Uncertain Perceptions: US Cold War Decision Making* (Ann Arbor, MI, University of Michigan Press, 1992), pp22–23.

29 Kelly, *A Theory of Personality*, p12.

30 Robert Jervis, *Perception and Misperception in International Politics* (Princeton NJ: Princeton University Press, 1976), p181.

31 Jervis, *Perception and Misperception*.

32 US House of Representatives Committee, *The Financial Crisis and the Role of Federal Regulators*, p3.

33 Speaking on *Meet the Press* on the 5th anniversary of the 9/11 attacks, US Vice-President Dick Cheney stated: 'The world is better off because Saddam Hussein is in jail instead of in power in Baghdad. It was the right thing to do and if we had it to do over again, we'd do exactly the same thing.' Dick Cheney, interview by Tim Russert, *Meet The Press*, 10 September 2006, www.msnbc.msn.com/id/14720480/page/4/.

34 This explains the Howard, Blair and Bush refusal to concede error on Iraq and provides an alternative to rationalist accounts that claim either the right (i.e. rational) decision was taken given the information at the time, employed by those supporting the coalition decision, or Iraq as another example of politics impeding an otherwise rational policy process.

35 And as described by Hall's analysis of the UK's change in economic philosophy under Thatcher. See Hall, 'Policy paradigms'.

36 Or, as Jennifer Sterling-Folker puts it: 'Actors are free to act as they wish, pursue any goals they desire, and to allow their interests and behaviors to be determined by the processes in which they are engaged. They are also free to die, but it is the choices they have made *vis-à-vis* themselves and others that determine that outcome, not anarchy itself.' Jennifer Sterling-Folker, 'Realist environment, liberal process, and domestic-level variables', *International Studies Quarterly*, 41 (1997), p19.

37 USSR leader Mikhail Gorbachev's reforms provided a clear influence on the ending of the Cold War and represented a major break with previous Soviet policy. Similarly, the influence of neo-conservative thinking in the Bush administration represents a decisive break with traditional realist approaches to foreign policy. Both examples indicate the extent to which different personalities and ideologies in the executive affect policy and decision making.

38 Alexander Wendt, 'Constructing international politics', *International Security*, 20 (1995), p72. According to Wendt, 'Where neorealist and constructivist structuralisms really differ, however, is in their assumptions about what structure is made of. Neorealists think it is made only of a distribution of material capabilities, whereas constructivists think it is also made of social relationships. Social structures have three elements: shared knowledge, material resources, and practices', p73.

39 Kenneth N. Waltz, *Theory of International Politics* (Reading, MA: Addison-Wesley, 1983 reprint), Ch. 1.

40 See Finnemore and Sikkink, 'Taking stock', p394; Wendt, 'Constructing international politics', p75; Jeffrey T. Checkel, 'The constructivist turn in international relations theory', *World Politics*, 50 (1998), pp324–348.

41 Checkel, 'The constructivist turn in international relations theory'.

42 Christian Reus-Smit, 'Constructivism', in *Theories of International Relations*, Scott Burchill, Andrew Linklater, Richard Devetak, Jack Donnelly, Terry Nardin, Matthew Paterson, Christian Reus-Smit and Jacqui True (eds), 4th edn (Basingstoke, UK: Palgrave Macmillan, 2009), pp221–222.

43 Brian Martin and Evelleen Richards, 'Scientific knowledge, controversy, and public decision-making', in *Handbook of Science and Technology Studies*, Sheila Jasanoff, Gerald E. Markle, James C. Peterson and Trevor J. Pinch (eds) (Newbury Park, CA: Sage, 1995), pp506–526.

44 Martin and Richards, 'Scientific knowledge'.

45 Finnemore and Sikkink, 'Taking stock', p393.

46 Finnemore and Sikkink, 'Taking stock'.

47 Checkel, 'The constructivist turn in international relations theory', p324.

48 Clifford Geertz, *The Interpretation of Cultures* (New York: Basic Books, 1973), Ch. 8.

49 Yves Surel, 'The role of cognitive and normative frames in policy making', *Journal of European Public Policy*, 7 (2000), p500.

50 Robert Putnam, 'Diplomacy and domestic politics: The logic of two level games', *International Organization*, 42 (1988), pp427–460.

51 Jervis, *Perception and Misperception*, p28.

52 Gideon Rose, 'Neoclassical realism and theories of foreign policy', *World Politics*, 51 (1998): p147.

53 See Hall, 'Policy paradigms', p275.

54 Jervis, *Perception and Misperception*, p25. Jervis also points out that during the Cuban missile crisis 'none of the leading [US] officials espoused views that were linked to his position within the government', p27.

55 See, for example, Snyder, Bruck and Sapin, *Foreign Policy Decision-Making (Revisited)* (New York: Palgrave Macmillan, 2002).

56 While Graham Allison's political actor model fits well with the competition that existed between senior staff in the Bush administration and can be seen as a characteristic of US executives in general, Allan Gyngell and Michael Wesley argue that US-derived models do not accurately describe the dynamics of executive government in Australia nor its relationship with the bureaucracy, both of which are described by Gyngell and Wesley as far more 'collegial' than in the US. See Allison and Zelikow *Essence of Decision* and Allan Gyngell and Michael Wesley, *Making Australian Foreign Policy* (Melbourne: Cambridge University Press, 2003). For an excellent account of the tensions within the Bush administration prior to the Iraq invasion, see Chris Dolan and David Cohen, 'The war about the war: Iraq and the politics of national security advising in the G. W. Bush administration's first term', *Politics & Policy*, 34 (March 2006), pp30–64.

Chapter 3 notes

1   W. E. Walker, P. Harrimoës, J. Rotmans, J. P. van der Sluijs, M. B. A. van Asselt, P. Janssen and M. P. Krayer von Krauss, 'Defining uncertainty: A conceptual basis for uncertainty management in model-based decision support', *Integrated Assessment*, 4 (2003), pp5–17.

2   Walker et al, 'Defining Uncertainty'. See also Pielke Jr, *The Honest Broker: Making Sense of Science in Policy and Politics* (New York: Cambridge University Press, 2000).

3   Walker et al, 'Defining Uncertainty', p12.

4   'There is no single most likely, "central", or "best-guess" scenario, either with respect to SRES [Special Report on Emission Scenarios] scenarios or to the underlying scenario literature. Probabilities or likelihood are not assigned to individual SRES scenarios. None of the SRES scenarios represents an estimate of a central tendency for all driving forces or emissions, such as the mean or median, and none should be interpreted as such.' Intergovernmental Panel on Climate Change (IPCC), *IPCC Special Report Emissions Scenarios: Summary for Policymakers* (Geneva: IPCC, 2000), p11.

5   IPCC, *Special Report Emissions Scenarios*, p3.

6   John Zillman, 'Our future climate', World Meteorological Day Address, Australian Bureau of Meteorology, 21 March 2003, www.bom.gov.au/announcements/media_releases/ho/20030320a.shtml.

7   Michael Smithson, 'The many faces and masks of uncertainty', in *Uncertainty and Risk: Multidisciplinary Perspectives*, Gabriel Bammer and Michael Smithson (eds) (London: Easthscan, 2008), p15.

8   Carol Silva and Hank Jenkins-Smith, 'The precautionary principle in context: US and EU scientists' prescriptions for policy in the face of uncertainty', *Social Science Quarterly*, 88 (2007): p649; see also Aaron Wildavsky and Karl Dake, 'Theories of risk perception: Who fears what and why?' *Daedalus*, 119 (1990): pp41–60; Eric Plutzer, Ardith Maney and Robert O'Connor, 'Ideology and elites' perceptions of the safety of new technology', *American Journal of Political Science*, 42 (1998): pp190–209.

9   Pielke Jr, *The Honest Broker*, pp63–64.

10 Pielke Jr, *The Honest Broker*, p23.

11 Catherine Althaus, 'A disciplinary perspective on the epistemological status of risk', *Risk Analysis*, 25 (2005), p568.

12 Michael Heazle, 'Lessons in precaution: The International Whaling Commission experience with precautionary management', *Marine Policy*, 30 (2006), pp496–509.

13 Silvio Funtowicz and Jerome R. Ravetz, 'Science for the post-normal age', *Futures*, 25 (1993), p744.

14 Thomas Kuhn characterized the practice of normal science as 'puzzle solving' where the puzzles (i.e. problems) are chosen, defined and solved according to the priorities and rules of the dominant paradigm, which invariably excludes problems thought to be unsolvable since the whole purpose of normal science, according to Kuhn, is to bring problems to a conclusion. Thus, Kuhn argued, the activity of normal science was analogous to puzzle solving because of normal science's preference for problems for which the solutions were known, or at least known to exist: '[O]ne of the things a scientific community acquires with a paradigm is a criterion for choosing problems that ... can be assumed to have solutions. To a great extent these are the only problems that the community will admit as scientific or encourage its members to undertake. Other problems, including many that previously had been standard, are rejected as metaphysical, as the concern of another discipline, or sometimes as just too problematic to be worth the time.' See Kuhn, *Structure of Scientific Revolutions*, pp36–39.

15 Jerome R. Ravetz, 'What is post-normal science?', *Futures*, 31 (1999), p647.

16 Funtowicz and Ravetz, 'Science for the post-normal age', pp739–755.

17 Stephen Kern, *A Cultural History of Causality: Science, Murder Novels, and Systems of Thought* (Princeton, NJ: Princeton University Press, 2004), Ch. 1.

18 Kern, *A Cultural History of Causality*, pp13–14.

19 Ravetz, 'The challenge beyond orthodox science', *Futures*, 34 (2002), pp200–203.

20 Any questioning of the IPCC's often alarming predictions on global warming or the research it cites by dissenting scientists, for example, is usually quickly dismissed with the scientists responsible labelled as 'sceptics' motivated by some ulterior motive (often ties to the energy industry). For an account of one scientist's experience as a 'sceptic' after questioning the IPCC's use of the 'hockey stick' graph in its 2001 report, see Garth Paltridge, 'The politicised climate of science', *Quadrant*, XLVIII (October 2004), http://quadrant.org.au/php/archive_details_list.php?article_id=961.

21 Alston Chase, 'Some cautionary remarks about the precautionary principle' (paper presented at 'Countdown to Kyoto': The Consequences of the Mandatory Global Carbon Dioxide Emissions Reductions, Australian APEC Study Centre, Canberra, 19–21 August 1997), p4, www.apec.org.au/docs/chase.pdf.

22 John Lemons, 'The conservation of biodiversity: Scientific uncertainty and the burden of proof', in *Scientific Uncertainty and Environmental Problem Solving*, John Lemons (ed.) (Oxford: Blackwell Science, 1996), pp206–231.

23 Lemons, 'The conservation of biodiversity', p221

24 Peter Harremoës, 'Can risk analysis be applied in connection with the precautionary principle?', in *Extracts and Summary from the Danish Environmental Protection Agency's Conference on the Precautionary Principle* (Danish Environmental Protection Agency, Ministry of Environment and Protection, Copenhagen, 29 May 1998), pp30–35.

25 See Ch. 7.

26 Julian Morris, 'Defining the precautionary principle', in *Rethinking Risk and the Precautionary Principle*, Julian Morris (ed.) (Oxford: Butterworth-Heinemann, 2000) pp1–21.

27 Morris, 'Defining the precautionary principle', p10.

28 Joel Tickner, Carolyn Raffensperger and Nancy Myers provide a useful list of precautionary principle definitions that have appeared in various international

treaties and declarations, beginning with the *Ozone Layer Protocol* and *Second North Sea Declaration* in 1987, in the appendix of their pro-precautionary piece entitled *The Precautionary Principle in Action: A Handbook*. See Joel Tickner, Carolyn Raffensperger and Nancy Myers, *The Precautionary Principle in Action: A Handbook* (Science and Environmental Health Network, n.d.), www.biotech-info.net/handbook.pdf.

29 Morris, 'Defining the precautionary principle', p5.
30 United Nations General Assembly, 'Annex I: Rio declaration on environment and development', in *Report of the United Nations Conference on Environment and Development* (Rio de Janeiro, 3–14 June 1992), A/CONF.151/26 (VOL. I), Distr. GENERAL, 2 August 1992, Principle 15.
31 *Wingspread Statement on the Precautionary Principle* (drafted at the Wingspread Conference on the Precautionary Principle convened by the Science and Environmental Health Network, 26 January 1998), www.sehn.org/wing.html.
32 Commission of the European Communities, *Communication from the Commission on the Precautionary Principle* (Brussels, 2000) p3, http://ec.europa.eu/dgs/health_consumer/library/pub/pub07_en.pdf.
33 Aaron Wildavsky, 'Trial and error versus trial without error', in *Rethinking Risk and the Precautionary Principle*, Julian Morris (ed.) (Oxford: Butterworth-Heinmann), p24.
34 The website *Spiked* surveyed '40 members of the international scientific community' in early 2003 on the question of 'what significant achievements would have been limited or prevented, if science at the time had been governed by the precautionary principle that dominates science today'? See Sandy Starr, 'Science, risk and the price of precaution', 1 May 2003, www.spiked-online.com/Articles/00000006DD7A.htm.
35 Chase, 'Some cautionary remarks about the precautionary principle', pp7–8.
36 Ronald Bailey 'Precautionary tale', *Reason*, 1 April 1999, http://reason.com/archives/1999/04/01/precautionary-tale/singlepage.
37 Daniel Bodansky, 'Scientific uncertainty and the precautionary principle', *Environment*, September 1991, p43.
38 Peter M. Haas, 'Introduction: Epistemic communities and international policy coordination', in *Knowledge, Power, and International Policy Coordination*, Peter M. Haas (ed.) (Columbia, SC: University of South Carolina Press, 1997), pp1–35.
39 Michael Heazle, 'Scientific uncertainty and the International Whaling Commission: An alternative perspective on the use of science in policy making', *Marine Policy*, 28 (September 2004), pp361–374; and *Scientific Uncertainty*.
40 Haas, 'Introduction', p3.
41 Haas, 'Introduction', p23.
42 Heazle, 'Scientific uncertainty and the International Whaling Commission;' and *Scientific Uncertainty*.
43 See, for example, Joseph M. Grieco, 'Anarchy and the limits of co-operation: A realist critique of the newest liberal institutionalism', *International Organization*, 42 (1998): pp485–508.
44 Peter M. Haas, *Saving the Mediterranean – The Politics of International Environmental Co-operation* (New York: Columbia University Press, 1990); and 'Banning chlorofluorocarbons: Epistemic community efforts to protect stratospheric ozone', in *Knowledge, Power, and International Policy Coordination*, Peter M. Haas (ed.) (Columbia, SC: University of South Carolina Press, 1997), pp187–224.

45 See, for example, David Toke, 'Epistemic communities and environmental groups', *Politics*, 19 (1999): pp97–102; Claire Dunlop, 'Epistemic communities: A reply to Toke', *Politics*, 20 (2000): pp137–144.

46 According to Haas: 'By our definition, what bonds members of an epistemic community is their shared belief or faith in the verity and the applicability of partic- ular forms of knowledge or specific truths… It also somewhat resembles Kuhn's broader sociological definition of a paradigm, which is "an entire constellation of beliefs, values, techniques, and so on shared by members of a given community" and which governs "not a subject matter but a group of practitioners."' Haas, 'Introduction', pp2–3.

47 For clear expositions of interest-based and other approaches, see Gail Osher- enko and Oran R. Young, 'The formation of international regimes: Hypotheses and cases', in *Polar Politics: Creating International Environmental Regimes*, Oran R. Young and Gail Osherenko (eds) (Ithaca, NY: Cornell University Press, 1993), pp1–21; Young and Osherenko, 'International regime formation: Findings, research priorities, and applications', in *Polar Politics*, pp223–261; Stephan Haggard and Beth A. Simmons, 'Theories of international regimes', *International Organization*, 41 (1987), pp491–517; Andreas Hasenclever, Peter Mayer and Volker Rittberger, *Theories of International Regimes* (New York: Cambridge University Press, 1997).

48 See Gwyn Prins and Steve Rayner, *The Wrong Trousers: Radically Rethinking Climate Policy* (James Martin Institute for Science and Civilization, University of Oxford and the MacKinder Centre for the Study of Long-Wave Events, London School of Economics, 2007).

49 For a good account of the growing criticism of the Washington Consensus during the late 1990s and early 2000s, see Iyanatul Islam, 'Globalisation, economic devel- opment and economists: Voices of dissent', in *Globalisation and the Asia-Pacific: Contested Perspectives and Diverse Experiences*, Iyanatul Islam and Moazzem Hossain (eds) (Cheltenham, UK: Edward Elgar, 2006), pp3–27.

50 Islam, 'Globalisation, economic development and economists'. See also Robert McCleery and Fernando De Paolis, 'The Washington Consensus: A post-mortem', *Journal of Asian Economics*, 19 (2008), pp438–446. See also Ch. 6's discussion of the Washington Consensus.

Chapter 4 notes

1 Richard K. Betts, 'Analysis, war, and decision: Why intelligence failures are inevi- table', *World Politics*, 31 (1978), pp61–89.

2 Betts, 'Analysis, war, and decision', p61.

3 John Howard speech to the Australian Federal Parliament, prior to Iraq invasion. Commonwealth of Australia, *Parliamentary Debates*, House of Representatives, Official Hansard 1, 4 February 2003, p10645.

4 Tony Blair, 'PM statement opening Iraq debate in parliament', 18 March 2003, www.number10.gov.uk/Page3294.

5 George W. Bush, 'Address to the Nation', 17 March 2003, www.whitehouse.gov/ news/releases/2003/03/print/20030317-7.html.

6 Betts, 'Analysis, war, and decision', p61.

7 Parliamentary Joint Committee on ASIO, ASIS and DSD, *Intelligence on Iraq's Weapons of Mass Destruction* (Commonwealth of Australia, 2004). See also US Senate Select Committee on Intelligence, *Report on Whether Public Statements Regarding Iraq by US Government Officials were Substantiated by Intelligence*

Information, 110th Congress, 2nd Session, 5 June 2008; and *Post-war Findings about Iraq's WMD Programs and Links To Terrorism and how they Compare with Pre-War Assessments*, 109th Congress, 2nd Session, 8 September 2006.

8 'Iraq: A war without intelligence', *Jane's Intelligence Digest*, 30 October 2003, www.janes.com/security/international_security/news/jid/jid031030_1_n.shtml.

9 Silvio Funtowicz and Jerome R. Ravetz, 'Science for the post-normal age', *Futures*, 25 (1993), p744. See Ch. 3.

10 Paul R. Pillar, 'Great expectations: Intelligence as savior', *Harvard International Review*, 27 (Winter 2006), pp18–19; see also Mark Lowenthal, *Intelligence: From Secrets to Policy*, 3rd edn (Washington, DC: CQ Press, 2006); and John Heidenrich, *The State of Strategic Intelligence: The Intelligence Community's Neglect of Strategic Intelligence* (Centre for the Study of Intelligence, CIA, June 2007), https://www.cia.gov/library/center-for-the-study-of-intelligence/csi-publications/csi-studies/studies/vol51no2/the-state-of-strategic-intelligence.html.

11 Brian Jones and John Morrison both have noted that the 9/11 attacks should be seen as a security failure given the inability of airport security screening to prevent the hijackers from boarding domestic flights with weapons and also the earlier strategic warnings of a possible terrorist attack in the US provided by the US intelligence community (personal correspondence with John Morrison, 30 September 2008; personal correspondence with Brian Jones, 3 October 2008). In this sense, though, a security failure represents a failure of policy in that policy makers did not react to the available strategic assessments by making tactical adjustments. Policy maker judgements of the threat posed by a WMD-armed Iraq again ignored the strategic consensus that not only did no immediate threat exist, but that the potential for Saddam's use of WMD (assuming they existed) would only be made likely by military action against his regime, which is precisely what occurred. In both cases, the strategic assessments have been demonstrated as more reliable than the contrary judgements of policy makers, informed as they were by differing priorities and values.

12 See, for example, Pillar, 'Great expectations', especially pp19–20; Richard Clarke, *Against All Enemies* (New York: Free Press, 2004); and Lowenthal, *Intelligence*, p3.

13 Lowenthal, *Intelligence*, p3.

14 US Senate Select Committee on Intelligence, *Report on Whether Public Statements Regarding Iraq by US Government Officials were Substantiated by Intelligence Information*.

15 See Heidenrich, *The State of Strategic Intelligence*.

16 See Heidenrich, *The State of Strategic Intelligence*.

17 The Kerr Group, 'Intelligence and analysis on Iraq: Issues for the intelligence community', 29 July 2004, 8, www.gwu.edu/~nsarchiv/news/20051013/kerr_report.pdf.

18 The many disputes over the IWC Scientific Committee's advice and what it means (or should mean) in relation to IWC policy is a clear example of this, as are the ongoing disputes over global warming science and policy. See Heazle, *Scientific Uncertainty*; and 'Lessons in Precaution'.

19 US Senate Select Committee on Intelligence, *Report on Whether Public Statements Regarding Iraq by US Government Officials were Substantiated by Intelligence Information*, pp48–49.

20 Parliamentary Joint Committee, *Intelligence on Iraq's Weapons of Mass Destruction*, pp32–33. The presentation of stronger and more assertive assessments by ONA, in contrast to the Defence Intelligence Organisation's (DIO) still more

measured language, coincided with the release of the UK dossier and also the US National Intelligence Estimate (NIE) and its accompanying White Paper (the White Paper was already largely completed by this time) the following month.

21 Parliamentary Joint Committee, *Intelligence on Iraq's Weapons of Mass Destruction*, pp31–38.

22 Paul R. Pillar, interview by author, Washington, DC, 29 August 2007.

23 Kerr Group, 'Intelligence and analysis on Iraq', p9.

24 Pillar, interview.

25 Mark Phythian, 'Locating failure: US pre-war intelligence on Iraqi weapons of mass destruction', in *America's 'War on Terrorism': New Dimensions in US Government and National Security*, John E. Owens and John W. Dumbrell (eds) (Lanham, MD: Lexington Books, 2008), pp199–201.

26 Frank Lewincamp, interview by author, Canberra, Australia, 13 February 2008.

27 President George W. Bush based the claims in his 2003 State of the Union address of Iraq's ongoing development of biological weapons and use of mobile labs on evidence from Curveball despite warnings from Germany, the UK and even from within the CIA that Curveball's information was unconfirmed and that he could have fabricated all of his statements in order to gain German residency. See Bob Drogan, *Curveball: Spies, Lies, and the Con Man Who Caused a War* (New York: Random House, 2007), especially pp129–146.

28 US Senate Select Committee on Intelligence, *Report of the Select Committee on Intelligence on the US Intelligence Community's Prewar Intelligence Assessments on Iraq*, 108th Congress, 2nd Session, 9 July 2004, p249.

29 United Nations Special Commission (in Iraq); United Nations Monitoring, Verification and Inspection Commission; International Atomic Energy Agency.

30 Parliamentary Joint Committee, *Intelligence on Iraq's Weapons of Mass Destruction*, p98.

31 Hans Blix, interview by author, Stockholm, Sweden, 20 August 2007. According to Dr Blix, after UNMOVIC had completed 700 inspections on 500 sites on the basis of the best available intelligence from the US and UK, which had revealed nothing to indicate the existence of WMD or WMD programmes, the feeling in UNSCOM at this time was, 'If this is the best, what's the rest?'

32 Rod Barton, interview by author, Canberra, Australia, 14 February 2008.

33 Testimony of Andrew Wilkie to the Inquiry into Intelligence on Iraq's Weapons of Mass Destruction, 22 August 2003. Commonwealth of Australia, Joint Committee on ASIO, ASIS and DSD, Official Committee Hansard (Canberra, 2003), pp38–39.

34 Parliamentary Joint Committee, *Intelligence on Iraq's Weapons of Mass Destruction*, p59; Greg Thielmann, interview by author, Washington, DC, 31 August 2007.

35 Paul Kerr, 'Controversy grows surrounding prewar intel', *Arms Control Today*, 33 (2003), pp17–19; Parliamentary Joint Committee, *Intelligence on Iraq's Weapons of Mass Destruction*, pp35–39.

36 See George Tenet with Bill Harlow, *At the Center of the Storm* (New York: Harper Collins, 2007), pp449–475.

37 According to Gett Harigel: 'The term "weapons of mass destruction" (WMD), used to encompass nuclear (NW), biological (BW), and chemical weapons (CW), is misleading, politically dangerous, and cannot be justified on grounds of military efficiency... Whereas protection with various degrees of efficiency is possible against chemical and biological weapons, however inconvenient it might be for military forces on the battlefield and for civilians at home, it is not feasible at all

against nuclear weapons. Chemical weapons have shown to be largely ineffective in warfare, biological weapons have never been deployed on any significant scale. Both types should be better designated as weapons of terror against civilians and weapons of intimidation for soldiers. Requirements on their transport system differ vastly from those for nuclear warheads. They are extremely unpopular. Stockpiling of biological weapons is not possible over a long time scale. Only nuclear weapons are completely indiscriminate by their explosive power, heat radiation and radioactivity, and only they should therefore be called a weapon of mass destruction'. Gett Harigel, 'The concept of weapons of mass destruction: Chemical and biological weapons, use in warfare, impact on society and environment' (paper presented at the Seventh ISODARCO-Beijing Seminar on Arms Control, Xi'an, China, 8–13 October 2000), p2; see also, Milton Leitenberg, *Assessing the Biological Weapons and Bioterrorism Threat* (Strategic Studies Institute, US Army War College, December 2005); Wolfgang K. H. Panofsky, 'Dismantling the concept of "weapons of mass destruction"', *Arms Control Today*, 28 (April 1998), pp3–8.

38 Susan Moeller, *Media Coverage of Weapons of Mass Destruction* (Center for International and Security Studies at Maryland, University of Maryland, 9 March 2004).

39 Kenneth Pollack, *The Threatening Storm: The Case for Invading Iraq* (New York: Random House, 2002).

40 US Senate Select Committee on Intelligence, *Report on Whether Public Statements Regarding Iraq by US Government Officials were Substantiated By Intelligence Information*, p82.

41 US Senate Select Committee on Intelligence, *Report on Whether Public Statements Regarding Iraq by US Government Officials were Substantiated By Intelligence Information*.

42 John Morrison, interview by author, Canterbury, UK, 20 August 2008.

43 *Iraq's Weapons of Mass Destruction: The Assessment of The British Government*, 24 September 2002, p5.

44 Parliamentary Joint Committee, *Intelligence on Iraq's Weapons of Mass Destruction*, pp129–130.

45 Brian Jones, interview by author, Winchester, UK, 19 August 2008.

46 Parliamentary Joint Committee, *Intelligence on Iraq's Weapons of Mass Destruction*, pp83–84; see also pp32–33. It is also interesting to note that the Howard-appointed Flood report on Australian intelligence agencies, led by former ONA head Philip Flood, minimized the divergence between ONA and DIO assessments, concluding that 'much of what separated ONA and DIO reporting on Iraq represents the different styles that typify ONA and DIO product'. See Philip Flood, *Report of the Inquiry into Australian Intelligence Agencies* (Commonwealth of Australia, 24 July 2004), p29.

47 Notable exception here is UNMOVIC whose assessment and reports neither assumed nor dismissed the existence of WMD in Iraq; Blix, interview. See also the so-called 'Cluster Document', UNMOVIC Working Document, 'Unresolved Disarmament Issues: Iraq's Proscribed Weapons Programmes', 6 March 2003, www.un.org/Depts/unmovic/documents/6mar.pdf.

48 Mark Danner, *The Secret Way to War: The Downing Street Memo and the Iraq War's Buried History* (New York: New York Review of Books, 2006).

49 According to former US Defense Intelligence Agency Senior Middle East Analyst Jeff White, the view that Saddam had been and would remain a problem was broadly held in the US intelligence community. The consensus was that while Saddam was 'predatory' and a threat to US interests in the region, he was not irrational; 'he

[Saddam] sometimes miscalculated but he wasn't crazy'. Jeff White, interview by author, Washington, DC, 27 August 2007.

50 George W. Bush, 'President Bush outlines Iraqi threat', remarks by the President on Iraq, Cincinnati, Ohio, 7 October 2002, http://georgewbush-whitehouse.archives. gov/news/releases/2002/10/20021007-8.html.

51 Gordon Mitchell, 'Team B intelligence coups', *Quarterly Journal of Speech*, 92 (2006): pp148–149.

52 According to Democrat Senator Gary Hart: 'In retrospect Team B's conclusions were wildly off the mark. Describing the Soviet Union, in 1976, as having "a large and expanding Gross National Product", it predicted that it would modernize and expand its military at an awesome pace. For example, it predicted that the Back-fire bomber "probably will be produced in substantial numbers, with perhaps 500 aircraft off the line by 1984". In fact, the Soviets had 235 in 1984.' Quoted in Mitchell, 'Team B intelligence coups', p150.

53 Maria Ryan, 'Filling in the "unknowns": Hypothesis-based intelligence and the Rumsfeld Commission', *Intelligence and National Security*, 21 (2006), pp286–315.

54 The Commission to Assess the Ballistic Missile Threat to the United States, *Executive Summary of the Report of the Commission to Assess the Ballistic Missile Threat to the United States*, 104th Congress, 15 July 1998, http://ftp.fas.org/irp/ threat/missile/rumsfeld/index.html; see also Ryan, 'Filling in the "unknowns"', pp301–304.

55 Greg Thielmann retired in 2002 as Director of the Strategic, Proliferation, and Military Affairs Office in the State Department's Bureau of Intelligence and Research.

56 Greg Thielmann, 'Rumsfeld reprise? The missile report that foretold the Iraq intelligence controversy', *Arms Control Today*, 33 (July/August 2003), pp3–8.

57 Thielmann, 'Rumsfeld reprise?'

58 See 'Sir John Chilcot's closing statement', 8 February 2010, www.iraqinquiry.org. uk/news/100208-closing-statement.aspx.

59 In a television interview with the Australian Broadcasting Corporation's (ABC) *The 7:30 Report* on 22 July 2004, John Howard defended his decision to support the US invasion of Iraq by saying: 'I accept that the existence of stockpiles of weapons has not eventuated, I accept that. But I can only say to you as I would say to anybody else, you make judgments on the basis of the information before you at the time'. John Howard, interview by Kerry O'Brien, 'Howard welcomes intelligence findings', *The 7:30 Report*, ABC Television, 22 July 2004, www.abc.net.au/7.30/ content/2004/s1159893.htm.

Chapter 5 notes

1 See Introduction.

2 Peter Hall, 'Policy paradigms, social learning, and the state: The case of economic policymaking in Britain', *Comparative Politics*, 25 (1993).

3 Speaking at Georgetown University in March 1997, Secretary of State Madeleine Albright made future US policy on Iraq contingent on Saddam's removal from power: 'We do not agree with the nations who argue that if Iraq complies with its obligations concerning weapons of mass destruction, sanctions should be lifted. Our view, which is unshakeable, is that Iraq must prove its peaceful intentions. It can only do that by complying with all of the Security Council Resolutions to which it is subject. Is it possible to conceive of such a government under Saddam

Hussein?... The evidence is overwhelming that Saddam Hussein's intentions will never be peaceful... Clearly, a change in Iraq's government could lead to a change in US policy. Should that occur, we would stand ready, in co-ordination with our allies and friends, to enter rapidly into a dialogue with the successor regime.' 'Preserving Principle and Safeguarding Stability: United States Policy Towards Iraq', Speech by US Secretary of State Madeleine Albright, at Georgetown University, Washington, DC, 26 March 1997. Quoted in UK House of Commons, *The Iraq Crisis* (Parliamentary Research Paper 98/28, February 1998), p8, www.parliament.uk/commons/lib/research/rp98/rp98-028.pdf.

4   The Howard government attracted considerable criticism, especially from the EU, when it demanded and received an 8 per cent *increase* on its 1990 emission levels during negotiations for the Kyoto Protocol. Prime Minister Howard later announced Australia would not ratify the Kyoto agreement in 2003.

5   The concept of 'securitization' was initially developed by Barry Buzan, Ole Waever and Jaap de Wilde of the Copenhagen School. In their book, *Security: A New Framework for Analysis*, they write: '"Security" is the move that takes politics beyond the established rules of the game and frames the issue either as a special kind of politics or as above politics. Securitization can thus be seen as a more extreme version of politicization. In theory, any public issue can be located on the spectrum ranging from nonpoliticized (meaning the state does not deal with it and it is not in any other way made an issue of public debate and decision) through politicized (meaning the issue is part of public policy, requiring government decision and resource allocation...) to securitized (meaning the issue is presented as an existential threat, requiring emergency measures and justifying actions outside the bounds of political procedure).' Barry Buzan, Ole Waever and Jaap de Wilde, *Security: A New Framework for Analysis* (Boulder: Lynne Reinner Publishers, 1998), pp23–24.

6   According to Buzan, Waever and de Wilde: 'In the case of security, textual analysis suggests that something is designated as an international security issue because it can be argued that this issue is more important than other issues and should take absolute priority. This is the reason we link the issue to what might seem a fairly demanding criterion: that the issue is presented as an existential threat, If one can argue that something overflows the normal political logic of weighing issues against each other, this must be the case because it can upset the whole process of weighing as such: "If we do not tackle this problem, everything else will be irrelevant (because we will not be here or will not be free to deal with it in our own way)".' Buzan, Waever and de Wilde, *Security*, p24.

7   Commission on Presidential Debates, 'October 11, 2000, Debate Transcript: The Second Gore-Bush Presidential Debate', 2009, www.debates.org/index.php?page=october-11-2000-debate-transcript.

8   Jim Fuller, 'US officials cite serious energy shortage', *Washington File*, US Department of State, 2 April 2001, http://usinfo.org/wf-archive/2001/010402/epf111.htm.

9   Quoted in PBS *Online NewsHour*, 'Bush and the environment', panel discussion, 29 March 2001, www.pbs.org/newshour/bb/environment/jan-june01/bushenv_3-29.html.

10 *The Age*, 2 December 2003.

11 John Howard, interview by Jonathan Holmes 'What price global warming?', programme transcript, *Four Corners*, ABC Television, 28 August 2006, www.abc.net.au/4corners/content/2006/s1726376.htm.

12 Roger Pielke Jr and Daniel Sarewitz, 'Wanted: Scientific leadership on climate', *Issues in Science and Technology*, 19 (2002), p27.

13 Senator Al Gore, quoted in Pielke Jr and Sarewitz, 'Wanted: Scientific leadership on climate'.

14 Lydia Saad, 'Increased number think global warming is "exaggerated"', 11 March 2009, www.gallup.com/poll/116590/increased-number-think-global-warming-exaggerated.aspx; Frank Newport, 'Americans: Economy takes precedence over environment', 29 March 2009, www.gallup.com/poll/116962/americans-economy-takes-precedence-environment.aspx.

15 Daniel Sarewitz, 'Science and environmental policy: An excess of objectivity', Center for Science, Policy and Outcomes (1999).

16 The argument put forward by Howard and others that nuclear energy should be an option for reducing greenhouse gas emissions also serves as an example of the precautionary principle dilemma. Is the risk of a nuclear accident more or less acceptable than the still unknown but *possible* risks posed by greenhouse gas emissions? Who decides and on what basis?

17 See, for example, Richard Baker, 'PM feels the heat', *The Age*, 25 February 2007; and William Nordhaus, 'The *Stern Review* on the economics of climate change', 17 November 2006, http://qed.econ.queensu.ca/pub/faculty/milne/872/SternReviewD2.pdf.

18 Partha Dasgupta, 'Comments on the Stern Review's economics of climate change', 11 November 2006, www.econ.cam.ac.uk/faculty/dasgupta/STERN.pdf. Nicholas Stern's cost-benefit analysis of the present versus future costs of acting and not acting to mitigate anthropogenic climate change attracted criticism from many economists due to:

1 its employment of a pure rate of time preference or social discount rate of almost zero (0.1 per cent) and an overall discount rate of only 1.4 per cent as opposed to the 4–6 per cent realm normally used when discounting future costs and benefits;

2 the report allegedly downplaying the real cost of spending 1 per cent of annual world GDP on mitigation and the sacrifice this will require, particularly among developed countries where it will more likely amount to 1.8 per cent of *each* economy's GDP annually; and

3 Stern's 'cherry picking' of worst case scenarios and damage estimates as the basis of his cost-benefit analysis.

See also, for example, Eric Neumayer, 'A missed opportunity: The Stern Review on climate change fails to tackle the issue of non-substitutable loss of natural capital', *Global Environmental Change*, 17 (2007), pp297–301; Nordhaus, 'The Stern Review on the economics of climate change'; and Roger Pielke Jr, 'Stern's cherry picking on disasters and climate change', *Prometheus*, 30 October 2006, http://sciencepolicy.colorado.edu/prometheus/archives/climate_change/000973sterns_cherry-picki.html.

19 Stephen Bocking, *Nature's Experts: Science, Politics, and the Environment* (New Brunswick, NJ: Rutgers University Press, 2004), p118.

20 Bocking, *Nature's Experts*, p126.

21 Princeton physicist and climate sceptic Freeman Dyson also sees conflicts regarding fundamental values as underpinning the competing scientific arguments regarding global warming's causes. Nicholas Dawidoff writes that: 'Beyond the specific points of factual dispute [regarding global warming science], Dyson has said that it all boils down to "a deeper disagreement about values" between those who think "nature knows best" and that any gross human disruption of the natural environment is evil,

and "humanists", like himself, who contend that protecting the existing biosphere is not as important as fighting more repugnant evils like war, poverty and unemployment'. Nicholas Dawidoff, 'The lonely prophet', *The Courier-Mail Weekend*, 18–19 April 2009, p23.

22 Ian Sanderson makes the same point with his observation: 'The legacy of the Enlightenment is proving robust against post-modernist attacks on notions of rationality. In spite of the "rage against reason" conducted in the name of post-structuralist deconstruction, the forces of optimism about the role of scientific inquiry in pursuit of progress still prevail.' Ian Sanderson, 'Evaluation, policy learning and evidence-based policy making', *Public Administration*, 80 (2002), p1.

23 Greg Marston and Rob Watts capture nicely the innate appeal and 'common sense logic' of 'evidence-based' policy making in their discussion of how policy makers continue to employ the term as a source of legitimacy for policy decisions despite the many problems and unanswered questions it evokes: 'Finding a clear definition of evidence-based policy is difficult. In much of the policy literature, the meaning is considered self-explanatory or is defined simply as the systematic appraisal and review of empirical research findings... It is difficult to imagine anyone arguing that policy should be based on anything but the best available evidence. The concept of evidence-based policy has an intuitive, common sense logic, which partly explains how it has become naturalized in a diverse range of policy settings... The term acts as a catch phrase for "scientific", "scholarly", and "rationality", which taken together can be understood as an attempt to modernize policy-making and professionalize human service practice.' Greg Marston and Rob Watts, 'Tampering with the evidence: A critical appraisal of evidence-based policy-making', *The Drawing Board: An Australian Review of Public Affairs*, 3 (2003), pp143–163.

24 Sarewitz, 'Science and environmental policy'.

25 Sarewitz, 'Science and environmental policy'.

26 Former Australian delegate to the IPCC John Zillman writes that: 'According to the [UNFCCC] Convention, "climate change" is that which is due to human activity and is in addition to natural variability. The IPCC WG1 [Working Group 1], on the other hand, regards "climate change" as including natural variations. Thus, when the IPCC says "climate has changed over the past century", it is simply saying the climate now is not the same as it was a century ago (whatever the cause) whereas the [UN]FCCC listener will reasonably interpret such a statement as the scientific community affirming that *human* influence has changed climate over the past century.' John Zillman, 'The IPCC: A view from the inside' (Australian APEC Study Centre, August 1997), www.apec.org.au/docs/zillman.pdf.

27 Roger Pielke Jr, 'Misdefining "climate change": Consequences for science and action', *Environmental Science and Policy*, 8 (2005), pp553–555.

28 Email call for conference participants received by the author 3 April 2009 from Mary Mansfield via the Climate Change Info Mailing List; sent by bounce-875604-330596@lists.iisd.ca.

29 In October 2007, a British High Court judge ruled that nine claims in Gore's documentary misrepresented the available scientific evidence. The film's claim that the sea would rise by 20ft in 'the near future' as a result of global warming was 'distinctly alarmist'. The judge ruled that it could be shown in UK schools but only if it were accompanied by appropriate teaching guidance and supervision to balance the film's 'one-sided' views. BBC News, 'Gore climate film's nine "errors"', 11 October 2007, http://news.bbc.co.uk/2/hi/uk_news/education/7037671.stm.

30 See Intergovernmental Panel on Climate Change (IPCC), 'Summary for poli-cymakers', in *Climate Change 2007: The Physical Science Basis Contribution of Working Group I to the Fourth Assessment Report of the Intergovernmental Panel on Climate Change*, 2007, p9, www.ipcc.ch/pdf/assessment-report/ar4/wg1/ar4-wg1-spm.pdf.

31 The frontline of the 'hockey stick' graph debate, where many of the scientific claims and counterclaims regarding the extent to which current warming is exceptional, can be found on the following websites, *Realclimate.org* and *Climateaudit.org*. A balanced perspective on the 'hockey stick' claims and other climate change debates can be found at *Prometheus* http://sciencepolicy.colorado.edu; See also Fred Pearce, 'Climate change: Menace or myth?', *New Scientist*, 12 February 2005, http://environment.newscientist.com/channel/earth/climate-change/mg18524861.400.

32 In 2008, US climate scientist Roger Pielke Sr and two colleagues released their conclusions from an online poll on attitudes among research active climate scientists (140 responses from 1807 invitations) to the IPCC's Fourth Assessment Report's, 2007) WG1 conclusions, which focused on the basis of the physical science underpinning the IPCC's findings. Their findings were that 'while there is strong agreement on the important role of anthropogenically-caused radiative forcing of CO_2 in climate change and with the largest group supporting the IPCC report, there is not a universal agreement among climate scientists about climate science as represented in the IPCC's WG1. The claim that the human input of CO_2 is not an important climate forcing is found to be false in our survey. However, there remains substantial disagreement about the magnitude of its impacts.' The paper the authors produced was rejected without peer review by *EOS* and without explanation by *Nature Precedings*, according to Pielke Sr, '... it is clear that the AGU *EOS* and *Nature Precedings* Editors are using their positions to suppress evidence that there is more diversity of views on climate, and the human role in altering climate, than is represented in the narrowly focused 2007 IPCC report'. See Roger Pielke Sr's website 'Climate Science: Roger Pielke Sr' for comments and also the paper by Fergus Brown, James Annan and Roger Pielke Sr, 'Is there agreement amongst climate scientists on the IPCC AR4 WG1?', 22 February 2008, http://pielkeclimatesci.wordpress.com/2008/02/22/is-there-agreement-amongst-climate-scientists-on-the-ipcc-ar4-wg1/.

33 Jenny Hogan, 'Only huge emission cuts will curb climate change', *New Scientist.com*, 3 February 2005, www.newscientist.com/article.ns?id=dn6964&print=true.

34 See David C. Lowe, 'Global change: A green source of surprise', *Nature*, 439 (12 January 2006), pp148–149.

35 Criticism of peer review among scientists and academics being biased and generally falling short of the ideal of objective and impartial assessment has been increasing, particularly in the context of climate change. As Sheila Jasanoff argues: 'Advocates of peer review tend to assume that the line between acceptable and unacceptable science is objectively verifiable, available to be discovered by any competent reviewer. Yet the empirical literature on peer review suggests almost the opposite: that standards for deciding what is acceptable are matters of negotiation and compromise, and that peer review is simply part of the process of construction by which scientists certify some claims and conventions as valid.' Jasanoff, *The Fifth Branch*, pp61–62. See also, Tony Gilland, 'IPCC: The dangers of enforcing "consensus"', *Spiked*, 15 October 2007, www.spiked-online.com/index.php?/site/article/3967/.

36 Not to mention our inability to *know* what either the global climate or we might be doing in 50 or 100 years time.

37 See, for example, Pielke Jr, 'Stern's cherry picking on disasters and climate change'.

38 US Senate, *Byrd-Hagel Resolution*, 105th Congress, 1st Session, S. Res. 98, 25 July 1997.
39 See Putnam, 'Diplomacy and domestic politics'.
40 Quoted in Geoffrey Lean and Christopher Silvester, 'Blair falls into line with Bush view on global warming', *The Independent*, 25 September 2005, www.independent.co.uk/environment/blair-falls-into-line-with-bush-view-on-global-warming-508336.html.
41 Peter Hartcher, 'Howard talks up breakaway climate group at summit', *The Sydney Morning Herald*, 17 November 2006, www.smh.com.au/news/environment/howard-talks-up-breakaway-climate-group/2006/11/16/1163266712683.html.
42 George W. Bush, 'President Bush's 2007 State of the Union Address (as delivered in the House Chamber)', *The Washington Post*, 23 January 2007, www.washington-post.com/wpdyn/content/article/2007/01/23/AR2007012301075.html.
43 Stephanie Peatling and Wendy Frew, 'Greenhouse battle handed to industry', *The Sydney Morning Herald*, 13 January 2006, www.smh.com.au/news/national/green-house-battle-handed-to-industry/2006/01/12/1136956303520.html.
44 Amanda Hodge and Samantha Maiden, 'Ferguson splits left on Kyoto', *The Australian*, 13 January 2006.
45 UK Mission to the UN, *Energy, Security and Climate*, UK Concept Paper, 23 April 2007, http://unfccc.int/files/application/pdf/ukpaper_securitycouncil.pdf.
46 Maria Julia Trombetta, 'Environmental security and climate change: Analysing the discourse', *Cambridge Review of International Affairs*, 21 (2008): pp585–602.
47 William Nordhaus, *A Question of Balance: Weighing the Options on Global Warming Policies* (New Haven, CT: Yale University Press, 2008), p22. It is also worth noting that UK emissions began increasing in the late 1990s under the Blair government.
48 Trombetta, 'Environmental security and climate change', pp599–601.
49 Michael Grubb notes that approximately half of the UK's emissions reduction in the 1990s can be attributed to the switch from coal to natural gas electrical generation. See Michael Grubb, 'Britannia waives the rules', *New Economy*, 9 (2002), p142.
50 John Howard, interviewed by Jonathan Holmes 'John Howard interview – energy', *Four Corners*, ABC Television, 12 September 2006, www.abc.net.au/4corners/content/2006/s1738726.htm. William Nordhaus makes a similar point in criticizing the use of base year emission targets: 'Base year emissions have become increasingly obsolete as the economic and political fortunes of different countries have changed. The 1990 base year penalizes efficient countries (like Sweden) or rapidly growing countries (such as Korea and the United States). It also gives a premium to countries with slow growth or with historically high carbon-energy use (such as Britain, Russia and Ukraine).' William Nordhaus, 'Life after Kyoto: Alternative approaches to global warming policies' (Yale University, 9 December 2005), www.econ.yale.edu/~nordhaus/kyoto_long_2005.pdf.
51 See Lorraine Elliot, 'Pragmatism, prosperity, and environmental challenges in Australia's foreign policy', in *Trading on Alliance Security: Australia in World Affairs 2001–2005*, James Cotton and John Ravenhill (eds) (South Melbourne: Oxford University Press, 2007), pp214–216.
52 Some critics of the science and economic advice used to support the Kyoto reductions even went so far as to suggest that European governments initially supported the protocol's implementation only because they believed that it would never come into force due to the opposition of the US and other like-minded governments. See,

for example, S. Fred Singer, *Climate Policy – from Rio to Kyoto: A Political Issue for 2000 – and Beyond* (Stanford University: Hoover Institution on War Revolution and Peace, 2000).

Chapter 6 notes

1 See Dolan and Cohen, 'The war about the war'; Ivo Daalder and James Lindsay, 'America unbound: The Bush revolution in foreign policy', *Brookings Review*, 21 (2003), pp2–6; James Mann, *Rise Of The Vulcans: The History of Bush's War Cabinet* (New York: Penguin Books, 2004), especially Chs 13–15; Jason Ralph, *Tony Blair's 'New Doctrine of International Community' and the UK Decision to Invade Iraq* (Polis Working Paper No. 20, School of Politics and International Studies, University of Leeds, August 2005); and Philip Stephens, *Tony Blair: The Making of a World Leader* (New York: Viking Penguin, 2004), Ch. 12.

2 The previous 'big idea' in economic theory had been that Keynesian-based notions of a 'mixed economy' (i.e. one that combined government activism and direction with market forces) were the most reliable guide to economic development and prosperity. See David Lindauer and Lant Pritchett, 'What's the big idea? The third generation of policies for economic growth', *Economia*, 3 (2002), pp1–39.

3 Michael Pusey, *Economic Rationalism In Canberra: A Nation Building State Changes its Mind* (Melbourne: Cambridge University Press, 1991).

4 Jamie Peck, 'Neoliberalizing states: Thin policies/hard outcomes', *Progress in Human Geography*, 25 (2001), p446.

5 See Tom Conley, *The Vulnerable Country* (Sydney: University of New South Wales Press, 2009), pp255–256.

6 According to Bailey, the EU agreed to an emissions trading scheme during the Kyoto Protocol negotiations only to persuade the US to accept emission targets under the agreement. Ian Bailey, 'Neoliberalism, climate governance and the scalar politics of EU emissions trading', *Area*, 39 (2007), p434; see also Michael Grubb with Christiaan Vrolijk and Duncan Brack, *The Kyoto Protocol: A Guide and Assessment* (London: Royal Institute of International Affairs, Energy and Environmental Programme and Earthscan, 1999), pp86–96.

7 See, for example, the following reports by the Australian Department of Foreign Affairs and Trade Economic Analytical Unit, *Globalisation: Keeping the Gains* (Canberra: Commonwealth of Australia, 2003); and also *Solomon Islands: Rebuilding an Island Economy* (Canberra: Commonwealth of Australia, 2004).

8 Robert Jervis, *Perception and Misperception* in International Politics (Princeton, NJ: Princeton University Press, 1976), p195.

9 Jervis, *Perception and Misperception*, p196.

10 Louis Uchitelle, 'World Bank economist felt he had to silence his criticism or quit', *The New York Times*, 2 December 1999, www.nytimes.com/1999/12/02/business/world-bank-economist-felt-he-had-to-silence-his-criticism-or-quit.html.

11 Uchitelle, 'World Bank economist felt he had to silence his criticism or quit'. According to Robert Hunter Wade: 'Wolfensohn badly wanted a second term, not least to consolidate his claim to the Nobel Peace Prize. By then Lawrence Summers was Treasury Secretary, the most powerful figure in the Clinton Cabinet by far. Summers had the main voice in the decision about Wolfensohn's second term. The assertive and intrusive Summers, himself a former chief economist of the Bank, made no secret that Wolfensohn was not his choice as president the first time around, and from the beginning had little compunction about telling

Wolfensohn what to do. Staff around Wolfensohn learned that a telephone call from Summers was likely to plunge their boss into a foul mood, especially because in the end Wolfensohn, no less pig-headed, has not often felt able to tell Summers when to get lost.' Robert Hunter Wade, 'US hegemony and the World Bank: The fight over people and ideas', *Review of International Political Economy*, 9 (2002), pp221–222.

12 'The Great Depression changed the economic discourse around the world. The working assumption was that market economies could not function on their own. Government had to intervene through regulations, intervention, and if needed by planning for the economy. In other words, the rule was that government intervention was needed and the exception was to leave the market to itself. The Reagan–Thatcher revolution strived for making free market the rule and government intervention the exception.' Kamran Dadkhah, *The Evolution of Macroeconomic Theory and Policy* (Berlin: Springer, 2009), p213. For an excellent account of Margaret Thatcher's embracing of Friedrich von Hayek's free market economic philosophy and its impact on economic policy in the UK, see Daniel Yergin and Joseph Stanislaw, *The Commanding Heights: The Battle Between Government and the Marketplace that is Remaking the Modern World* (New York: Simon & Schuster, 1998), pp92–124.

13 See Peter Hall, 'Policy paradigms, social learning, and the state: The case of economic policymaking in Britain', *Comparative Politics*, 25 (1993).

14 For example, the extensive deregulation and privatization in Australia and New Zealand during the 1980s under Labor governments. See also Paul Kelly, *The March of the Patriots* (Melbourne: Melbourne University Press, 2009).

15 Lindauer and Pritchett, 'What's the big idea?', pp7–8.

16 John Williamson, 'A short history of the Washington Consensus' (paper commissioned by Fundacion CIDOB for a conference, 'From the Washington Consensus towards a new Global Governance', Barcelona, 24–25 September 2004), www.iie.com/publications/papers/williamson0904-2.pdf.

17 Lindauer and Pritchett, 'What's the big idea?'.

18 See Mann, *Rise of the Vulcans*.

19 In Australian and New Zealand politics, the Labor Party, as in Great Britain, traditionally has represented left of centre political ideology and policies (although some factions within the Labor Party historically have taken extreme leftist positions). But, since the late 1970s, the Australian and New Zealand Labor parties have taken a much more conservative view on a range of economic and social policies, such has been the influence of conservative economic thinking over the last two decades. In Australia, deregulation, privatization and other 'neo-liberal' economic reforms began under the Hawke Labor government in the early 1980s; similar reforms began in New Zealand during this period under a Labor government.

20 Branko Milanovic, interview by author, Washington, DC, 30 August 2007.

21 See the Clinton administration's 1998 National Security Strategy; US Government, *A National Security Strategy for a New Century* (Washington, DC: The White House, October 1998).

22 Milanovic, interview; Ravi Kanbur, interview by author, Brisbane, Australia, 30 October 2007.

23 John Williamson, 'What should the World Bank think about the Washington Consensus?', *The World Bank Research Observer*, 15 (August 2000), pp251–264; Williamson, 'A short history of the Washington Consensus'.

24 US Government, *A National Security Strategy for a New Century*, piv.

25 Mark Beeson and Iyanatul Islam, 'Neoliberalism and East Asia: Resisting the Washington Consensus' (School of Political Science and International Studies Publications, University of Queensland, 2003), http://eprint.uq.edu.au/archive/00000626/.
26 Hunter Wade, 'US hegemony and the World Bank'.
27 Dani Rodrik, 'After neo-liberalism, what?', 2002, www.newrules.org/docs/after-neolib/rodrik.pdf.
28 Rodrik, 'After neo-liberalism, what?'.
29 Dani Rodrik, 'Goodbye Washington Consensus, hello Washington confusion? A review of the World Bank's economic growth in the 1990s: Learning from a decade of reform', *Journal of Economic Literature*, XLIV (December 2006), p974.
30 Lindauer and Pritchett, 'What's the big idea?', p15; Rodrik, 'Goodbye Washington Consensus, hello Washington confusion?', p980.
31 Rodrik, 'Goodbye Washington Consensus, Hello Washington confusion?', p974.
32 Relatively few criticisms of the Washington Consensus principles existed until after the 1997 Asian financial crisis. Following the 1997 crisis, and the IMF's widely criticized responses to it, internal criticism of both the Bretton Woods institutions and US Treasury influence rapidly increased, peaking in 2002–2003. See, for examples, the list of articles critically analyzing World Bank/IMF policy between 1994 and 2006 on the Global Policy Forum website: Global Policy Forum, 'General analysis on internal critics of the World Bank and the IMF', 2009, www.globalpolicy.org/socecon/bwi-wto/critics/generalindex.htm.
33 Williamson, 'A short history of the Washington Consensus'.
34 See Joseph Stiglitz, 'What I learned at the world economic crisis', *New Republic*, 222 (17 and 24 April 2000), pp56–60.
35 See Richard S. Eckaus's comments in Lindauer and Pritchett, 'What's the big idea?', pp31–32.
36 US Government, *The National Security Strategy of the United States of America* (Washington, DC: The White House, September 2002), pv.
37 See, for example, Robert I. Rotberg, 'Failed states in a world of terror', *Foreign Affairs*, 81 (2002), pp127–140.
38 See also Martin Griffiths' discussion of how the 9/11 attacks fundamentally altered the relationship between 'core' and 'periphery' states. Martin Griffiths, 'American Power', in *The Rise of Anti-Americanism*, Brendon O'Connor and Martin Griffiths (eds) (New York: Routledge, 2006), pp105–120.
39 Michael Wesley, 'The state of the art on the art of state building', *Global Governance*, 14 (2008), pp369–385.
40 See, for example, Hunter Wade, 'US hegemony and the World Bank'.
41 Joseph Stiglitz, 'Iraq's next shock will be shock therapy', *Project Syndicate*, February 2004, www.project-syndicate.org/commentary/stiglitz42.

Chapter 7 notes

1 Ulrich Beck, 'From industrial society to the risk society: Questions of survival, social structure and ecological enlightenment', *Theory, Culture & Society*, 9 (February 1992), p101.
2 Robert Gallucci, interview by author, Washington, DC, 30 August 2007.
3 Gallucci, interview.
4 James March and Johan Olsen, *Rediscovering Institutions: The Organizational Basis of Politics* (New York: Free Press, 1989), pp30–31.
5 Bernard Crick, *In Defence of Politics* (London: Continuum, 2000), p18.

6 Gallucci, interview.
7 Michael Heazle, 'Scientific uncertainty and the International Whaling Commission: An alternative perspective on the use of science in policy making', *Marine Policy*, 30 (2006), Ch. 6.
8 Heazle, *Scientific Uncertainty*, pp137–138, 148–149.
9 See New Zealand, Opening Statement at 46th Annual Meeting of the International Whaling Commission, Puerto Vallarta, May 1994.
10 International Whaling Commission (IWC), *Thirty-Third Report* (Cambridge: IWC, 1983), p40.
11 As Greg Donovan, the IWC Scientific Editor, has noted, the original wording of the moratorium only stated that 'catch limits for the killing of whales for commercial purposes shall be zero' but before the vote was taken the extra wording including the comprehensive assessment and the 'establishment of other catch limits' was added. The extra wording was added, in Donovan's view, 'perhaps to indicate to the whaling countries that the proposal [the moratorium] seriously considered the possibility of whaling resuming'. See the preface of Greg P. Donovan (ed.), *The Comprehensive Assessment of Whale Stocks: The Early Years*, Special Issue 11 (Cambridge: IWC, 1989).
12 Donovan, *The Comprehensive Assessment of Whale Stocks*, preface.
13 'Report of the special meeting of the Scientific Committee on Planning for a Comprehensive Assessment of Whale Stocks', in Donovan, *The Comprehensive Assessment of Whale Stocks*, p3.
14 The two basic management objectives provided for by the ICRW are:

1 that whale species are not hunted to extinction; and
2 that the maximum sustainable harvest is achieved.

But as the IWC's Scientific Editor Greg Donovan points out, these two objectives represent management extremes and require clarification in terms of how one is balanced against the other. Thus, the role of the Scientific Committee in defining and conducting the comprehensive assessment was to provide the commission with specific options based on various 'trade-offs' between these two basic objectives. Donovan, however, also describes the 'setting of objectives and the relative weight given to those objectives (the trade-offs)' as a process that requires 'political rather than scientific decisions'. Donovan, *The Comprehensive Assessment of Whale Stocks*, p7.
15 Philip Hammond, 'Letter of resignation to the IWC' (IWC/2.1, 26 May 1993).
16 See Douglas Butterworth, 'Science and sentimentality', *Nature*, 357 (18 June 1992), pp532–534; and Kalland, 'Whose whale is that?', p167.
17 Kalland, 'Whose whale is that?', p167.
18 Butterworth, 'Science and sentimentality', p532.
19 See Johan Tønnessen and Arne Johnsen, *The History of Modern Whaling* (Berkeley: University of California Press, 1982); and Heazle, *Scientific Uncertainty*.
20 Speaking at the National Press Club in Canberra in early March 2003, Prime Minister Howard rejected regime change in Iraq as the basis for Australian support for US military action: 'Well, I would have to accept that if Iraq had genuinely disarmed, I couldn't justify on its own a military invasion of Iraq to change the regime. I've never advocated that.' See John Howard, 'John Howard's address on Iraq to the National Press Club', 13 March 2003, www.australianpolitics.com/news/2003/03/03-03-13.shtml. See also Catherine McGrath, 'PM seeks public support for Iraq stand', *The World Today*, ABC Radio, 30 January 2003, www.abc.net.au/worldtoday/stories/s773045.htm.

21 Howard, 'John Howard's address on Iraq to the National Press Club'.
22 Pielke Jr, *The Honest Broker*.

Chapter 8 notes

1 Bernard Crick, *In Defence of Politics* (London: Continuum, 2000), p18.
2 Richard Clarke, *Against All Enemies* (New York: Free Press, 2004); Tenet, *At the Center of the Storm*; and Ron Suskind, *The Price of Loyalty: George W. Bush, the White House, and the Education of Paul O'Neill* (New York: Simon & Schuster, 2004).
3 'States like these, and their terrorist allies, constitute an axis of evil, arming to threaten the peace of the world. By seeking weapons of mass destruction, these regimes pose a grave and growing danger. They could provide these arms to terrorists, giving them the means to match their hatred. They could attack our allies or attempt to blackmail the United States. In any of these cases, the price of indifference would be catastrophic.' George W. Bush, 'State of the Union Address', 29 January 2002, http://transcripts.cnn.com/2002/ALLPOLITICS/01/29/bush.speech.txt/.
4 Mark Danner, *The Secret Way to War: The Downing Street Memo and the Iraq War's Buried History* (New York: New York Review of Books, 2006).
5 BBC, *The Road to War – The Inside Story*, April 2003, screened on ABC Australia's *Four Corners*, 26 May 2003.
6 In a letter published in January 1998 on the neo-conservative website 'Project For The New American Century', 18 neo-conservative, or neo-conservative aligned, academics, policy commentators and members of past administrations dating back to President Ford urged President Clinton to take military action against Saddam Hussein, arguing that: 'Given the magnitude of the threat, the current policy, which depends for its success upon the steadfastness of our coalition partners and upon the cooperation of Saddam Hussein, is dangerously inadequate. The only acceptable strategy is one that eliminates the possibility that Iraq will be able to use or threaten to use weapons of mass destruction. In the near term, this means a willingness to undertake military action as diplomacy is clearly failing. In the long term, it means removing Saddam Hussein and his regime from power. That now needs to become the aim of American foreign policy.' The list of names endorsing the letter included several later appointments to George W. Bush's administration including John Bolton, Richard Armitage, Paul Wolfowitz and Donald Rumsfeld, *Project for the New American Century*, 26 January 1998, www.newamericancentury.org/iraqclintonletter.htm.
7 Pillar, interview.
8 Blix, interview.
9 White, interview.
10 Dominic de Villepin, interviewed on BBC, *The Road to War – The Inside Story*, April 2003.
11 Colin Powell, 'Transcript of Powell's UN presentation', *CNN.com*, 6 February 2003, http://edition.cnn.com/2003/US/02/05/sprj.irq.powell.transcript/.
12 Greg Thielmann, personal correspondence with author, 14 September 2008.
13 Powell, 'Transcript of Powell's UN presentation'.
14 Parsons, *Public Policy*, p42
15 See, for example, Paul R. Pillar, 'Intelligence, policy, and the war in Iraq', *Foreign Affairs* (March/April 2006): pp15–27; Garry Woodard, 'We now know about going to war in Iraq', October, 2007, www.mup.com.au/uploads/files/acmo/WoodardGoingToWarInIraqEssay.pdf.

16 As John Dryzeck has noted: 'The more complex a problem or situation, the greater the number of plausible interpretations of it, and so the greater the number of frames that can be brought to bear.' Dryzek, 'Policy analysis and planning', p223.

17 Steven Ney, *Resolving Messy Policy Problems: Handling Conflict in Environmental, Transport, Health and Ageing Policy* (London: Earthscan, 2009), p34. See also Dryzek, 'Policy analysis and planning'.

18 International Institute for Sustainable Development, *Earth Negotiations Bulletin*, 12 (29 September 2009), www.iisd.ca/download/pdf/enb12429e.pdf.

19 Russell, *Sceptical Essays*, p12.

20 Gwyn Prins et al, *How to Get Climate Policy Back on Course* (Institute for Science, Innovation and Society, University of Oxford, and the Mackinder Programme for the Study of Long Wave Events, London School of Economics, 6 July 2009), p5, www.eci.ox.ac.uk/research/climate/cop15/oxford/content/technical/pdfs/Climate-policy-back-on-course.pdf.

21 Prins et al, *How to Get Climate Policy Back on Course*, p10.

22 Roger Pielke Jr et al, 'Lifting the taboo on adaptation', *Nature*, 445 (8 February 2007), pp597–98.

23 See, for example, Michael Wara, *Measuring the Clean Development Mechanism's Performance and Potential* (The Program on Energy and Sustainable Development, Stanford University, Working Paper No. 56, July 2006); Nick Davies, 'Abuse and incompetence in fight against global warming', *The Guardian*, 2 June 2007, www.guardian.co.uk/environment/2007/jun/02/energy.business/print; Economist Debates, 'Carbon offsets', *The Economist*, 4 December 2008, www.economist.com/debate/days/view/249.

24 Michael Heazle, 'Energy and human security in the Asia Pacific', in *Energy Security in Asia*, Michael Wesley (ed.) (London: Routledge, 2006), pp209–221.

25 An additional strategic dimension to the development of alternative energy technologies, albeit a more hawkish one, is the effect a drop in oil prices, due to decreasing demand, would have on 'recalcitrant' states such as Iran and also Middle Eastern sources of funding for transnational terrorist groups; renewable energy development would also help reduce the increasing dependence of European states on Russian oil and gas.

26 Bodansky, Daniel (2010) 'The Copenhagen Climate Change Conference – A post-mortem', *American Journal of International Law*, vol 104, http://ssrn.com/abstract=1553167.

Chapter 9 notes

1 Michael Heazle, 'Lessons in precaution: The International Whaling Commission experience with precautionary management', *Marine Policy*, 28 (2004).

2 Daniel Sarewitz, 'Science and environmental policy: An excess of objectivity', Center for Science, Policy and Outcomes (1999).

3 Robert Gallucci, interview by author, Washington, DC, 30 August 2007.

Bibliography

Age, The (2003) 'I will not ratify Kyoto Protocol: PM, 2 December, www.theage.com.au/cgi-bin/common/popupPrintArtical.pl?path=/articles/2003/12/02/1070351578736.html

Allison, Graham and Phillip Zelikow, *Essence of Decision: Explaining the Cuban Missile Crisis*, 2nd edn, New York: Longman, 1999

Althaus, Catherine, 'A disciplinary perspective on the epistemological status of risk', *Risk Analysis*, 25 (2005), pp567–588

Australian Department of Foreign Affairs and Trade Economic Analytical Unit, *Globalisation: Keeping the Gains*, Canberra: Commonwealth of Australia, 2003

Australian Department of Foreign Affairs and Trade Economic Analytical Unit, *Solomon Islands: Rebuilding an Island Economy*, Canberra: Commonwealth of Australia, 2004

Bailey, Ian, 'Neoliberalism, climate governance and the scalar politics of EU emissions trading', *Area*, 39 (2007), pp431–442

Bailey, Ronald, 'Precautionary tale', *Reason*, 1 April 1999, http://reason.com/archives/1999/04/01/precautionary-tale/singlepage

Baker, Richard, 'PM feels the heat', *The Age*, 25 February 2007

BBC, *The Road to War – The Inside Story*, April 2003, screened on ABC Australia's *Four Corners*, 26 May 2003

BBC News, 'Gore climate film's nine "errors"', 11 October 2007, http://news.bbc.co.uk/2/hi/uk_news/education/7037671.stm

Beck, Ulrich, 'From industrial society to the risk society: Questions of survival, social structure and ecological enlightenment', *Theory, Culture & Society*, 9 (February 1992), pp97–123

Beeson, Mark and Iyanatul Islam, 'Neoliberalism and East Asia: Resisting the Washington Consensus', School of Political Science and International Studies Publications, University of Queensland, 2003, http://eprint.uq.edu.au/archive/00000626/

Betts, Richard K., 'Analysis, war, and decision: Why intelligence failures are inevitable', *World Politics*, 31 (1978), pp61–89

Blair, Tony, 'PM statement opening Iraq debate in parliament', 18 March 2003, www.number10.gov.uk/Page3294

Bocking, Stephen, *Nature's Experts: Science, Politics, and the Environment*, New Brunswick, NJ: Rutgers University Press, 2004

Bodansky, Daniel, 'Scientific uncertainty and the precautionary principle', *Environment*, September 1991, pp4–5, 43–44

Bodansky, Daniel, 'The Copenhagen Climate Change Conference: A post mortem', 12 February 2010, *Social Science Research Network*, http://papers.ssrn.com/sol3/papers.cfm?abstract_id=1553167.

Brown, Fergus, James Annan and Roger Pielke Sr, 'Is there agreement amongst climate scientists on the IPCC AR4 WG1?', 22 February 2008, http://pielkeclimatesci.wordpress. com/2008/02/22/is-there-agreement-amongst-climate-scientists-on-the-ipcc-ar4-wg1/

Bush, George W., 'State of the Union Address', 29 January 2002, http://transcripts.cnn. com/2002/ALLPOLITICS/01/29/bush.speech.txt/

Bush, George W., 'President Bush outlines Iraqi threat', remarks by the President on Iraq, Cincinnati, Ohio, 7 October 2002, http://georgewbush-whitehouse.archives. gov/news/releases/2002/10/20021007-8.html

Bush, George W., 'Address to the Nation', 17 March 2003, www.whitehouse.gov/ news/releases/2003/03/print/20030317-7.html

Bush, George W., 'President Bush's 2007 State of the Union Address (as delivered in the House Chamber)', *The Washington Post*, 23 January 2007, www.washingtonpost. com/wpdyn/content/article/2007/01/23/AR2007012301075.html

Butterworth, Douglas, 'Science and sentimentality', *Nature*, 357 (18 June 1992), pp532–534

Buzan, Barry, Ole Waever and Jaap de Wilde, *Security: A New Framework for Analysis*, Boulder: Lynne Reinner Publishers, 1998

Cannon, Carl M., 'Untruth and consequences', *The Atlantic*, 299 (January–February 2007), pp56–67

Carr, E. H., *What is History?*, Oxford: Oxford University Press, 1961

Chase, Alston, 'Some cautionary remarks about the precautionary principle', paper presented at 'Countdown to Kyoto': The Consequences of the Mandatory Global Carbon Dioxide Emissions Reductions, Australian APEC Study Centre, Canberra, 19–21 August 1997, www.apec.org.au/docs/chase.pdf

Checkel, Jeffrey T., 'The constructivist turn in international relations theory', *World Politics*, 50 (1998), pp324–348

Cheney, Dick, interview by Tim Russert, *Meet the Press*, 10 September 2006, www. msnbc.msn.com/id/14720480/page/4/

Chollet, Derek H. and James M. Goldgeier, 'The scholarship of decision-making: Do we know how we decide?', in *Foreign Policy Decision-Making (Revisited)*, Richard C. Snyder, H. W. Bruck and Burton Sapin (eds), New York: Palgrave Macmillan, 2002, pp153–180

Clarke, Richard, *Against All Enemies*, New York: Free Press, 2004

Commission of the European Communities, *Communication from the Commission on the Precautionary Principle*, Brussels, 2000, http://ec.europa.eu/dgs/health_ consumer/library/pub/pub07_en.pdf

Commission on Presidential Debates, 'October 11, 2000, debate transcript: The second Gore-Bush Presidential Debate', 2009, www.debates.org/index.php?page=october-11-2000-debate-transcript

Commonwealth of Australia, Joint Committee on ASIO, ASIS and DSD, Official Committee Hansard, Canberra, 23 August 2003

Commonwealth of Australia, *Parliamentary Debates*, House of Representatives, Official Hansard 1, Monday, 4 February 2003

Conley, Tom, *The Vulnerable Country*, Sydney: University of New South Wales Press, 2009

Crick, Bernard, *In Defence of Politics*, 5th edn, London: Continuum, 2000

Daalder, Ivo and James Lindsay, 'America unbound: The Bush revolution in foreign policy', *Brookings Review*, 21 (Fall 2003), pp2–6

Dadkhah, Kamran, *The Evolution of Macroeconomic Theory and Policy*, Berlin: Springer, 2009

Danner, Mark, *The Secret Way to War: The Downing Street Memo and the Iraq War's Buried History*, New York: New York Review of Books, 2006

Dasgupta, Partha, 'Comments on the Stern Review's economics of climate change', 11 November 2006, www.econ.cam.ac.uk/faculty/dasgupta/STERN.pdf

Daston, Lorraine, 'Scientific error and the ethos of belief', *Social Research*, 72 (Spring 2005), pp1–28

Davies, Nick, 'Abuse and incompetence in fight against global warming', *The Guardian*, 2 June 2007, www.guardian.co.uk/environment/2007/jun/02/energy.business/print

Dawidoff, Nicholas, 'The lonely prophet', *The Courier Mail Weekend*, 18–19 April 2009

Dolan, Chris and David Cohen, 'The war about the war: Iraq and the politics of national security advising in the G. W. Bush administration's first term', *Politics & Policy*, 34 (March 2006), pp30–64

Donovan, Greg P. (ed.), *The Comprehensive Assessment of Whale Stocks: The Early Years*, Special Issue 11, Cambridge: IWC, 1989

Drogan, Bob, *Curveball: Spies, Lies, and the Con Man Who Caused a War*, New York: Random House, 2007

Dryzeck, John, 'A post-positivist policy analytic travelogue', *The Good Society*, 11 (2002), pp32–36

Dryzek, John, 'Policy analysis and planning: From science to argument', in *The Argumentative Turn in Policy Analysis and Planning*, Frank Fischer and John Forester (eds), Durham, NC: Duke University Press, 1993, pp213–232

Dunlop, Claire, 'Epistemic communities: A reply to Toke', *Politics*, 20 (2000), pp137–144

Economist Debates, 'Carbon offsets', *The Economist*, 4 December 2008, www.economist.com/debate/days/view/249

Elliot, Lorraine, 'Pragmatism, prosperity, and environmental challenges in Australia's foreign policy', in *Trading on Alliance Security: Australia in World Affairs 2001–2005*, James Cotton and John Ravenhill (eds), South Melbourne: Oxford University Press, 2007, pp213–228

Ezrahi, Yaron, *The Descent of Icarus*, Cambridge, MA: Harvard University Press, 1990

Finnemore, Martha and Kathryn Sikkink, 'Taking stock: The constructivist research program in international relations and comparative politics', *Annual Review of Political Science*, 4 (2001), pp391–416

Fischer, Frank and John Forester (eds), *The Argumentative Turn in Policy Analysis and Planning*, Durham, NC: Duke University Press, 1993

Flood, Philip, *Report of the Inquiry into Australian Intelligence Agencies*, Commonwealth of Australia, 24 July 2004

Freeden, Michael, *Ideologies and Political Theory: A Conceptual Approach*, Oxford: Oxford University Press, 1996

Frewer, Lynn and Brian Salter, 'Public attitudes, scientific advice and the politics of regulatory policy: The case of BSE', *Science and Public Policy*, 29 (April 2002), pp137–145

Fuller, Jim, 'US officials cite serious energy shortage', *Washington File*, US Department of State, 2 April 2001, http://usinfo.org/wf-archive/2001/010402/epf111.htm

Funtowicz, Silvio and Jerome R. Ravetz, 'The good, the true, and the post-modern', *Futures* 24(10) (December 1992), pp963–976

Funtowicz, Silvio and, Jerome R. Ravetz, 'Science for the post-normal age', *Futures*, 25 (September 1993), pp739–755

Geertz, Clifford, *The Interpretation of Cultures*, New York: Basic Books, 1973

Gilland, Tony, 'IPCC: The dangers of enforcing "consensus"', *Spiked*, 15 October 2007, www.spiked-online.com/index.php?/site/article/3967/

Global Policy Forum, 'General analysis on internal critics of the World Bank and the IMF', 2009, www.globalpolicy.org/socecon/bwi-wto/critics/generalindex.htm

Goldenberg, Maya J., 'On evidence and evidence-based medicine: Lessons from the philosophy of science', *Social Science and Medicine*, 62 (2006), pp2621–2632

Goldstein, Judith and Robert O. Keohane, 'Ideas and foreign policy: An analytical framework', in *Ideas and Foreign Policy: Beliefs, Institutions, and Political Change*, Judith Goldstein and Robert O. Keohane (eds), Ithaca, NY: Cornell University Press, 1993, pp3–30

Grieco, Joseph M., 'Anarchy and the limits of co-operation: A realist critique of the newest liberal institutionalism', *International Organization*, 42 (1988), pp485–508

Griffiths, Martin, 'American power', in *The Rise of Anti-Americanism*, Brendon O'Connor and Martin Griffiths (eds), New York: Routledge, 2006, pp105–120

Grubb, Michael, 'Britannia waives the rules', *New Economy*, 9 (2002), pp139–142

Grubb, Michael, with Christiaan Vrolijk and Duncan Brack, *The Kyoto Protocol: A Guide and Assessment*, London: Royal Institute of International Affairs, Energy and Environmental Programme and Earthscan, 1999

Gyngell, Allan and Michael Wesley, *Making Australian Foreign Policy*, Melbourne: Cambridge University Press, 2003

Haas, Peter M., *Saving the Mediterranean – The Politics of International Environmental Co-operation*, New York: Columbia University Press, 1990

Haas, Peter M., 'Introduction: Epistemic communities and international policy coordination', in *Knowledge, Power, and International Policy Coordination*, Peter M. Haas (ed.), Columbia, SC: University of South Carolina Press, 1997, pp1–36

Haas, Peter M., 'Banning chlorofluorocarbons: Epistemic community efforts to protect stratospheric ozone', in *Knowledge, Power, and International Policy Coordination*, Peter M. Haas (ed.), Columbia, SC: University of South Carolina Press, 1997, pp187–224

Haas, Peter M. (ed.), *Knowledge, Power, and International Policy Coordination*, Columbia, SC: University of South Carolina Press, 1997

Habermas, Jurgen, *Toward a Rational Society*, London: Heinemann Educational Books, 1971

Haggard, Stephan and, Beth A. Simmons, 'Theories of international regimes', *International Organization*, 41 (1987), pp491–517

Hajer, Maarten, 'Policy without polity? Policy analysis and the institutional void', *Policy Sciences*, 36 (2003), pp175–195

Hall, Peter, 'Policy paradigms, social learning, and the state: The case of economic policymaking in Britain', *Comparative Politics*, 25 (April 1993), pp275–296

Hammond, Philip, 'Letter of resignation to the IWC', IWC/2.1, 26 May 1993

FCO (2002) *Iraq's Weapons of Mass Destruction: The Assessment of The British Government*, 24 September 2002, Foreign and Commonwealth Office, London, p5, www.fco.gov.uk/resources/en/pdf/pdf3/fco_iraqdossier

Harigel, Gett, 'The concept of weapons of mass destruction: Chemical and biological weapons, use in warfare, impact on society and environment', paper presented at the Seventh ISODARCO-Beijing Seminar on Arms Control, Xi'an, China, 8–13 October 2000

Harremoës, Peter, 'Can risk analysis be applied in connection with the precautionary principle?', in *Extracts and Summary from the Danish Environmental Protection Agency's Conference on the Precautionary Principle*, Danish Environmental

Protection Agency, Ministry of Environment and Protection, Copenhagen, 29 May 1998, pp30–35

Hartcher, Peter, 'Howard talks up breakaway climate group at summit', *The Sydney Morning Herald*, 17 November 2006, www.smh.com.au/news/environment/howard-talks-up-breakaway-climate-group/2006/11/16/1163266712683.html

Hasenclever, Andreas, Peter Mayer and Volker Rittberger, *Theories of International Regimes*, New York: Cambridge University Press, 1997

Heazle, Michael, 'Scientific uncertainty and the International Whaling Commission: An alternative perspective on the use of science in policy making', *Marine Policy*, 28 (September 2004), pp361–374

Heazle, Michael, 'Energy and human security in the Asia Pacific', in *Energy Security in Asia*, Michael Wesley (ed.), London: Routledge, 2006, pp209–221

Heazle, Michael, 'Lessons in precaution: The International Whaling Commission experience with precautionary management', *Marine Policy*, 30 (2006), pp496–509

Heazle, Michael, *Scientific Uncertainty and the Politics of Whaling*, Seattle: University of Washington Press, 2006

Heidenrich, John, *The State of Strategic Intelligence: The Intelligence Community's Neglect of Strategic Intelligence*, Centre for the Study of Intelligence, CIA, June 2007, www.cia.gov/library/center-for-the-study-of-intelligence/csi-publications/csi-studies/studies/vol51no2/the-state-of-strategic-intelligence.html

Hodge, Amanda and Samantha Maiden, 'Ferguson splits left on Kyoto', *The Australian*, 13 January 2006

Hogan, Jenny, 'Only huge emission cuts will curb climate change', *New Scientist.com*, 3 February 2005, www.newscientist.com/article.ns?id=dn6964&print=true

Hoppe, Robert, 'Policy analysis, science and politics: From "speaking truth to power" to "making sense together"', *Science and Public Policy*, 26 (1999), pp201–210

Howard, John, interview by Jonathan Holmes, 'John Howard interview – energy', *Four Corners*, ABC Television, 12 September 2006, www.abc.net.au/4corners/content/2006/s1738726.htm

Howard, John, interview by Jonathan Holmes, 'What price global warming?', programme transcript, *Four Corners*, ABC Television, 28 August 2006, www.abc.net.au/4corners/content/2006/s1726376.htm

Howard, John, interview by Kerry O'Brien, 'Howard welcomes intelligence findings', *The 7:30 Report*, ABC Television, 22 July 2004, www.abc.net.au/7.30/content/2004/s1159893.htm

Howard, John, 'John Howard's address on Iraq to the National Press Club', 13 March 2003, www.australianpolitics.com/news/2003/03/03-03-13.shtml

Hunter Wade, Robert, 'US hegemony and the World Bank: The fight over people and ideas', *Review of International Political Economy*, 9 (2002), pp215–243

Intergovernmental Panel on Climate Change (IPCC), *IPCC Special Report Emissions Scenarios: Summary for Policymakers*, Geneva: IPCC, 2000

Intergovernmental Panel on Climate Change (IPCC), 'Summary for policymakers', *Climate Change 2007: The Physical Science Basis Contribution of Working Group I to the Fourth Assessment Report of the Intergovernmental Panel on Climate Change*, 2007, www.ipcc.ch/pdf/assessment-report/ar4/wg1/ar4-wg1-spm.pdf

International Energy Agency (IEA), CO_2 *Emissions from Fuel Combustion*, Paris: IEA, 2009

International Energy Agency (IEA), 'R&D statistics', 2009, www.iea.org/Textbase/stats/rd.asp

International Institute for Sustainable Development, *Earth Negotiations Bulletin*, 12 (29 September 2009), www.iisd.ca/download/pdf/enb12429e.pdf

International Whaling Commission (IWC), *Thirty-Third Report*, Cambridge: IWC, 1983

'Iraq: A war without intelligence', *Jane's Intelligence Digest*, 30 October 2003, www.janes.com/security/international_security/news/jid/jid031030_1_n.shtml

Islam, Iyanatul, 'Globalisation, economic development and economists: Voices of dissent', in *Globalisation and the Asia-Pacific: Contested Perspectives and Diverse Experiences*, Iyanatul Islam and Moazzem Hossain (eds), Cheltenham, UK: Edward Elgar, 2006, pp3–27

Jasanoff, Sheila, *The Fifth Branch: Science Advisers as Policymakers*, Cambridge, MA: Harvard University Press, 1990

Jervis, Robert, *Perception and Misperception in International Politics*, Princeton, NJ: Princeton University Press, 1976

Kalland, Arne, 'Whose whale is that? Diverting the commodity path', in *Elephants and Whales: Resources for Whom?*, Milton M. R. Freeman and Urs P. Kreuter (eds), Amsterdam: Gordon and Breach, 1994, pp159–186

Kelly, George A., *A Theory of Personality: The Psychology of Personal Constructs*, New York: W. W. Norton and Company, 1963

Kelly, Paul, *The March of the Patriots*, Melbourne: Melbourne University Press, 2009

Kern, Stephen, *A Cultural History of Causality: Science, Murder Novels, and Systems of Thought*, Princeton, NJ: Princeton University Press, 2004

Kerr, Paul, 'Controversy grows surrounding prewar intel', *Arms Control Today*, 33 (2003), pp17–21

Kuhn, Thomas, *The Structure of Scientific Revolutions*, 3rd edn, Chicago: University of Chicago Press, 1996

Lasswell, Harold, 'The emerging conception of the policy sciences', *Policy Sciences*, 1 (1970), pp3–14

Lean, Geoffrey and Christopher Silvester, 'Blair falls into line with Bush view on global warming', *The Independent*, 25 September 2005, www.independent.co.uk/environment/blair-falls-into-line-with-bush-view-on-global-warming-508336.html

Leitenberg, Milton, *Assessing the Biological Weapons and Bioterrorism Threat*, Strategic Studies Institute, US Army War College, December 2005

Lemons, John, 'The conservation of biodiversity: Scientific uncertainty and the burden of proof', in *Scientific Uncertainty and Environmental Problem Solving*, John Lemons (ed.), Oxford: Blackwell Science, 1996, pp206–231

Lindauer, David and Lant Pritchett, 'What's the big idea? The third generation of policies for economic growth', *Economia*, 3 (2002), pp1–39

Lindblom, Charles E., 'The science of muddling through', *Public Administration Review*, 19 (1959), pp79–88

Lindblom, Charles E., 'Still muddling, not yet through', *Public Administration Review*, 39 (1979), pp517–526

Lowe, David C., 'Global change: A green source of surprise', *Nature*, 439 (12 January 2006), pp148–149

Lowenthal, Mark, *Intelligence: From Secrets to Policy*, 3rd edn, Washington, DC: CQ Press, 2006

Mann, James, *Rise of the Vulcans: The History of Bush's War Cabinet*, New York: Penguin Books, 2004

March, James and Johan Olsen, *Rediscovering Institutions: The Organizational Basis of Politics*, New York: Free Press, 1989

Marston, Greg and Rob Watts, 'Tampering with the evidence: A critical appraisal of evidence-based policy-making', *The Drawing Board: An Australian Review of Public Affairs*, 3 (2003), pp143–163

Martin, Brian and Evelleen Richards, 'Scientific knowledge, controversy, and public decision-making', in *Handbook of Science and Technology Studies*, Sheila Jasanoff, Gerald E. Markle, James C. Peterson and Trevor J. Pinch (eds), Newbury Park, CA: Sage, 1995, pp506–526

McCalla, Robert B., *Uncertain Perceptions: US Cold War Crisis Decision Making*, Ann Arbor, MI: University of Michigan Press, 1992

McCleery, Robert and Fernando De Paolis, 'The Washington Consensus: A post-mortem', *Journal of Asian Economics*, 19 (2008), pp438–446

McGrath, Catherine, 'PM seeks public support for Iraq stand', *The World Today*, ABC Radio, 30 January 2003, www.abc.net.au/worldtoday/stories/s773045.htm

Mearsheimer, John, 'A realist reply', *International Security*, 20 (1995), pp82–93

Mitchell, Gordon, 'Team B intelligence coups', *Quarterly Journal of Speech*, 92 (2006), pp144–173

Moeller, Susan, *Media Coverage of Weapons of Mass Destruction*, Center for International and Security Studies at Maryland, University of Maryland, 9 March 2004

Morris, Julian, 'Defining the precautionary principle', in *Rethinking Risk and the Precautionary Principle*, Julian Morris (ed.), Oxford: Butterworth-Heinmann, 2000, pp1–21

Neumayer, Eric, 'A missed opportunity: The Stern Review on climate change fails to tackle the issue of non-substitutable loss of natural capital', *Global Environmental Change*, 17 (2007), pp297–301

Newport, Frank, 'Americans: Economy takes precedence over environment', 19 March 2009, www.gallup.com/poll/116962/americans-economy-takes-precedence-environment.aspx

New Zealand, Opening Statement at 46th Annual Meeting of the International Whaling Commission, Puerto Vallarta, May 1994

Ney, Steven, *Resolving Messy Policy Problems: Handling Conflict in Environmental, Transport, Health and Ageing Policy*, London: Earthscan, 2009

Nieman, Max and Stephen J. Stambough, 'Rational choice theory and the evaluation of public policy', *Policy Studies Journal*, 26 (1998), pp449–465

Nordhaus, William, 'Life after Kyoto: Alternative approaches to global warming policies', Yale University, 9 December 2005, www.econ.yale.edu/~nordhaus/kyoto_long_2005.pdf

Nordhaus, William, 'The Stern Review on the economics of climate change', 17 November 2006, http://qed.econ.queensu.ca/pub/faculty/milne/872/SternReviewD2.pdf

Nordhaus, William, *A Question of Balance: Weighing the Options on Global Warming Policies*, New Haven, CT: Yale University Press, 2008

OECD, *National Accounts of OECD Countries Volume I: Main Aggregates 1996–2007*, Paris: OECD, 2009

OECD, *Main Science and Technology Indicators*, vol. 2009/1, Paris: OECD, 2009

Osherenko, Gail and Oran R. Young, 'The formation of international regimes: Hypotheses and cases', in *Polar Politics: Creating International Environmental Regimes*, Oran R. Young and Gail Osherenko (eds), Ithaca, NY: Cornell University Press, 1993, pp1–21

Paltridge, Garth, 'The politicised climate of science', *Quadrant*, XLVIII (October 2004), http://quadrant.org.au/php/archive_details_list.php?article_id=961

Panofsky, Wolfgang K. H., 'Dismantling the concept of "weapons of mass destruction"', *Arms Control Today*, 28 (April 1998), pp3–8

Panofsky, Wolfgang K. H., 'Dismantling the concept of "Weapons of Mass Destruction"', *Arms Control Today*, 28 (April 1998), pp3–8

Parliamentary Joint Committee on ASIO, ASIS and DSD, *Intelligence on Iraq's Weapons of Mass Destruction*, Commonwealth of Australia, 2004

Parsons, Wayne, *Public Policy: An Introduction to the Theory and Practice of Policy Analysis*, Aldershot, UK: Edward Elgar Publishing, 1995

PBS *Online NewsHour*, 'Bush and the environment', PBS *Online NewsHour*, 29 March 2001, www.pbs.org/newshour/bb/environment/jan-june01/bushenv_3-29.html

Pearce, Fred, 'Climate change: Menace or myth?' *New Scientist*, 12 February 2005, http://environment.newscientist.com/channel/earth/climate-change/mg18524861.400

Peatling, Stephanie and Wendy Frew, 'Greenhouse battle handed to industry', *The Sydney Morning Herald*, 13 January 2006, www.smh.com.au/news/national/greenhouse-battle-handed-to-industry/2006/01/12/1136956303520.html

Peck, Jamie, 'Neoliberalizing states: Thin policies/hard outcomes', *Progress in Human Geography*, 25 (2001), pp445–455

Phythian, Mark, 'Locating failure: US pre-war intelligence on Iraqi weapons of mass destruction', in *America's 'War on Terrorism': New Dimensions in US Government and National Security*, John E. Owens and John W. Dumbrell (eds), Lanham, MD: Lexington Books, 2008, pp185–208

Pielke Jr, Roger, 'Misdefining "climate change": Consequences for science and action', *Environmental Science and Policy*, 8 (2005), pp548–561

Pielke Jr, Roger, 'Stern's cherry picking on disasters and climate change', *Prometheus*, 30 October 2006, http://sciencepolicy.colorado.edu/prometheus/archives/climate_change/000973sterns_cherry_picki.html

Pielke Jr, Roger, *The Honest Broker: Making Sense of Science in Policy and Politics*, New York: Cambridge University Press, 2007

Pielke Jr, Roger and Daniel Sarewitz, 'Wanted: Scientific leadership on climate', *Issues in Science and Technology*, 19 (Winter 2002), pp27–30

Pielke Jr, Roger, Gwyn Prins, Steve Rayner and Daniel Sarewitz, 'Lifting the taboo on adaptation', *Nature*, 445 (8 February 2007), pp597–598

Pillar, Paul R., 'Great expectations: Intelligence as savior', *Harvard International Review*, 27 (Winter 2006), pp16–21

Pillar, Paul R., 'Intelligence, policy, and the war in Iraq', *Foreign Affairs* (March/April 2006), pp15–27

Plutzer, Eric, Ardith Maney and Robert O'Connor, 'Ideology and elites' perceptions of the safety of new technology', *American Journal of Political Science*, 42 (1998), pp190–209

Pollack, Kenneth, *The Threatening Storm: The Case for Invading Iraq*, New York: Random House, 2002

Powell, Colin, 'Transcript of Powell's UN presentation', *CNN.com*, 6 February 2003, http://edition.cnn.com/2003/US/02/05/sprj.irq.powell.transcript/

Prins, Gwyn and Steve Rayner, *The Wrong Trousers: Radically Rethinking Climate Policy*, James Martin Institute for Science and Civilization, University of Oxford and the MacKinder Centre for the Study of Long-Wave Events, London School of Economics, 2007

Prins, Gwyn, Malcolm Cook, Christopher Green, Mike Hulme, Atte Korhola, Eija Riitte Korhola, Roger Pielke Jr, Steve Rayner, Akihiro Sawa, Daniel Sarewitz, Nico Stehr and Hans van Storch, *How to Get Climate Policy Back on Course*, Institute for Science, Innovation and Society, University of Oxford, and the Mackinder Programme for the Study of Long Wave Events, London School of Economics, 6

July 2009, www.eci.ox.ac.uk/research/climate/cop15/oxford/content/technical/pdfs/Climate-policy-back-on-course.pdf

Project for the New American Century, 26 January 1998, www.newamericancentury.org/iraqclintonletter.htm

Pusey, Michael, *Economic Rationalism In Canberra: A Nation Building State Changes its Mind*, Melbourne: Cambridge University Press, 1991

Putnam, Robert, 'Diplomacy and domestic politics: The logic of two level games', *International Organization*, 42 (1988), pp427–460

Ralph, Jason, *Tony Blair's 'New Doctrine of International Community' and the UK Decision to Invade Iraq*, Polis Working Paper No. 20, School of Politics and International Studies, University of Leeds, August 2005

Ravetz, Jerome R., 'What is post-normal science?', *Futures*, 31 (1999), pp647–653

Ravetz, Jerome R., 'The challenge beyond orthodox science', *Futures*, 34 (2002), pp200–203

Reus-Smit, Christian, 'Constructivism', in *Theories of International Relations*, 4th edn, Scott Burchill, Andrew Linklater, Richard Devetak, Jack Donnelly, Terry Nardin, Matthew Paterson, Christian Reus-Smit and Jacqui True (eds), Basingstoke, UK: Palgrave Macmillan, 2009, pp212–236

Rodrik, Dani, 'After neo-liberalism, what?', 2002, www.newrules.org/docs/afterneolib/rodrik.pdf

Rodrik, Dani, 'Goodbye Washington Consensus, hello Washington confusion? A review of the World Bank's economic growth in the 1990s: Learning from a decade of reform', *Journal of Economic Literature*, XLIV (December 2006), pp973–987

Rose, Gideon, 'Neoclassical realism and theories of foreign policy', *World Politics*, 51 (1998), pp144–172

Rotberg, Robert I., 'Failed states in a world of terror', *Foreign Affairs*, 81 (2002), pp127–140

Russell, Bertrand, *Sceptical Essays*, New York: Barnes and Noble, 1961

Ryan, Maria, 'Filling in the "unknowns": Hypothesis-based intelligence and the Rumsfeld Commission', *Intelligence and National Security*, 21 (2006), pp286–315

Saad, Lydia, 'Increased number think global warming is "exaggerated"', 11 March 2009, www.gallup.com/poll/116590/increased-number-think-global-warming-exaggerated.aspx

Sanderson, Ian, 'Evaluation, policy learning and evidence-based policy making', *Public Administration*, 80 (2002), pp1–22

Sarewitz, Daniel, 'Science and environmental policy: An excess of objectivity', Center for Science, Policy and Outcomes – Columbia University, 1999, www.cspo.org/products/articles/excess.objectivity.html

Sarewitz, Daniel, 'How science makes environmental controversies worse', *Environmental Science and Policy*, 7 (2004), pp385–403

Shore, Cris and Susan Wright, *Anthropology of Policy: Critical Perspectives on Governance and Power*, London and New York: Routledge, 1997

Silva, Carol and Hank Jenkins-Smith, 'The precautionary principle in context: US and EU scientists' prescriptions for policy in the face of uncertainty', *Social Science Quarterly*, 88 (2007), pp640–664

Singer, S. Fred, *Climate Policy – From Rio to Kyoto: A Political Issue for 2000 – and Beyond*, Hoover Institution on War Revolution and Peace, Stanford University, 2000

Smithson, Michael, 'The many faces and masks of uncertainty', in *Uncertainty and Risk: Multidisciplinary Perspectives*, Gabriel Bammer and Michael Smithson (eds), London: Earthscan, 2008, pp13–26

Snyder, Richard C., H. W. Bruck and Burton Sapin (eds), *Foreign Policy Decision-Making (Revisited)*, New York: Palgrave Macmillan, 2002

Starr, Sandy, 'Science, risk and the price of precaution', 1 May 2003, www.spiked-online.com/Articles/00000006DD7A.htm

Stephens, Philip, *Tony Blair: The Making of a World Leader*, New York: Viking Penguin, 2004

Sterling-Folker, Jennifer, 'Realist environment, liberal process, and domestic-level variables', *International Studies Quarterly*, 41 (1997), pp1–25

Stiglitz, Joseph, 'What I learned at the world economic crisis', *New Republic* 222 (17 and 24 April 2000), pp56–60

Stiglitz, Joseph, 'Iraq's next shock will be shock therapy', *Project Syndicate*, February 2004, www.project-syndicate.org/commentary/stiglitz42

Stone, Deborah, *Policy Paradox*, New York: W. W. Norton & Company, 2002

Surel, Yves, 'The role of cognitive and normative frames in policy making', *Journal of European Public Policy*, 7 (2000), pp495–512

Suskind, Ron, *The Price of Loyalty: George W. Bush, the White House, and the Education of Paul O'Neill*, New York: Simon & Schuster, 2004

Suskind, Ron, *The One Percent Doctrine*, New York: Simon & Schuster, 2006

Tenet, George, with Bill Harlow, *At the Center of the Storm*, New York: HarperCollins, 2007

The Commission to Assess the Ballistic Missile Threat to the United States, *Executive Summary of the Report of the Commission to Assess the Ballistic Missile Threat to the United States*, 104th Congress, 15 July 1998, http://ftp.fas.org/irp/threat/missile/rumsfeld/index.html

The Kerr Group, 'Intelligence and analysis on Iraq: Issues for the intelligence community', 29 July 2004, www.gwu.edu/~nsarchiv/news/20051013/kerr_report.pdf

Thielmann, Greg, 'Rumsfeld reprise? The missile report that foretold the Iraq intelligence controversy', *Arms Control Today*, 33 (July/August 2003), pp3–8

Tickner, Joel, Carolyn Raffensperger and Nancy Myers, *The Precautionary Principle In Action: A Handbook*, Science and Environmental Health Network, n.d. www.biotech-info.net/handbook.pdf

Toke, David, 'Epistemic communities and environmental groups', *Politics*, 19 (1999), pp97–102

Tønnessen, Johan and Arne Johnsen, *The History of Modern Whaling*, Berkeley: University of California Press, 1982

Torgerson, Douglas, 'Contextual orientation in policy analysis: The contribution of Harold D. Lasswell', *Policy Sciences*, 18 (1985), pp241–261

Trombetta, Maria Julia, 'Environmental security and climate change: Analysing the discourse', *Cambridge Review of International Affairs*, 21 (2008), pp585–602

Uchitelle, Louis, 'World Bank economist felt he had to silence his criticism or quit', *The New York Times*, 2 December 1999, www.nytimes.com/1999/12/02/business/world-bank-economist-felt-he-had-to-silence-his-criticism-or-quit.html

UK House of Commons, *The Iraq Crisis*, Parliamentary Research Paper 98/28, February 1998, www.parliament.uk/commons/lib/research/rp98/rp98-028.pdf

UK Mission to the UN, *Energy, Security and Climate*, UK Concept Paper, 23 April 2007, http://unfccc.int/files/application/pdf/ukpaper_securitycouncil.pdf

United Nations General Assembly, 'Annex I: Rio Declaration on Environment and Development', *Report of the United Nations Conference on Environment and Development* (Rio de Janeiro, 3–14 June 1992), A/CONF.151/26 (VOL. I), Distr. GENERAL, 2 August 1992

UNMOVIC Working Document, 'Unresolved Disarmament Issues: Iraq's Proscribed Weapons Programmes', 6 March 2003, www.un.org/Depts/unmovic/documents/6mar.pdf

US Government, *A National Security Strategy for a New Century*, Washington, DC: The White House, October 1998

US Government, *The National Security Strategy of the United States of America*, Washington, DC: The White House, September 2002

US House of Representatives Committee on Oversight and Government Reform, *The Financial Crisis and the Role of Federal Regulators*, Preliminary Hearing Transcript, 111th Congress, 23 October 2008

US Senate, *Byrd-Hagel Resolution*, 105th Congress, 1st Session, S. Res. 98, 25 July 1997

US Senate Select Committee on Intelligence, *Report of the Select Committee on Intelligence on the US Intelligence Community's Prewar Intelligence Assessments on Iraq*, 108th Congress, 2nd Session, 9 July 2004

US Senate Select Committee on Intelligence, *Post-war Findings about Iraq's WMD Programs and Links to Terrorism and How They Compare with Pre-War Assessments*, 109th Congress, 2nd Session, 8 September 2006

US Senate Select Committee on Intelligence, *Report on Whether Public Statements Regarding Iraq by US Government Officials were Substantiated by Intelligence Information*, 110th Congress, 2nd Session, 5 June 2008

Walker, W. E., P. Harrimoës, J. Rotmans, J. P. van der Sluijs, M. B. A. van Asselt, P. Janssen and M. P. Krayer von Krauss, 'Defining uncertainty: A conceptual basis for uncertainty management in model-based decision support', *Integrated Assessment*, 4 (2003), pp5–17

Waltz, Kenneth N., *Theory of International Politics*, Reading, MA: Addison-Wesley, 1983 reprint

Wara, Michael, *Measuring the Clean Development Mechanism's Performance and Potential*, The Program on Energy and Sustainable Development, Stanford University, Working Paper No. 56, July 2006

Weller, Patrick, *Don't Tell the Prime Minister*, Melbourne: Scribe Publications, 2002

Wendt, Alexander, 'Constructing international politics', *International Security*, 20 (1995), pp71–81

Wesley, Michael, 'The state of the art on the art of state building', *Global Governance*, 14 (2008), pp369–385

Wildavsky, Aaron, 'Trial and error versus trial without error', in *Rethinking Risk and the Precautionary Principle*, Julian Morris (ed.), Oxford: Butterworth-Heinemann, 2000, pp22–45

Wildavsky, Aaron and Karl Dake, 'Theories of risk perception: Who fears what and why?', *Daedalus*, 119 (Fall 1990), pp41–60

Williamson, John, 'What should the World Bank think about the Washington Consensus?' *The World Bank Research Observer*, 15 (August 2000), pp251–64

Williamson, John, 'A short history of the Washington Consensus', paper commissioned by Fundacion CIDOB for a conference, 'From the Washington Consensus towards a new Global Governance', Barcelona, 24–25 September 2004, www.iie.com/publications/papers/williamson0904-2.pdf

Wingspread Statement on the Precautionary Principle, drafted at the Wingspread Conference on the Precautionary Principle convened by the Science and Environmental Health Network, 26 January 1998, www.sehn.org/wing.html

Woodard, Garry, 'We now know about going to war in Iraq', October 2007, www.mup.com.au/uploads/files/acmo/WoodardGoingToWarInIraqEssay.pdf

Woodward, Bob, *State of Denial: Bush at War Part III*, New York: Simon & Schuster, 2006

Yergin, Daniel and Joseph Stanislaw, *The Commanding Heights: The Battle Between Government and the Marketplace that is Remaking the Modern World*, New York: Simon & Schuster, 1998

Young, Oran R. and Gail Osherenko, 'International regime formation: Findings, research priorities, and applications', in *Polar Politics: Creating International Environmental Regimes*, Oran R. Young and Gail Osherenko (eds), Ithaca, NY: Cornell University Press, 1993, pp223–261

Young, Oran R. and Gail Osherenko (eds), *Polar Politics: Creating International Environmental Regimes*, Ithaca, NY: Cornell University Press, 1993

Zillman, John, 'The IPCC: A view from the inside', Australian APEC Study Centre, August 1997, www.apec.org.au/docs/zillman.pdf

Zillman, John, 'Our future climate', World Meteorological Day Address, Australian Bureau of Meteorology, 21 March 2003, www.bom.gov.au/announcements/media_releases/ho/20030320a.shtml

Interviews and correspondence

Barton, Rod, interview by author, Canberra, Australia, 14 February 2008

Blix, Hans, interview by author, Stockholm, Sweden, 20 August 2007

Gallucci, Robert, interview by author, Washington, DC, 30 August 2007

Jones, Brian, interview by author, Winchester, UK, 19 August 2008

Jones, Brian, Personal correspondence with author, 3 October 2008

Kanbur, Ravi, interview by author, Brisbane, Australia, 30 October 2007

Lewincamp, Frank, interview by author, Canberra, Australia, 13 February 2008

Milanovic, Branko, interview by author, Washington, DC, 30 August 2007

Morrison, John, interview by author, Canterbury, UK, 20 August 2008

Morrison, John, personal correspondence with author, 30 September 2008

Pillar, Paul R., interview by author, Washington, DC, 29 August 2007

Thielmann, Greg, interview by author, Washington, DC, 31 August 2007

Thielmann, Greg, personal correspondence with author, 14 September 2008

White, Jeff, interview by author, Washington, DC, 27 August 2007

Index